Pau Hana

PAU HANA

PLANTATION LIFE
AND LABOR IN HAWAII
1835–1920

RONALD TAKAKI

UNIVERSITY OF HAWAII PRESS
Honolulu

First printing 1983
Second printing 1984
Paperback edition 1984

TITLE PAGE ILLUSTRATION COURTESY OF
HAWAII STATE ARCHIVES

Library of Congress Cataloging in Publication Data

Takaki, Ronald T., 1939–
  Pau Hana : plantation life and labor in Hawaii, 1835–
1920.

  Bibliography: p.
  1. Sugar workers—Hawaii—Koloa—History. 2. Sugar-
cane industry—Hawaii—Koloa—History. 3. Plantations—
Hawaii—Koloa—History. 4. Hawaii—Emigration and
immigration—History. I. Title.
HD8039.S86U64 1983   331.7'63361'0996941   83–10225
ISBN 0–8248–0865–7

For

Kasuke and Katsu Okawa
Issei Pioneers

Richard Okawa
and
Catherine Okawa Takaki

Contents

Preface

The idea for this book was initially suggested to me by my uncle, Richard Okawa. A few years ago, while I was on sabbatical in Hawaii to complete a book on nineteenth-century American race relations, I often stopped by his home in Moiliili to "talk story." One afternoon, as I told him about my writing, I suddenly noticed his eyes light up, and he asked me excitedly in lyrical pidgin English: "Hey, why you no go write a book about us?" My grandfather had come to Hawaii as a contract laborer in 1886, and my mother had been born on the Hawi Plantation in Kohala. Here, surely, was a story worthy of serious scholarly attention, my Uncle insisted. So I replied: "Why not?"

As I read through the literature on Hawaii, I was surprised to discover that a book on the plantation labor experience did not exist. There were general histories such as works by Gavan Daws and Lawrence Fuchs, and specialized studies of particular ethnic groups such as monographs by Clarence Glick on the Chinese, Ernest Wakukawa on the Japanese, Wayne Patterson on the Koreans, and Mary Dorita on the Filipinos. But there was no study of plantation life and labor from a historical and multiethnic perspective.

Pau Hana was written to address this need. Seeking to add a new dimension and an Asian American perspective to the existing rich body of immigration and labor history written by scholars like Oscar Handlin and Herbert Gutman, this work also reminds us that not all of America's immigrants came from Europe and the history of labor in this country was not wholly continental. Entitled *Pau Hana*, which means "finished working" in Hawaiian, this study examines the experiences of plantation laborers—Hawaiians, Chinese, Norwegians, Germans, Portuguese, Japanese, Koreans, Filipinos—in the islands.

Based on an extensive examination of available primary sources, my research offered me an opportunity to develop an intimate understanding of the working people of Hawaii's past—to learn about the plantation labor experience from Japanese newspapers, letters written by Norwegian contract laborers in the 1880s, diaries of Portuguese and Japanese immigrants, interviews of Korean and Portuguese laborers, oral histories of Chinese and Filipino workers, pamphlets of labor unions, and Hakka and Portuguese folk songs as well as the plantation work songs, or *hole hole bushi*, of Japanese laborers. My research also enabled me to gain access to the inner sanctum of the planters' association and the world of corporate power. I examined the confidential business correspondence of plantation managers and corporate agencies such as Castle and Cooke, C. Brewer and Company, Theo. H. Davies and Company, and American Factors, which all handled the needs of the plantations, including the need for the supply and control of labor. In the course of my investigation, I accumulated several pounds of photocopied documents (diaries of plantation managers, reports, letters, and business memos—some marked "private") that revealed much about the strategies and policies of plantation managers to develop a multiethnic work force, and that also told me much about the day-to-day lives of the workers.

What happened in Hawaii was not an isolated occurrence: sugar plantation economies and societies were developed in many other parts of the world, including Louisiana, British Guiana, Cuba, Puerto Rico, and Jamaica. Like other sugar-producing areas, Hawaii was part of what Immanuel Wallerstein has described as the "modern world system," for it was a semi-peripheral country producing a cash crop for export to a core country. But where the American South, the West Indies, and Latin America depended on slave labor to raise cane, Hawaii relied on free or wage labor.

This study of the plantation labor experience in Hawaii is organized topically: the origins and development of the sugar industry from its beginnings at Koloa to the formation of the "Big Five," the immigration and the making of a multiethnic working class in the islands, the experiences of laboring men and women at the point of production, the transplantation of institutions and traditions from the old countries and the emergence of a new language and families in the camps, and finally the individual and collective responses of laborers to the plantation system. Between 1835 and 1920 planters had developed the sugar kingdom and inducted workers of many nationalities into a new world of labor and production; workers, in turn, had transformed both the economic and political terrain and created a new society in the islands. By 1920 the industry was reaching beyond sugar to pineapple production and toward tourism, and the laborers were beginning to feel a new consciousness—an identity of themselves as settlers, as locals, and an understanding of the need for a politics that transcended ethnicity.

Today Hawaii is well known as a society of diverse cultures and ethnic groups. In fact politicians and promoters for the Hawaii Visitors Bureau regularly boast about this rich intermingling of different peoples and cultures in the islands. But, as cement towers crowd the Waikiki shoreline, as condominiums replace the camps of plantation laborers at Kaanapali, and as multinational corporations convert cane fields into tennis courts and golf courses for tourists, we often forget how and why this diversity developed and its plantation origins. Hopefully *Pau Hana* will help us remember.

A Note of Appreciation

Mahalo to the many people who helped to make *Pau Hana* a reality. Barnes Riznik of the Grove Farm Plantation Museum allowed me virtually to camp for almost two weeks in his archives, where I gathered a little mountain of information. David Kittelson and Michaelyn Chou of the Hawaiian Collection in the University of Hawaii Library issued me a stack permit and personally made certain I did not overlook important materials and documents. Don J. Heinz, director of the Hawaiian Sugar Planters' Association, granted me permission to work in the HSPA Archives, and Librarian Mary Matsuoka carried to my table armloads of scrapbooks for me to examine.

Ruben Alcantara, John Liu, Greg Mark, and Wayne Patterson provided valuable bibliographical assistance during the initial stages of my research.

Dana Takaki helped me scan miles of plantation documents on microfilm and photocopy scores of newspaper articles.

Thuy Truong transferred or handcopied data from books and documents to thousands of 3" x 5" notecards.

Marjie Barrows proofread the typescript and also made some stylistic suggestions.

Wei-Chi Poon helped me with the Hakka translations.

Linda Oamilda, director of the Waipahu Cultural Garden Park, guided me around the Waipahu Plantation; Major Okada, Tadao Okada, and many other friends of the WCGP generously invited me to share their potluck lunches (without "mongoose hekka") and "talk story" with them about plantation life in the old days.

Raymond and Nancy Len listened to what I had to say about the project and extended their encouragement.

Franklin Odo consistently provided wise advice from the beginning to the end of the project. H. Brett Melendy and Ed Beechert took time away from their own writing to read an early draft of the manuscript and offer comments. Alexander Saxton pointed out places where the study would benefit from additional information and elaboration. Roberto Haro helped me work out some of the ideas for the book, as we jogged around the perimeter of the Berkeley campus, and also gave the manuscript his critical reading. Lawrence Friedman thoughtfully read the manuscript and convinced me to make several important changes. Jere Takahashi systematically criticized the manuscript chapter by chapter. Donald Worster gently urged me to rethink some of the "big questions." Carol Takaki tirelessly read and re-read the manuscript in its various drafts, and meticulously noted the passages that needed more clarity or greater felicity of expression.

Iris Wiley contacted me shortly after I had begun working on this book and patiently provided support and encouragement until I was pau. Kathleen Matsueda helped to transform the study from typescript to book.

Finally, mahalo to Uncle Richard Okawa for his suggestion.

Isogu pau hana
Mibi no ha ga karamu
Korobya mi o sasu
Kibi no iga

In the rush at *pau hana*
I get caught in cane leaves,
When I stumble and fall,
They prickle, they jab.

(Work Song of Japanese Plantation Laborers)

Prologue:
Pau Hana

Most of them are gone. Buried in forlorn and windswept cemeteries near sandy beaches and rocky shorelines on the edges of the cane fields, they seem to be a forgotten people, their lonely and weathered tombstones standing like erect and voiceless guards. But many of the old plantation laborers still remain; they linger in their pau hana years. For most of their lives, they had worked in the hot cane fields and the rumbling sugar mills. Now, in their final years, they rest and remember.

Many decades ago, they had left their homes in faraway lands—China, Portugal, Japan, Korea, the Philippines, and other places—to labor on the plantations of Hawaii. Now, in the evenings, they try to recall the old country, the village, the mountain behind it, the nearby river, and the farm, but they find their memories fading. In the mornings, they still wake up early, as they did in the old days when the five A.M. plantation siren sounded to announce the beginning of the workday. But they do not have to hurry now: lunas will no longer rout them out of bed and march them to the fields. They feel the aches and pains of bodies worn and damaged from long years of backbreaking plantation labor. They live quietly, some of them in cramped eight-by-eight-foot rooms in Chinatown, all of their life's possessions stuffed on shelves and under beds. Their faces wrinkled and their shoulders bent, they finger and study yellowed photographs of themselves—young, energetic, and hopeful.

Sometimes they feel out of place, for they know they belong to a passing era—the vanishing world of plantation Hawaii. They watch the islands changing so fast: the expansion of resort hotels and new subdivisions with all "da same kine" houses into the cane fields they once plowed and harvested, the conversion of the Kahuku sugar mill into a museum for tourists, and the construction of luxurious condominiums, which block the old paths to beaches where they once fished and picked *'opihi*. "No can go fish over there no more—'kapu' and 'private property' signs now all over the place," they complain. In the distance, they see the ubiquitous building cranes silhouetted against the skyline and anxiously note the spread of concrete highrises: "Almost no can see Punchbowl and Diamond Head anymore." Periodically they hear 747s shriek across the blue sky, descending to debouch millions of visitors in paradise.

Time seems to move slowly for the oldtimers; no longer do plantation sirens measure their days. They sit on park benches in Aala Park and Ala Moana and talk story. "R'memba da one time," one of them begins, gesturing wildly, his hands so beautifully expressive and his voice so lilting. Others quickly join the conversation. "Our stories should be listened to by the young people. It's for their sake. We really had a hard time, you know." "We had to work in the canefields, cutting cane, being afraid, not knowing the language. We didn't know how to use the tools or what their names were. When any *haole* or Portuguese luna came, we got frightened and thought we had to work harder or get fired." "Yes, and us women, before going off to work, we had to wear skirts, long-sleeved *kasuri* shirts, hats, handkerchiefs tied on, *kyahan*, and *tabis*. Even getting dressed properly for work was a big job." And as the old people reminisce about the earlier days of plantation life and labor, they know they can claim an important place in the history of Hawaii. In the midst of all the talking an old man, vividly recalling the mountains of cane he had cut and carried, proudly exclaims: "With my bare hands and calloused heart and patience, I helped build Hawaii."[1]

I

The Sugar Kingdom:
The Making of Plantation Hawaii

"An Entering Wedge"

One day in 1835, the natives of Koloa on the island of Kauai were surprised to see a white man wandering through their village, "a mere hamlet, seldom visited by even a missionary." They had seen white men before: in 1778 many of the natives had traveled to Waimea, sixteen miles away, to get a glimpse of Captain James Cook; or had heard stories about how he had sailed into the bay in two huge ships with billowing white sheets, how his men had carried awesome weapons of fire and destruction, and how they had left a dreadful disease with native women. Many of the natives still possessed souvenirs of Cook's visit, the iron nails they had ripped from his landing boats and the butcher's cleaver one of them had stolen.[1]

As the Koloa natives curiously watched their new visitor, they compared William Hooper of Boston to the other *haoles* 'outsiders' living on Kauai: the merchants in Waimea shipping the fragrant sandalwood to China and supplying whaling vessels with water and provisions, and the missionaries building a new church and spreading Christianity among the natives. But the people of Koloa did not realize that Hooper, more than the merchants and the missionaries, represented the beginning of a new era in the history of Hawaii. Sent to Koloa by Ladd and Company of Honolulu to establish the first sugar cane plantation in the Sandwich Islands, Hooper was there to remake Hawaii in an American image: to advance the market civilization of the United States beyond Indian lands and Mexican territory to a new Pacific frontier, undermining in the process native Hawaiian society and the people's traditional relationship with their land.[2]

Though he was only twenty-six years old, Hooper keenly understood the significance of his venture in Koloa. Two years earlier

WILLIAM HOOPER
"I laid out a piece of land supposed to contain 12 acres
to be cultivated with cane."

Hooper, Peter Brinsmade, and William Ladd had landed in Honolulu and opened a mercantile trading house they named Ladd and
Company. The company had leased from King Kamehameha III
980 acres of land for the cultivation of sugar cane on the east side
of the Waihohonu Stream in Koloa for fifty years at $300 a year.
The company had also secured permission to hire natives to work
on the plantation. It had agreed to pay a tax for each man
employed to Kauikeaouli, the king of the Hawaiian islands, and
Kaikioewa, the governor of Kauai, and to pay the workers satisfactory wages. The king and governor, in return, would exempt the
workers from any taxation, except the tax paid by their employer.[3]

As Hooper surveyed the newly leased land and the natives to be
inducted into his work force, he certainly thought Koloa was a fit-
ting place for the beginning of the sugar industry in the islands,
for the place name itself means "Great Cane" (*ko* 'cane' and *loa*
'great'). Everywhere Hooper looked, wild cane flourished on the

fertile land of Koloa, nourished by rains that fell on towering Kahili Mountain, almost always shrouded in mist, and then swept southward ten miles toward the plains of Koloa and finally toward the beaches of Poipu. Far away from American civilization, initially Hooper lived in a grass hut and was obliged to eat *taro*, a root which the natives pounded into *poi*; he even jokingly described himself as becoming a *"real kanaka."* Anxious to start his operations, Hooper wrote in his diary on 11 September 1835: "Koloa, Island of Kauai, S. Islands, obtained from Govr. Kekeiova [Kaikioewa], the use of 25 kanakas at two dollars each per month." The next day, he "laid out a piece of land supposed to contain 12 acres to be cultivated with cane." Two days later, "twenty three of the twenty five kanakas hired from the Govr. made their appearance on the plantation at sunrise & commenced work after breakfast"; in the course of the day, they removed the grass from about two acres.[4]

Within one year the young man from Boston had transformed both the land and native society in Koloa. On 12 September 1836, he proudly listed his accomplishments: twenty-five acres of cane under cultivation, twenty houses for the natives, a house for the superintendent, a carpenter's shop, a blacksmith's shop, a mill dam, a sugar house, a boiling house, and a sugar mill. Pleased with the progress of his plantation, Hooper recorded in his diary his thoughts on the meaning of the Koloa experience:

> Just one year to day since I commenced work on this plantation, during which I have had more annoyances from the chiefs and difficulty with the natives (from the fact of this land being the first that has ever been cultivated, on the plan of *free* labour, at these islands) than I ever tho't it possible for one white man to bear, nevertheless I have succeeded in bringing about a place, which if followed up by other foreign residents, will eventually emancipate the natives from the miserable system of "chief labour" which ever has existed at these Islands, and which if not broken up, will be an effectual preventitive to the progress of civilization, industry and national prosperity. . . . The tract of land in Koloa was [developed] after much pain . . . for the purpose of breaking up the system aforesaid or in other words to serve as an entering wedge . . . [to] upset the whole system.[5]

A sense of mission lay behind Hooper's energetic enterprise. More than profits were at stake. In building his plantation, Hooper

KOLOA PLANTATION, 1841
"The tract of land in Koloa was [developed] . . . to serve as an
entering wedge."

viewed himself as a white man, as a pathfinder or vanguard of civilization, introducing the system of free labor in order to emanci-
pate the natives from the miserable system of " 'chief labour.' "
For young Hooper, the Koloa Plantation was an "entering wedge"
designed to irrevocably split apart traditional Hawaiian society.

As they watched Hooper begin his enterprise, the natives of
Koloa must have felt a profound ambivalence. They undoubtedly
were very apprehensive about his new operation, fearful of the
negative effects the plantation system would have on their culture
and way of life. They also saw him as a haole and identified him
with the destruction of the sandalwood forests, with the denuding
of the *'āina* 'land', and with the sailors who were infecting native
women with venereal diseases. But the natives also must have
hoped Hooper would offer them an escape from the old Hawaiian
system of exploitation and fear. The king owned all of the lands,
and chiefs holding land did so for payment of loyal services and
dues. The common people or *makaainana*, in order to have use of
small tracts of land, had to labor for the king or local chiefs, the
ali'i. *Kapus*, or tabus, strictly enforced by the *ilamuku*, or police,
severely restricted their activities and ambitions. The Hawaiian
historian David Malo, educated by missionaries and forty-two
years old when Hooper founded the Koloa Plantation, reported
that the commoners were subjected to hard labor, heavy taxation,
and cruelty. If they were lax in performing labor for their chief,

they were expelled from the land or even subject to a death penalty. They held the chiefs in "great dread," and lived in a state of "chronic fear." Theirs was a "life of weariness . . . constantly burdened by one exaction after another."[6]

Seeking to improve their lot, twenty-three natives went to work for Hooper on 13 September 1835. But two days later, they suddenly stopped working. "The kanakas having discovered the chiefs were to pay and not me," Hooper wrote in his diary, "concluded that 'all work and no pay' was poor business, therefore spent most of the forenoon in idleness." Apparently Hooper's workers thought they were to be paid through their chiefs and, doubtful they would be paid at all, refused to work. They were quickly offered an "inducement"—direct payment of "one real," or 12 1/2 cents per day—and "they sprang to it, and at sundown finished their stint." Workers were given food and shelter, in addition to their wages.[7]

But Hooper did not pay his workers in reals or cash. Rather he issued coupons or script, pieces of cardboard on which he wrote amounts for 12 1/2, 25, and 50 cents and which his workers could exchange for goods only at his plantation store. Thus Hooper was able to both pay his workers and make a profit from their purchases. Periodically Hooper ran out of coupons. On 15 November 1837, for example, he wrote to Ladd and Company: "I am excessively annoyed for want of money; had to knock off laying bricks today, to make some." He also found himself looking for new consumer goods for his workers to buy with their coupons. On 23 February 1836 he asked Ladd and Company to send him clothing to sell to the natives: "Their great desire seems to be to get a suit of clothes to show off. In this I intend to gratity them so soon as they shall have earned it. I beg you therefore . . . to purchase say 20 suits of cheap thin clothing, various sizes." But in early 1838 Hooper wrote to his company: "What shall we pay off our men with? Calico, etc., they are tired of. Can't you get up something?" And a year later, he noted how the natives had purchased a sufficient supply of fabric and how the plantation store needed other items to sell to them. In this process, Hooper had created both a wage-earning labor force and a consumer class dependent on a plantation-owned market which had to expand consumer needs constantly.[8]

Native families, reported Hooper's neighbor James Jarvis, readily "volunteered" to have their taxes paid for them and to work for the Koloa Plantation for wages. They were drawn into Hooper's labor force with "the inducement of regular wages, good houses, and plenty of food, when compared with their usual mode of living." Hooper's work force increased from twenty-five in September 1835 to forty in May 1836. In March 1838 Hooper noted that one hundred men, women, and children looked to him for their "daily Poe [poi]."[9]

Among Hooper's workers were native women. Employed to strip the cane and assist in grinding and boiling operations, they proved to be such capable workers that Hooper wrote to Ladd and Company on 12 June 1838: "I am in want of no more Sugar Boys. The women on the plantation now make good ones and it is best that I should keep them constantly at work." They were not only worked constantly but were also paid less than the men: women received only 6 cents per day while the men received 12 1/2 cents. Hooper's justification for this dual-wage system was that it kept the women employed and allowed them to make "more than enough to support their families."[10]

On the plantation, Hooper's laborers found themselves in a new world of modern industrial agriculture. They no longer cultivated their traditionally held small plots of land, sharing their crops with the aliʻi. They no longer directed their own labors, making their own decisions regarding what to plant and when to work, rest, or go fishing. As plantation laborers, they found their time controlled by unfamiliar workday sounds, schedules, and rhythms. "At sunrise the laborers are turned out by the ringing of the bell," Jarvis wrote, "and work till sunset, sufficient time being allowed for their meals. At night they are assembled and paid by a sort of bank note, considered as good as money all over the island and redeemable in goods on Saturday." The workers, Hooper reported to Ladd and Company, "meet me in the field at six in the morning, work till 7 1/2—go to breakfast & return to work till 12 1/2—an hour at dinner & then work till sundown at which time I pay them off in paper. . . . Friday is allotted to them to take care of their Tarrow [taro] Patches & Saturday to cook their Grub." Where previously they had planned their time and activities by the movements of the sun, now they awoke by the ringing of the plantation bell, and a clock determined when they would eat, work, rest, and work again. And their days were organized into weeks, with weekdays for working and weekends for tending their gardens.[11]

As plantation workers, they performed a myriad of tasks. Under

Hooper's direction, they first cleared grass from tracts of land for cane cultivation and used a plough pulled by oxen to prepare the soil for the planting of cane cuttings. When one of the oxen died from overwork, Hooper replaced the ox with men. "At one time," Jarvis reported, "in lieu of cattle, he was obliged to employ forty natives, to drag a plough." Hooper filled his diary with descriptions of plantation work tasks. On 25 November 1835 he wrote: "This day the natives finished planting one strip of cane." 20 June 1836: "Men engaged in stripping the dry leaves from cane." 9 August 1836: "Holeing for and Planting cane—clearing land." 27 March 1837: "Commenced the day with 47 natives—Hoeing cane, laying out ground & etc." 13 November 1837: "The natives continued cutting cane." 16 November 1837: "The natives engaged cutting cane." 2 December 1837: "Commenced cutting cane."[12]

In addition to their work in the fields, plantation laborers erected buildings, bridges, and dams, as well as operated the mill. Hooper recorded the construction of a factory in the middle of the cane fields of Koloa in diary entries beginning 9 May 1836: "This commenced with 40 men to build a dam for a sugar mill to go by water power." May 11: "Continued with our men on Dam. . . ." May 18: "Finished Dam, now employed [men] in setting up Mill." May 28: "Employed 6 men to put up frame for Sugar Mill." May 31: "All hands to work thatching Mill House." August 4: "Natives finished the wall made for new water wheel. . . ." Working with two white carpenters, Manuel and Antoine, the laborers finished building the sugar mill. On 10 November 1836 Hooper proudly wrote to Ladd and Company: "I set the mill in operation on Monday noon. It works admirably taking four men to keep it supplied with cane, or rather to feed it. There is no stop to it. . . . The natives are completely taken 'aback' and consider the Mill as one of the 'seven wonders.' " A month later he was pleased to report that the natives working in the mill were efficiently extracting juice from the cane.[13]

Drawn away from their own lands and traditional homes, Hooper's native workers had entered a new plantation community. They lived on the plantation, in houses allotted to them by Hooper. Assigned plots of land to cultivate crops for their own food and allowed time on weekends to work their gardens, they received from Hooper a barrel of fish every third week. This system in which the workers supplemented their own subsistence needs enabled Hooper to minimize both wages and production costs. On Saturdays, Hooper's workers went to the plantation store to sell vegetables and crafts and to purchase goods with their coupons. Market day on the Koloa Plantation was filled with excitement and noise. According to Jarvis,

> at sunrise the little shops on the plantation are opened, to redeem the paper money, and purchase such articles as the natives bring for sale. Crowds of them in the rudest attire, or no attire at all, early throng the house. One brings vegetables, another fish, fine tapas, mats, curiosities, in short, any thing and every thing which they suppose the *haole* (foreigner), to want. Women leading fat pigs, which . . . they take in their arms and press to their bosoms to still their deafening lamentations, join the throng; while dog and fowl add their voices to the dulcet strain.[14]

Plantation workers not only labored, lived, and shopped on the Koloa Plantation, they also received medical care. Initially Hooper himself attended to the medical needs of his workers. On 29 April 1836 he reported to Ladd and Company: "They are often ailing. . . . They are troubled with sore eyes etc etc which need & ought to have advice & medicine." The next year Hooper contracted the services of a Dr. Lafore. In a letter to the doctor dated 16 October 1837 Ladd and Company wrote: "In reference to your inquiry on Sat. last, as to what amt. might be expected from us, for medical attendance on the natives in our employ, we have only to repeat that it would be exceedingly gratifying to us to have you as a neighbor and for all medical attendance on those in our employ, we should expect to pay you, by the year, the price to be decided by yourself, at its commencement or termination." What Hooper was developing on the Koloa Plantation was a system of capitalist paternalism that would embrace the total needs of plantation workers and set a pattern for planter-worker relationships in Hawaii.[15]

Though they were dependent on Hooper for their "daily Poe" and other needs, native workers refused to give him the control and loyalty he expected. Time and again Hooper was exasperated because he was unable to exact satisfactory obedience and sustained labor from his workers. Throughout his Koloa diary, he described his workers as undependable, as children, as "dull asses," and as "Indians." His letters to Ladd and Company chronicled the frustrations he felt as the supervisor of recalcitrant laborers. On 23

February 1836, he complained: "It requires the concentrated patience of an hundred Jobs to get along with these natives . . . [their] obedient masks of loyalty . . . [hiding their] dissatisfaction" and repugnance toward plantation labor. 21 September 1836: "Cane grows rapidly, some of it astonishingly—my natives are on their oars." 3 October 1836: "I would write more on this sheet but my men are, as usual, on their oars in my absence." 26 October 1836: "The natives do but little when my back is turned." 10 December 1836: "The native laborers need to be broken in [but] when that will be *I* can not tell." 12 May 1838: "A gang of Sandwich Island men are like a gang of School Boys. When their master is with them they mind their lessons, but when he is absent it is 'hurra boys.' They display so little interest for their employment that it makes my *heart ache.*"[16]

Hooper's laborers required constant surveillance or else they would not work. They became skillful pretenders; next-door-neighbor Jarvis often "amusingly" watched them practice their art of deception. While working in the fields, natives were always ready to deceive their employer and escape from work, he reported. If an overseer left for a moment, down they would squat and pull out their pipes. Then the "longest-winded fellow" would begin a story, an improvisation in which he would entertain everyone with "vulgar" humor and often "mimic the haole." As soon as the overseer came within sight, they would seize their spades and quickly "commence laboring with an assiduity" that baffled description and "perhaps all the while not strain a muscle."[17]

But Hooper did not find their behavior amusing. Irritated and impatient, he castigated his native workers for their inefficiency and doubted they would ever become useful as plantation workers. Their habits and customs, handed down to them from their forefathers and preserved so tenaciously would remain "the great obstacle to their employment" as agricultural wage laborers. Centuries, at least, Hooper lamented, would intervene before they would understand that it was a part of their "duty" to serve "their masters faithfully." He conceded that there were many good men among the natives who would take hold and turn themselves into "white kanakas" for one or two years; but he had no confidence that their patience would hold out. As long as the plantation depended on native labor, the superintendent would have to be a *"Slave Driver."*[18]

Hooper employed white overseers to help him supervise his native workers. He discovered that sometimes the overseers themselves needed to be broken in, to be introduced to a system of stern plantation discipline. On one occasion, a recently hired overseer named Titcomb overheard some workers expressing dissatisfaction with their wages. Reporting the incident to Ladd and Company, Hooper wrote:

> It seems that he secreted himself long side of his tea stick fence to hear the conversation of some natives in a house nearby—by it, he learned that the natives were on the morrow to demand 25 cts. per day—no mistake—so down he came to find out what was to be done. I very calmly told him that if he would take a whip and undertake to drive off the natives from his land, he would in my opinion have experience enough to last him a month. I have heard nothing more since.[19]

Frustrated because he could not convert the natives into docile and efficient modern agricultural workers, Hooper began employing Chinese laborers. He had first noticed their presence in Waimea: there a few of them were grinding wild cane, brought to them by natives, in a small sugar mill owned by William French. After visiting this mill in the spring of 1835, Hooper wrote to Ladd and Company:

> I have seen the Chinese sugar works in successful operations; although extremely crude, yet they are doing well. They have worked 6 days in the week ever since its first establishment, making abt 210 lb sugar per day & molasses by the cord. They could make four times as much by increasing the size of kettles. Mr. F. is much elated with its success and from what I learn from Mr. Whitney you may expect a Host of Chinese. . . . Mr. French's establishment at Waimea is a great eye sore to the natives. They have to work *all* the time— and no regard is paid to their complaints for food, etc., etc. Slavery is nothing to it.

Shortly after the construction of his own mill, Hooper projected the need for Chinese labor. "We may deem it," he advised Ladd and Company, "at a future day, necessary to locate some halfdozen Chinese on the land, if the establishment grows it will require them. The Supt. cannot feed the mill, boil the juice, make the sugar, etc etc, and to trust it to the natives is worse than nothing— they are alas, children, boys, and always will be."[20]

In a letter to Ladd and Company dated 1 December 1838 Hooper insisted that "a colony of Chinese would, probably, put the plantation in order, to be perpetuated, sooner and with less trouble than any other class of husbandmen." By this time, several Chinese were already working for Hooper; they had probably been recruited from French's mill, which had been put out of business due to competition from the Koloa mill. A pattern of ethnic labor segmentation was already evident, for Hooper tended to assign his Chinese laborers to the mill and Hawaiian laborers to the fields. In Hooper's view, the Chinese had more experience in milling and were more reliable as factory operatives than the Hawaiians. The Chinese were also placed in separate living quarters. Unlike the native workers, who lived on the plantation with their families in individual houses, the Chinese workers were single men and were housed together in a barrack-type structure. In April 1838 Hooper informed Ladd and Company that a large building had been erected for the "Chinamen." "They are highly pleased," he added, "and by their fixtures on doors I should suppose they intend to spend their days in it." Thus Chinese workers, too, now looked to Hooper for their "daily Poe." Early in 1839 Hooper ordered from Ladd and Company a supply of rice.[21]

But the use of Chinese workers did not mean the end of labor difficulties. Hooper's workers, Hawaiian and Chinese, found new ways to resist management and avoid work. Some of the natives shoplifted merchandise from the plantation store. On 28 January 1837 Hooper angrily scribbled into his diary: "[Detected] the natives stealing—therefore paid out no goods today." Three days later he wrote: "5 natives taken before Hukiko [Hukiku, the headman at Koloa]—convicted of stealing and sentenced to work on the roads." But by this time, some of his workers had devised a more ingenious way to acquire goods from the plantation store. As the natives learned how to read and write from a young schoolmaster in the village, some of them utilized their newly acquired knowledge and skills to make artful reproductions of Hooper's medium of exchange. The counterfeit coupons, according to Jarvis, were "so strikingly like the original, imitating the signatures with scrupulous exactness, that it was some time before the fraud was detected."[22]

But the fraud was eventually discovered. On 11 June 1836, Hooper, surprised and dismayed, wrote in his diary: "Some native

KOLOA PLANTATION SCRIPT
"If the ground work is fine waved
lines, or a delicate net work, and
the border highly wrought, we
doubt if we shall be troubled with
counterfeits from the Chinese."

has attempted to counterfeit the papers which I issued for dollars."
Some of the counterfeiters were Chinese. Hooper realized that unless the problem were checked, the counterfeit conspiracy could
undermine his entire enterprise. His laborers would have little incentive to work, for they would have their own source of script.
Determined to outwit his workers, Hooper asked Ladd and Company to have paper bills printed in Boston. In a letter to the printer
dated 15 November 1837 Ladd and Company gave instructions to
have the currency printed from a copper plate in order to be certain it could not be duplicated: "If the ground work is fine waved
lines, or a delicate net work, and the border highly wrought, we
doubt if we shall be troubled with counterfeits from the Chinese or
any other source." But it took time to order the printed currency
from Boston and have it sent to Hawaii. Meanwhile on 5 January
1839 Hooper again found counterfeit coupons in circulation and
urged Ladd and Company to hurry the order for the printed money: "I send you up a specimen of what I suppose to be *native* ingenuity in shape of counterfeit money. I have six reals of it." Acknowledging its genuine appearance, Hooper confessed: "I would
not swear it was not mine." Finally, three months later, Hooper
was relieved to receive the bank bills printed in Boston, which he
considered "very nicely executed."[23]

The founding of the Koloa Plantation had been a very trying experience for Hooper. The new land did not yield easily. The rainy seasons, with their howling winds and pelting showers, forced him to stay indoors, and the enveloping dampness aggravated his rheumatism. Cut off from family and friends and from the security and comfort of Boston, he suffered from intense isolation, finding his new life in Koloa lonesome and "dull as death." And the people of the new land had not been as pliant as he had hoped: they were difficult to manage and often drove him to despair. They seemed to resist him at almost every point. They were also more intelligent than he had assumed, able to avoid work and to extract extra compensation in creative and devious ways. Physically exhausted from his constant struggle with his workers, Hooper vented his frustrations to Ladd and Company in 1838: "No galley slave looks forward to the day when he is to be made free with half so much satisfaction as I do when I shall bid a *final* adieu to intercourse with Hawaiians! Gracious Anticipations!"[24]

A year later Hooper was granted his wish, but he left behind him, in Koloa, a place transformed. In a sense Hooper may remind us of William Shakespeare's Prospero *(The Tempest)* and Mark Twain's Connecticut Yankee. Both Prospero and the Yankee, Hank Morgan, viewed themselves as men of civilization involved in an heroic struggle against primitive society. Prospero had settled on an island and inducted a native, Caliban, into his service, his work force; and Hank Morgan had traveled to another island, Arthurian England, where he had imposed a modern industrial order. Reflecting the expansionist culture portrayed in Prospero and Morgan, Hooper had migrated to an island. There, employing native labor, he had cleared the wild grass from the land in order to plant ordered rows of cane and altered the very character of the tiny hamlet of Koloa, bringing to it the dark smoke and the loud and dissonant mechanical sounds of a modern factory. Seeking both to earn corporate profits for Ladd and Company and to liberate natives from their traditional society, he had integrated economic and moral motives. He had removed natives from their farms and villages to his plantation and offered them housing, medical care, and a store stocked with consumer goods. More important, Hooper had opened the way for the development of a corporate-dominated sugar economy and a paternalistic racial and class hierarchy in the islands.

Elsewhere in the world—Jamaica, Cuba, Haiti, Puerto Rico—white men had already established plantations for the cultivation of sugar cane. But while they had enslaved both the indigenous and imported populations as agricultural workers, Hooper had employed both natives and Chinese as free or wage-earning laborers in order to produce sugar as a cash crop. His invoices for 1837–1838 showed that he had shipped to Honolulu 30 tons of sugar and 170 barrels of molasses—a small but nonetheless portentous beginning of a new plantation economy which would penetrate traditional Hawaiian society like an "entering wedge."

"King Sugar"

After William Hooper's departure the Koloa Plantation continued to increase its production of sugar and also began to attract widespread attention. On 30 September 1846 the *Sandwich Island News*, reporting the plantation's profitable sugar output, welcomed the introduction of the new sugar industry into the Hawaiian economy. Four years later the Reverend Daniel Dole visited the Koloa Plantation and was impressed with its success. "The plantation," he reported to a friend, "has been very profitable the past year; the sugar made being worth $20,000 and the expenses being less than 1/2 this sum." In 1857 the Koloa Plantation received international recognition when *De Bow's Review* of New Orleans published an article on the Sandwich Islands, which described the operation and the potential of the Koloa Plantation: "It employs one hundred native and twenty Chinese field laborers, and produces about two hundred tons of sugar per annum; with proper machinery it is capable of yielding five hundred."[25]

As Hooper had hoped, the Koloa Plantation was drawing foreign investors into the sugar business and spawning other plantations in the islands. In 1864, on a windward promontory opposite a small off-shore island that would come to be called "Chinaman's Hat" because of its shape, the first sugar plantation on the island of Oahu was founded. In her memoirs, Elizabeth Wilder recalled how her father and husband had moved their families to Kualoa where they erected a stone chimney for the sugar mill: "Fields were fenced and ploughed for the cane, small flumes were put up, Chinese coolies imported as laborers. . . ." The same year, the *Pacific Commercial Advertiser* excitedly described a similar development occurring on the island of Maui: "What a change has taken place in Waikapu within two years! Where there were a few taro-patches . . . a village has sprung up, with its sugar mill and buildings, its waving cane fields and busy laborers, scattering industry, thrift and contentment everywhere. Here, where a few hundred dollar's worth of taro was formerly raised, fifty thousand dollars worth of sugar may now annually be made and sent to market."[26]

The cultivation of cane was spreading rapidly throughout the archipelago, from Kauai to the Big Island. Like Cuba and Puerto Rico, Hawaii had the essential natural conditions for growing sugar cane: rich soil, warm climate, and an abundance of water. Aware of Hawaii's agricultural potential, the editor of the *Pacific Commercial Advertiser* predicted in 1864 that sugar would be the "great staple of the islands." On Kauai alone, there were eight plantations by 1877: Koloa, Lihue, Kilauea, Hanalei, Grove Farm, Eleele, Kapaa, and Kawaihau. Surveying the proliferation of plantations and the rise of the new industry, the editor of the *Hawaiian Gazette* proclaimed: "It is apparent that Sugar is destined most emphatically to be 'King.' "[27]

One of the crucial developments that led to the enthronement of "King Sugar" was the Great Mahele of 1848, which destroyed the traditional system of land ownership in Hawaii. Previously, all lands were owned by the king, and foreigners were not permitted to purchase or lease land on terms that would justify large capital investments. The lease of land to Ladd and Company for the Koloa Plantation was an exception. During the 1840s American missionaries promoted the idea of private landownership for commoners as a means of encouraging them to become thrifty and industrious; American businessmen meanwhile pressed for changes that would allow them to secure land on a long-term basis. In 1846 American advisers successfully persuaded the Hawaiian government to appoint a Board of Land Commissioners headed by a planter to register land claims and to settle land disputes. The Board revolutionized landownership in the islands when it instituted the 1848 Great Mahele (division), which apportioned the lands of Hawaii to the crown, government, chiefs, and people. Then in 1850 the government enacted a land law extending to foreign residents the right to acquire and hold land fee simple. Subsequently lands under private ownership were rapidly transferred from the native population to the haoles: land speculators and sugar growers paid minimal sums for large tracts of land to chiefs eager to get rich quickly, and acquired smaller holdings through the courts from commoners unfamiliar with western concepts of land and new legal requirements such as applications for land deeds and payment of land taxes. By 1890, three out of four privately held acres were owned by haoles or their corporations. Forty years later the census revealed the continuance of this concentration of land under white ownership. It showed that of the 5,955 farm units, 633 were owned, managed, or leased by haoles, 510 by Hawaiians, 4,191 by Japanese, and 335 by Chinese. But haole individuals and corporations controlled 2,579,733 acres, which were, according to Lawrence Fuchs, more than 16 times the acreage controlled by Hawaiians and part-Hawaiians, more than 45 times Japanese-American holdings, and more than 140 times the amount of land held by Chinese.[28]

The availability of land for the expansion of sugar cultivation was timely: in 1848 the discovery of gold in California and the new influx of population on the Pacific coast created a new market for food products shipped from Hawaii. For example, exports to California from the Port of Koloa from 1 July 1850 to 30 June 1851 included 1 goat, 50 cattle, 130 swine, 542 turkeys, 1,017 fowls, 75 barrels of onions, 360 barrels of sweet potatoes, 1,000 barrels of squashes, 40 barrels of yams, 353 gallons of syrup, 2,851 gallons of molasses, and 26,063 pounds of sugar. Celebrating the bonanza the California gold rush had brought to the islands, the Royal Hawaiian Agricultural Society depicted the new prosperity: "Our coffee and sugar no longer remain piled in our warehouses. Our fruits and vegetables no longer decay in the spot where they were grown. We are not even compelled to seek for them a market, but clamorous purchasers come to our very doors and carry off our supplies."[29]

The boom quickly subsided after 1851, however, and the demand for Hawaiian foodstuffs was neither as steady nor reliable as the Royal Hawaiian Agricultural Society had so optimistically predicted. Ten years later, however, the Civil War in the United States boosted the price of sugar from 4 cents per pound in 1861 to a high of 25 cents in 1864. Sugar production responded quickly to the new prices, and sugar exports increased from 572 to 8,865 tons. A more important turning point for the profitability of sugar occurred in 1875, when the United States and Hawaii concluded the Reciprocity Treaty. Under the terms of the treaty, Hawaii was granted the right to export sugar, duty free, to the United States. The treaty set off an investment hysteria in Hawaii. "It may be said that the speculation in cane-growing is becoming quite a *furore*, not to say that it is rapidly progressing towards the incipient stage of a regular mania," the *Pacific Commercial Advertiser* reported in 1877. "Thus we hear, upon all sides, of persons heretofore engaged in multifarious businesses, professional men, clerks, employers, in short, individuals representing all classes of the community—talking of making a venture in cane culture."[30]

The "mania" was not economically irrational. Reciprocity returned huge profits to the Hawaiian sugar planters: it enabled them to sell their duty-free sugar in the tariff-protected American sugar market at the duty-paid price rather than a discounted price, adding two cents per pound duty to their sugar and raising their margin of profit. In 1898 the annexation of Hawaii to the United States guaranteed Hawaiian access to the duty-protected American sugar market and the continuation of high profits for the Hawaiian sugar industry. Cousequently the industry paid enormous dividends. Plantations usually averaged more than 10 percent in annual dividends on capitalization, and some of them exceeded this rate of return. The Hawaiian Commercial and Sugar Company paid annual dividends of 16 percent or more during a nine-year period; the Kekaha Plantation paid a 45 percent dividend in 1911, 40 percent in 1916, and 49 percent in 1920. The Lihue Plantation, incorporated in 1892 at $700,000, doubled the value of its capital stock within six years. In 1910 it paid a dividend of 100 percent and raised its capitalization to over two million dollars. Six years later the Lihue Plantation paid a 60 percent dividend, and represented a capitalization of three million dollars.[31]

Due to the Great Mahele, the Gold Rush, the American Civil War, and the Reciprocity Treaty, the Hawaiian sugar industry experienced meteoric success. Sugar production increased from Hooper's 30 tons for 1837–1838 to 375 tons in 1850, 572 tons in 1860, and 9,392 tons in 1870. Ten years later sugar production soared to 31,792 tons and continued to climb to 129,899 tons in 1890, 298,544 tons in 1900, 518,127 tons in 1910, and 556,871 tons in 1920. The value of exported sugar in 1877 was $1,800,248; in 1920 it had risen to $119,490,663. Sugar was Hawaii's most important export, virtually its only export: in 1897, for example, sugar exports represented $15.4 million out of an export total of $16.2 million. The number of laborers and of acres under sugar cultivation paralleled the expansion of sugar production. Between 1875 and 1910 the plantation work force increased more than thirteen times, from 3,260 to 43,917. Meanwhile cultivated plantation lands multiplied nearly eighteen times, or from 12,000 acres to 214,000 acres, and the number of plantations jumped from 20 to 52.[32]

Corporate consolidation accompanied this tremendous growth of the sugar industry. Five corporations dominated sugar production in Hawaii: of the total tonnage of sugar produced in 1920, American Factors controlled 29 percent, C. Brewer 26 percent, Alexander and Baldwin 23 percent, Castle and Cooke 10 percent, and T. H. Davies 6 percent. These corporations, known as the "Big Five," also developed extensive control in all other areas of the Hawaiian economy, including pineapple production, the retail merchandise business, electric power, telephone communication, railroad transportation, steamship lines, banking, and later the tourist industry. The sugar kingdom contained a formidable network of corporations—the California and Hawaiian Sugar Refinery, Bank of Hawaii, Inter-Island Steam Navigation Company, Matson Navigation Company, Oahu Railroad and Land Company, Honolulu Rapid Transit Company, Honolulu Gas Company, Hawaiian Electric Company, and Liberty House.[33]

The pattern of corporate consolidation and control that developed in Hawaii prompted the United States Commissioner of Labor to report in 1905: "Directly or indirectly all industries in the territory of Hawaii are dependent upon the sugar industry—the social, the economic, and the political structure of the islands is built upon a foundation of sugar." And six years later, journalist Ray Stannard Baker described the awesome extent of corporate domination of Hawaii: "Hawaii has been called . . . the Paradise of the Pacific. But it is a paradise not only of natural beauties and wonders; it is also a paradise of modern industrial combination. In no part of the United States is a single industry so predominant as the sugar industry is in Hawaii, and nowhere else, perhaps, has the centralized control of property reached a state of greater perfection." But to achieve such perfection, such predominance, the sugar industry required a vast supply of labor. William Hooper had projected such a need and had initiated the development of a multiethnic and transnational plantation labor system. To expand their acreage and production, planters inducted into their work force not only laborers from Hawaii but also from China, Japan, Portugal, Norway, Germany, Korea, Puerto Rico, the Philippines, and even Russia.[34]

II
The Uprooted

The Making of a Multiethnic Society

"Get labor first," planters said, "and capital will follow." But they found that labor was scarce in the islands, and the need for it became their most worrisome preoccupation. Due mainly to the ravishes of diseases brought to Hawaii by foreigners, the indigenous population had precipitously decreased from 300,000 in 1778 to 71,000 in 1853. Many Hawaiians were also leaving the islands to work in California, and planters feared such emigration was reducing further the supply of local labor. In 1850 the king tried to aid the distressed planters by prohibiting emigration to California, declaring that the native population was diminishing and that the labor shortage was a serious problem for the planters. Planters also tried to induct Hawaiians coercively into their labor force. In 1869 the editor of the *Pacific Commercial Advertiser* demanded the strict enforcement of the vagrancy law in order to expand the supply of native laborers: "If only we could compel our idlers, loafers or vagrants . . . to work, for their own good, and for the good of the kingdom, we would at once have a supply of perhaps 5,000 able-bodied men and women."[1]

But planters knew that the 1850 prohibition of emigration and the enforcement of the vagrancy law would not solve their labor problem, and they had already begun to scour the world in search of new sources of labor. As early as 1850 they founded the Royal Hawaiian Agricultural Society and called for the introduction of "coolie labor from China to supply the places of the rapidly decreasing native population." Shortly after the arrival of the first Chinese contract laborers in 1852, the president of the society predicted: "We shall find Coolie labor to be far more certain, systematic, and economical, [sic] than that of the native. They are prompt at the call of the bell, steady in their work, quick to learn, and . . . will accomplish more [than Hawaiian laborers]." In 1874 planters argued that the decrease in the native population had intensified the demand for labor and boosted wages. "The planter now pays an average of $8 per month with food," they calculated; "or say $12 is the whole average cost of every plantation hand in the country, which is somewhat more than the price of labor in Mauritius, the Philippine Islands, Java, Cuba, and other sugar producing countries." By this time sugar growers had begun to import thousands of Chinese to expand their labor force and keep wages low; but the Chinese did not turn out to be the final solution to the labor problem in Hawaii. Planters found that the Chinese did not usually remain on the plantations: after they had completed the terms of their labor contracts, most of them returned to China or moved to Honolulu. Faced with the need to import Chinese continuously to maintain the size of their work force, planters sent recruiters to other countries in Asia, as well as Europe, to find more permanent and reliable laborers.[2]

In their worldwide search for labor, planters viewed workers as commodities necessary for the operation of the plantation. They depended on the Honolulu agencies or mercantile houses such as Theo. H. Davies and Company, Castle and Cooke, and H. Hackfeld and Company (renamed American Factors during World War I) to meet their various plantation needs. In their business correspondence, they submitted requisitions, lists of orders for men and materials.

On 22 August 1889, for example, Theo. H. Davies and Company sent C. McLennan, manager of the Laupahoehoe Plantation, a memorandum that acknowledged receipt of an order for:

tobacco
portuguese labourers. We have ordered 20 men for you.
lumber
7 ft. iron bar
wool mattress
olive oil

On 2 July 1890, the Davies Company wrote McLennan regarding an order for bonemeal, canvas, "Japanese laborers," macaroni, and a "Chinaman." A letter from the Davies Company to McLennan on 3 January 1898 confirmed a list of orders, which included: "DRIED BLOOD [fertilizer]." "LABORERS. We will book your order for 75 Japanese to come as soon as possible." "MULES & HORSES." Similar memoranda filled the business correspondence of other agencies. On 12 October 1894 William G. Irwin wrote to George C. Hewitt of the Hutchinson Plantation to acknowledge receipt of orders for pipe coverings, insulators, bolts, bone meal (300 tons), and Chinese labor (40 men). A letter dated 5 May 1908 from the vice president of H. Hackfeld and Company to George Wilcox of Grove Farm Plantation had itemized sections, listed alphabetically, for "Fertilizer" and "Filipinos."[3]

Although planters placed orders for labor as they would a commodity or tool, they were not unaware of the workers' nationalities or ethnicities. In fact they systematically developed an ethnically diverse plantation working class in order to create divisions among their laborers and therefore reinforce management control. Robert Hall, manager of the Niulii Plantation, complained about the frequent occurrence of strikes on plantations where workers were mostly of one nationality, and recommended a "judicious mixture [of nationalities to] . . . modify the effect of a strike." Manager George F. Renton of the Hawi Plantation warned his fellow planters that strikes would occur as long as workers could combine, and urged them to employ as many nationalities as possible on each plantation and thus "offset" the power of any one nationality. George H. Fairfield, manager of the Makee Sugar Company, stated the planters' divide-and-rule strategy even more bluntly: "Keep a variety of laborers, that is different nationalities, and thus prevent any concerted action in case of strikes, for there are few, if any, cases of Japs, Chinese, and Portuguese entering into a strike as a unit."[4]

During the early 1880s, as sugar planters increasingly relied on Chinese laborers, they realized they had created another problem —a predominantly Chinese working class. To correct this imbalance, they introduced Portuguese workers. "We need them," the *Planters' Monthly* declared, "especially as an offset to the Chinese; not that the Chinese are undesirable—far from it—but we lay great stress on the necessity of having our labor mixed. By employing different nationalities, there is less danger of collusion among laborers, and the employers . . . secure better discipline." Meanwhile the Hawaiian government apprehensively noticed that the Chinese had become a large alien element, constituting one-fourth of the population in the islands. In 1883 the government restricted

Chinese entry to six hundred immigrants in any consecutive three-month period. Three years later the entry of all unskilled Chinese was prohibited. But by then planters had already begun the massive importation of Japanese laborers, as "the principle check upon the Chinese, in keeping down the price of labor."[5]

Within a few years, however, the majority of the plantation laborers were Japanese, and the planters suddenly found themselves switching back to Chinese workers. Fearful the Japanese were "getting too much of an upper hand in the labor market" of the islands, planters renewed the importation of Chinese to reduce their dependency on Japanese labor. They thought "discipline would be easier and labor more tractable if Chinese were present or obtainable in sufficient numbers to play off against the Japanese in case of disputes." In their business correspondence, planters stated frankly the political purpose for importing Chinese labor. George C. Hewitt, manager of the Hutchinson Plantation, wrote to William G. Irwin and Company on 16 March 1896: "Our order for *40 Japs*—given you in our letter of the 6th inst., is now *void*. 25 Chinese, which are expected to arrive in April will fill all our back orders for labor to date." A few months later, H. Hackfeld and Company informed George Wilcox of the Grove Farm Plantation: "Regarding the proportion of Chinese and Japanese laborers we beg to advise, that the Hawaiian Sugar Planters' Association and the Bureau of Immigration have agreed upon 2/3rd of the former and 1/3 of the latter. For your *private* information we mention, that the reason for this increasing the percentage of the Chinese laborers is due to the desire of breaking up the preponderance of the Japanese element."[6]

In 1900, however, planters could no longer import Chinese laborers, for Hawaii had been annexed to the United States and federal laws prohibiting Chinese immigration had been extended to the new territory. Worried the "Japs" were "getting too numerous," planters scrambled for new sources of labor. "There is a movement on foot," wrote the director of H. Hackfeld and Company to George Wilcox of the Grove Farm Plantation on 22 December 1900, "to introduce Puerto Rican laborers, as also some Italians, Portuguese, and Negroes from the South. . . . We would ask you to let us know at your earliest convenience how many laborers of each nationality you need." Planter John Hind had already visited the Southern states and had returned "fully convinced of the feasibility of bringing Negroes to the islands as field hands." And in 1901, two hundred Blacks from Tennessee were brought to Hawaii.[7]

By then sugar growers had already begun to scan the horizon of the labor market in Asia, and to view Korea as a potential new source of labor. On 19 November 1896, for example, Theo. H. Davies and Company wrote to C. McLennan: "It has been proposed that the planters should have another source from which to obtain Asiatic laborers, lest the supply of Chinese or Japanese should be interfered with so that it might become impossible for us to get any one or either nationality. The source from which it is suggested that we get a new supply is Corea." Shortly after the annexation of Hawaii, sugar planters and their business agents in Honolulu developed a plan to import a trial shipment of Koreans and "pit" them against the "excess of Japanese." The introduction of Koreans, planters stated in their correspondence, was necessary in order to make certain the Japanese laborers would not be "so independent in their relations with their managers and bosses" and would not attempt to form "a combination to put up wages."[8]

Determined to "mix the labor races" and develop a work force divided "about equally between two Oriental nationalities," planters began to import Korean laborers in 1902. A month after the arrival of 102 Koreans in January 1903, Walter Giffard, secretary and treasurer of William G. Irwin and Company, predicted: "The Korean immigration scheme which has been inaugurated will in due course give us an element which will go far towards not only assisting labor requirements but will be of great service in counteracting the evil effects in the labor market caused by too great a preponderance of Japanese." The director of Theo. H. Davies and Company wrote McLennan: "Corean laborers must be introduced here in small numbers so that we may not be depending so exclusively on Japanese." More importantly, he added, the Koreans were "not likely to combine with the Japanese at any attempt at strikes." The manager of the Hutchinson Sugar Plantation, angry at Japanese workers for demanding higher wages and leaving the plantation for the mainland, asked William G. Irwin and Company to send him Korean laborers soon: "In our opinion, it would be advisable, as soon as circumstances permit, to get a large number of Koreans in the country at say $12.50 a month, and drive the Japs out."[9]

But the sugar planters' hopes to use Koreans to drive out the "Japs" were dashed in 1905 when the Korean government terminated Korean emigration. A year later, after a Japanese strike at Waipahu on Oahu, the editor of the *Pacific Commercial Advertiser* urged planters to find an alternative source of Asian labor: "To discharge every Jap and put on newly-imported laborers of another race would be a most impressive object lesson to the little brown men on all the plantations." A few months later, the sugar planters sent Albert F. Judd to the Philippines to initiate the importation of Filipino laborers, and, on 20 December 1906, he personally led the first fifteen Filipinos down the gangplank of the S. S. *Doric* in Honolulu. As he displayed them on the dock, Judd announced: If the Filipino were treated right, he would be a "first-class laborer," "possibly not as good as the Chinaman or the Jap, but steady, faithful and willing to do his best for any boss for whom he has a liking." The manager of the Olaa Plantation, where the first Filipino laborers were sent, reported that he was pleased with the newcomers and recommended that more Filipinos be added to the plantation's labor force in order to bolster the "Filipino colony."[10]

Planters followed the course charted for them by Judd. The Gentlemen's Agreement of 1907 restricted the migration of Japanese laborers to the United States, and the Japanese strike of 1909 demonstrated to the planters their dangerous dependency on a predominantly Japanese work force. Consequently sugar growers saw the Philippines, which had been annexed to the United States at the end of the Spanish–American War in 1898, as the only available source of a permanent labor supply. Recruiting Filipinos by the thousands, planters used them in the same way as they had earlier used the Chinese and Koreans: to control and discipline Japanese plantation workers. The manager of the Hawaiian Agricultural Company, for example, complained to C. Brewer and Company about the high wages the Japanese on his plantation were demanding. On 7 August 1913, he wrote to the agency in Honolulu: "If possible for you to arrange it I should very much like to get say 25 new Filipinos to put into our day gang. . . . In this way perhaps we can stir up the Japs a bit." Twenty days later he wrote again to C. Brewer and Company, stating he was very pleased to receive the shipment of thirty Filipinos, and hoped he could use them to bring the Japanese workers to "their senses."[11]

The multiracial labor supply, which planters had developed for economic and political purposes, had far reaching effects on the ethnicity of society in Hawaii. This relationship between the recruitment of labor and the ethnicity of the population may be seen in a study of employment and population patterns. In 1872 Hawaiians and part-Hawaiians constituted 82.8 percent of the total plantation work force of 3,846, while the Chinese represented only 11.5 percent (446 laborers). Within ten years, however, the Chinese had replaced the Hawaiians as the primary source of labor: 49.1 percent (5,037 laborers) were Chinese, and only 25.1 percent (2,575 laborers) were from the native population. During the 1880s Japanese laborers quickly outnumbered the Chinese: the Japanese labor population increased dramatically from 0.1 percent of the work force (15 laborers) in 1882 to 63.3 percent (13,019) in 1892 to 73.4 percent (31,029) in 1902. Meanwhile Portuguese laborers, numbering only 637 in 1882, constituted 12.3 percent of the work force (2,526 laborers) in 1892 and 6.3 percent (2,669 laborers) in 1902. A year later, Koreans entered plantation employment, and within five years, 4.5 percent of the entire work force (2,125 laborers) were Korean. Only a small handful of Filipinos (141, or 0.3 percent of all laborers) worked on the plantations in 1908. By 1912 Filipino laborers constituted 9.7 percent of the plantation work force; eight years later, 29.4 percent of plantation laborers (13,061) were Filipino.

Population patterns followed patterns of labor recruitment. In 1853 Hawaiians and part-Hawaiians represented 97.1 percent of the population, or 71,019 out of 73,137 inhabitants, while Caucasians represented only 2.2 percent or 1,600, and Chinese only 0.5 percent or 364. In 1890 each group constituted 45.1 percent, 6.9 percent, and 18.6 percent, respectively, while two new groups, the Japanese and the Portuguese, each formed 14 percent of island society. Thirty years later Hawaiians and part-Hawaiians made up only 16.3 percent of the population, while Caucasians represented 7.7 percent, Chinese 9.2 percent, Japanese 42.7 percent, Portuguese 10.6 percent, Puerto Ricans 2.2 percent, Koreans 1.9 percent, and Filipinos 8.2 percent.

At the center of the making of modern Hawaii with its diversity of races and ethnic cultures was the sugar industry. In their prodigious search for foreign laborers and in their pursuit of a strategy to divide and control, planters had created a multiracial and multiethnic society in the islands. Most of the laborers were recruited from Asia—China, Japan, Korea, and the Philippines; thousands more came from Portugal and Puerto Rico, and several hundred others from Germany and Norway. Wherever their places of origin, all of them had to make the crossing to the islands—a voyage that took them far away from their homelands and represented the beginnings of a new people and a new Hawaii. Desperate, courageous, and hopeful, they left their homes, families, the graves of their ancestors, and familiar landmarks—particular trees, rocks, and hills that had circumscribed their world and their existence. Theirs was a radical action. Many of them had never even stepped beyond the boundaries of their villages; little in their experience had prepared them for the passage to Hawaii or for plantation labor there. Yet they uprooted themselves. Though they were recruited by the agencies to fill orders placed by the planters and to be pitted against each other, they came for their own reasons. As they traveled across seemingly endless watery prairies toward the islands, they carried their own visions of the new land and their future.

Tan Heung Shan

Long before they had heard about Hawaii as a place to find work on sugar plantations, the people of the province of Kwangtung in China had referred to the islands as "Tan Heung Shan" or the 'Fragrant Sandalwood Hills.' They thought the islands had mountains covered with thick forests of sandalwood trees, which they imported to make incense for their temples. Their demand for the scented wood was so great that it kept a small fleet of American ships busy plying the water routes between China and Hawaii in the early nineteenth century. Some of the Chinese worked as sailors on these trading vessels and made their way to the islands. Drifting from job to job, they eventually found themselves entering the plantation work force.

Meanwhile, in their homeland, certain developments set off a massive exodus from Kwangtung to countries all over the world, including the United States and the Kingdom of Hawaii. The thousands of Chinese who went to Hawaii to labor on the plantations were fleeing from turmoil, which seemed ubiquitous in their war-torn province. They had witnessed the violence of the Opium War of 1839–1842 as the British East India Company forcefully imposed the drug trade in China. They had also experienced the ravages of the Taiping Rebellion from 1850–1864, and reeled from the destruction of some twenty million people. In the 1860s they had suffered from the internecine strife between the Punti and Hakka clans over possession of the fertile delta lands.

In this world of political and social chaos, where suffering was often intensified by famine and flood, many people of Kwangtung listened intently to stories about Hawaii and wondered whether they would be able to find a better future in Tan Heung Shan. Many years later in Hawaii, an old Chinese immigrant remembered the hardships of life in the old country:

> There were four in our family, my mother, my father, my sister and me. We lived in a two room house. One was our sleeping room and the other served as parlor, kitchen and dining room. We were not rich enought to keep pigs or fowls, otherwise, our small house would have been more than overcrowded.
>
> How can we live on six baskets of rice which were paid twice a year for my father's duty as a night watchman? Sometimes the peasants have a poor crop then we go hungry. During the day my father would do other small jobs for the peasants or carpenters. My mother worked hard too for she went every day to the forest to gather wood for our stove. . . .
>
> Sometimes we went hungry for days. My mother and me would go over the harvested rice fields of the peasants to pick the grains they dropped. . . . We had only salt and water to eat with the rice.[12]

Another Chinese immigrant recalled how a violent feud had impoverished his family and forced him into contract labor:

> In a bloody feud between the Chang family and the Oo Shak village we lost our two steady workmen. Eighteen villagers were hired by Oo Shak to fight against the huge Chang family, and in the battle two men lost their lives protecting our pine forests. Our village, Wong Jook Long, had a few resident Changs. After the bloodshed, we were called for our men's lives, and the greedy, impoverished villagers grabbed fields, forest, food and everything, including newborn pigs, for payment. We were left with nothing, and in disillusion we went to Hong Kong to sell ourselves as contract laborers.[13]

Leaving their farms and villages, the Chinese migrants traveled on foot or small boats to the ports of Canton, Whampoa, Macao, and Hong Kong. There they learned from notices posted in the streets that laborers were needed in Hawaii and that they could find work in the islands for much better wages than in China. The migrants were mostly men, for the plantations wanted male laborers and Hawaii was viewed by the migrants as a place to earn money rather than to settle and raise families. Recruited as contract laborers by emigration brokers representing Hawaiian sugar planters, the migrants were taken to the wharves and found themselves struggling through huge crowds to board the ships.[14]

"Everyone was afraid that he would be left behind," said one migrant, "so as soon as the way was opened everyone just rushed to get on board and when he was finally aboard he was all out of breath." On the ship, they found themselves standing in a cramped steerage with hundreds of other laborers. Many of them became seasick and nauseous, and the steerage was soon transformed into an intolerably foul smelling cage. At night they were allowed on deck where they gasped for fresh air and slept on mats. Always they feared the possibility of a smallpox contagion.[15]

The voyage by sail took fifty-six days, sometimes as long as seventy days. But finally Chinese passengers sighted the mountains of the famous sandalwood islands. They felt relief and excitement, then frustration and impatience, as they learned that arrival did not mean the end of confinement. They disembarked and were placed directly in quarantine facilities, where they were kept under observation for smallpox. Sometimes the quarantine grounds were overcrowded, and on one occasion, 597 Chinese passengers were forced to remain on board their diseased-infected ship for an unbearable two months after it had reached Honolulu. In 1881 750 Chinese laborers bound for the Spreckelsville Plantation arrived on board the German steamer *Lydia*. Informed they would be placed in quarantine, the passengers refused to leave the ship and became mutinous. Finally an armed force was sent on board to quell the disturbance: 60 resisters were arrested and the rebellious Chinese were forcefully transferred to quarantine.

After the long wait in quarantine, Chinese laborers were taken into Honolulu. There they were sometimes allowed to practice gymnastics; according to the *Pacific Commercial Advertiser*, the Chinese transported to the islands on board the *Petronila* were such skilled gymnasts they would have put to "the blush" many of the local sports enthusiasts. The Chinese who had arrived by the *Lasker* in 1880 wore traditional clothing and new white felt hats.

One newly arrived Chinese worker was surprised to see that most of the people in Honolulu were either white or brown. He did not understand what they were saying, but he realized by the sounds that there were "two different languages—one was spoken by the white men and the other by the brown people." In 1879 a group of Chinese laborers found themselves welcomed by King Kalakaua himself. *"I would there were twenty millions more of them,"* the king declared. "With Chinese ingenuity, industry, and cheap labor, we shall be able to compete in trade with the rest of the nations in the struggle for national existence."[16]

After their arrival in the city, Chinese workers were herded into a labor market for assignment to the plantations. They were marched to a yard near the customhouse and guarded by soldiers. The planters and their agents inspected the laborers and made their selections. The Chinese laborers were then made to sign labor contracts that specified the period of service required, wages, board, housing, medical care, and other terms. A labor contract of 1870, for example, stated:

Honolulu, Hawaiian Islands

_____1870

I _____ Party of the first part, a native of China, a free and voluntary Passenger to the Sandwich Islands, do bind myself to labor on any of the said Islands, at any work that may be assigned me, by the Party of the Second part, or their agents, upon the terms and in the manner within specified, for the term of Five Years from this date.

_____ Party of the second part, do agree and bind themselves, or agents, to conform fully to the within Agreement,

Witness_____ Signed_____

_____ Signed_____

MEMORANDUM OF AGREEMENT by the Agent of the Hawaiian Government.

No Contract can be made in Hongkong.

All Emigrants must go as Free Passengers.

Each Emigrant shall be given him, 1 heavy Jacket, 1 light Jacket, 1 Water-proof Jacket, 2 pair Pants, 1 pair Shoes, 1 pair Stockings, 1 Hat, 1 Mat, 1 Pillow, 1 Blanket.

A Present of Ten Dollars to be paid the day before the ship sails. In no instance will any deduction from wages be made for Clothes or Money advanced in Hongkong.

A free passage to Sandwich Islands, with food, water, and Medical care, given each Emigrant.

The Master to pay all Government personal Taxes.

All Children to be taught in the Public Schools, free of any expense to the Parents.

Each Man to receive $6 for each month labor performed of 26 days.

Each Woman to receive $5 for each month labor performed of 26 days.

The wages to be paid in Silver, upon the first Saturday after the end of the month.

No labor shall be exacted upon the Sabbath, only in case of emergency, when it shall be paid for extra.

All emigrants who are employed as House Servants, when their duties compel them to labor Sundays and evenings, shall receive for men 7 dollars per month, for women 6 dollars per month.

Three days Holiday shall be given each Emigrant at Chinese New Year and a present of $2.

These three days time to be counted the same as if employed.

In all cases, the Master to provide good and sufficient food and comfortable House Room.

In case of Sickness, Medical attendance and care free.

No wages during illness.

Each Emigrant to find his own Bed clothing.

Each Emigrant, upon arrival in the Sandwich Islands, to sign a contract (to work for such Master as may be chosen for him by the Government Agent) for the term of Five Years from the time of entering upon his duties, to work faithfully and cheerfully according to the laws of the Country, which compel both Master and Servant to fulfill their Contracts.

Families shall not be separated, the Government particularly desire that men will take their wives.

Every Emigrant shall have all the rights and protection under the law that are given to any Citizen of the Country.

At the expiration of the five years each Emigrant has a right to remain in the Country, or to leave it.

> Saml. G. Wilder
> H. H. M. Commissioner of
> Immigration.[17]

The Chinese who had signed labor contracts in Honolulu had traveled over 4,000 miles to work in the cane fields and sugar mills of Hawaii, far away from their families and homes in Kwangtung. As they stood on the shores of Tan Heung Shan and gazed at the sea toward China, they felt a wave of nostalgia sweep through them. Many kept hearing the voices of loved ones left behind and the folksong of their wives waiting for their return: "Yet jook, yee jook" 'One admonition, two admonition.'

> Ngai k'iou gnia, li k'oi ho fei saa fui li
> Ngai moun dout li pi chjang che dwon chong dout
> Ngai chee si mong gnia hang hao youn
> Sam nian chew nen jie fui ka
> Ngai k'iou gnia, put yao ben sim
> Gnia yao jow goo ka t'in
> Mi kae gngt fet pan kae gnet ki sin fui li
> Gni fet sam nian noui ngai si mong fon niang gnia fui ka

> I beg of you, after you depart, to come back soon,
> Our separation will be only a flash of time;
> I only wish that you would have good fortune,
> In three years you would be home again.

> Also, I beg of you that your heart won't change,
> That you keep your heart and mind on taking care of your family;
> Each month or half a month send a letter home,
> In two or three years my wish is to welcome you home.[18]

The Chinese laborers came as *wah kui* 'sojourners', hoping to return to Kwangtung in five years. From the other side of the world, came Portuguese laborers—seeking not only "good fortune" but also a place to stay.

Terra Nova

As a nine-year-old child living in the Azores in 1881, a Portuguese boy was taken by his father to visit friends every night. Many years later, in Hawaii, he recalled how they talked for long hours and how he had heard them repeatedly say: "Terra Nova, go Terra Nova." He knew his father was planning to leave the Azores Islands, located in the Atlantic Ocean eight hundred miles away from the Portuguese mainland, but he did not know where the new land or Hawaii was. His mother told him it was "some place across the sea [where] . . . plenty of Portuguese was going and get own land and get money to send children to school." His parents sold everything in their home and one day, his father went to a rich man's house and signed papers. But his uncle warned his father: "John, you crazy go 'Terra Nova!' The people [there] just like wild animals. They going eat you up." But the boy's father did not want to remain in the Azores where a poor man had to work so hard and his children "no go to school." He saw that the rich men had splendid homes with hot houses for their pineapples and pretty flowers. They treated poor men like him as if they were "just like nothing," and thought everything was "all right" in the Azores. But everything was not all right for John, and in 1883 he took his family to the new land.[19]

Only six years earlier, William Hillebrand had opened the way for Portuguese immigration to Terra Nova. While visiting the Madeira Islands of Portugal, he wrote a letter to the Hawaiian Minister of the Interior. The Portuguese, he reported, would make excellent plantation workers and help meet Hawaii's need for labor: "Sober, honest, industrious, and peaceable, they combine all the qualities of a good settler, and with all this, they are inured to your climate. Their education and ideas of comfort and social requirements are just low enough to make them contented with the lot of an isolated settler and its attendant privations. . . ." The Portuguese, planters thought, could be imported into the islands as families and offer the sugar industry a more "industrious," "peaceable," and stable work force than the Chinese. By November 1877 the first group of Portuguese had been recruited as contract laborers. They had agreed to work in Hawaii for three years, in return for wages of ten dollars a month (ten hours of labor each day for 26 days), daily rations, lodging, garden ground, medical care, and transportation to the islands. "They are a cleanly looking, well-behaved set, with the old fashioned polite manners of the Portuguese and Spanish races," the *Pacific Commercial Advertiser* announced shortly after their arrival in Honolulu. Comparing the Portuguese to the Chinese immigrants, the newspaper added: "The more we have of this sort of immigration the better. They are, as a race . . . temperate, painstaking, thrifty and law abiding people. They come here to stay, and they do not send their earnings out of the country, as do some other nationalities."[20]

During the 1880s thousands of Portuguese made the crossing to Hawaii. One of them recorded his experiences on board the *Tho-*

mas Bell. On the day his ship was scheduled to sail, João Baptista d'Oliveira wrote in his diary:

November 8, 1887. It was two o'clock in the afternoon. I had just said goodbye to my family, and was approaching the beach of Funchal when I met some of my friends who had come to bid me farewell. Trying to conceal my tears by looking away from them, my eyes rested on some boats being launched which were carrying families who were to board the THOMAS BELL. Hurriedly excusing myself, I soon became a part of them. . . . The ship was now leaving the Port of Funchal. I went up aft . . . leaned against the rail and gazed at the land, knowing in my heart that I would never see it again.

November 9. Going down below deck, I met some of the immigrants and inquired as to how they had passed the night. Some had not fared badly, but others had been quite seasick and had severe headaches.

December 21. We were again becalmed. Not a cloud in the sky was visible. The men and women all went to do their laundry, as was their custom.

At 2:30 the steward caught another albatross . . . and he cleaned it. . . . Some said, "Thanks to God, for things are coming our way. Today, the day of *Santo Thome*, we killed a *porca da Festa* [the pig for Christmas] which was excellent. The enthusiasm was so great that while they were preparing this tasty dish, we heard one of the bachelors singing this song:

> Longe da minha terra,
> (Far from my land,)
> E aqui sem consolacao,
> (And here without consolation,)
> Meu peito receio encerra
> (My heart conceals its apprehension)
> por verse em solidao
> (Because of being in solitude)

> Paciencia. Nao importa.
> (Patience. It doesn't matter.)
> Fadario irei cumprir.
> (I shall wait on fate.)
> Hoje vou-me divertir
> (Today I shall have a good time)
> Por Ver a morte da porca.
> (Seeing the death of a pig.)

Todos folgao de contentos,
(All rejoice and are content,)
E a alegria em todos e,
(Everyone is happy,)
Todos lembrao seus parentes,
(All remember their relatives,)
N'este dia de Sao Thome.
(On this day of St. Thomas.)

January 20. At dawn there was terrific storm, and at nine o'clock a strong wind was accompanied by a heavy rain. . . . The ship's tossing increased and again we had fears of a watery grave.

March 18. At dawn the wind was the same and the heat just as intense. By 6 P.M. the passengers had already stretched out their bedding on the deck. . . . No one could remain below the deck because of the heat and the "soldados ingleses" [red-coats, or bed-bugs] who were bleeding us. They were with us in such great numbers that our bunks were literally decorated with these magnificent soldiers. Their odor was exquisite, a rival to the best of perfumes.

April 11. The news at the break of day was most heartening. We were told that we would be able to see Hawaii as soon as the day cleared. Eager for the first glimpse of our destination, we lined the rails in anticipation of that long-awaited moment. We have been aboard this ship for 155 days now. Small wonder that such a glimpse would create such a stir! And when we did see the outline in the far distance, excitement was everywhere.

At 8 A.M. they buried at sea a two-year old child, the son of Victorino Martin. This unfortunate child had been ill for a long time.

April 12. The islands of Hawaii and Maui were clearly visible at dawn. Gathered at the prow were many passengers who did not forget to thank God for His kindness to them. . . . At 9 A.M. Oahu appeared in view, and at sunset we saw two other islands, Lanai and Molokai.

April 13. It was about 10 A.M. when a tug-boat named *Eweo* arrived and led us into port. . . . At twelve noon, we were visited by many Portuguese. Then all of the passengers brought their luggage up to the deck. It was like Judgment Day for most of us; for once, food was of no importance. Our only concern was to gain entrance into "heaven. . . ."

April 14. It was 4 P.M. when we finally set foot on terra firma, and saw many dark-skinned women who are called "*Canecas*. . . ." One hundred and fifty six days aboard the *Thomas Bell!* What the future

holds for us, God only knows. May he be with us to guide us in the
days that lie ahead![21]

And so Hawaii drew them to its shores. The islands were so far
away from their country that the Portuguese immigrants had to
live on their ships for nearly half a year to get there, to convert the
ships into temporary homes. But what terrible homes they were!
Outside, stormy seas made them sick and threatened to send them
to "watery graves." Inside, below deck, bed-bugs bit and bled
them. Still 11,057 of them, including large numbers of women and
children, migrated to Hawaii between 1877 and 1888. Another
657 came in 1895 and 5,500 between 1906 and 1913. They refused to allow men of wealth in the old country to abuse them, to
treat them "just like nothing." Determined to be something, to own
land, to have their children educated in school, they pulled up
their roots and left their homes to seek a new beginning in a place
they affectionately and hopefully called Terra Nova.

Norwegian Summer

In the fall of 1880, as Chinese and Portuguese laborers boarded
ships bound for Hawaii, Norwegians in the town of Drammen
read newspaper announcements inviting them to emigrate as contract laborers to the Sandwich Islands. The suggestion of migrat-
ing to the other side of the world must have been a startling idea to
the people of Drammen, yet they found themselves drawn to the
announcement placed in their newspapers by Christian L'Orange,
an agent for Castle and Cooke. Many of them were suffering from
economic hardships, and already thousands of their fellow countrymen had emigrated to the United States in search of land and
employment. Within a few weeks, the agent had enlisted 629 Norwegians: 294 unmarried men and boys (over twelve years of age),
53 unmarried women and girls, 78 married couples, and 126 children.[22]

As contract laborers, they had agreed to work in Hawaii for a
three-year period, ten hours a day in the field or twelve hours a day
in the mill for twenty-six days a month. They would be transported to the islands, and there they would be paid monthly wages of
nine dollars and given board, lodging, and medical care for themselves and their families. If they failed to meet the terms of their

contract, however, they would face severe penalties: they could be forced by the courts to pay their employers for loss of work time and to serve double the time lost or as much as one month's extra service. Continued refusal to work would lead to imprisonment. The contract contained terms which the Norwegians considered restrictive, even oppressive, but they were given assurances that life on the plantation would be pleasant, even prosperous. They were told informally they could expect to have free pasture for a cow and a horse. And if they were able laborers, they would eventually have an opportunity to get land for cultivation on a share basis.[23]

Hopeful they would have a chance for a new start in the Sandwich Islands, the Norwegian contract laborers sailed from Drammen in two ships, the *Beta* on 27 October 1880 and the *Musca* on 23 November 1880. According to one eye-witness account, passengers boarding the *Musca* found themselves on a particularly fine looking iron ship of about 700 tons, with berths for 225 persons installed between the decks. When they went down through the hatch into this "floating barracks," they became immersed in "a dimly lit scene of confusion." Men, women, and children were crowded together in different groups. Some of the passengers were kneeling before the ship's chests and writing last farewells to their families and friends; others were passing the time before departure with "a friendly game of cards, or an open flirtation." Worried fathers were tending the babies, while mothers were trying to make the cramped quarters comfortable. Accompanying all of this activity were the "penetrating and irritating screams of small savages, and the melancholy tones of a cast-off violin." Then the passengers saw a pastor coming on board to hold a departure service, and gathered around him. As they listened to the pastor give his blessing and warm farewell, they began to cry, and one couple quickly asked him to marry them before they set sail. The pastor granted them special permission to marry without first reading the banns at church, and conducted the wedding ceremony in the ship's cabin, with the *Musca*'s doctor as the witness. The newlyweds were then assigned space with the rest of the married couples at the center of the storage deck. The unmarried women were located in the quarters aft, and the single men forward.[24]

The passage to Hawaii was an extremely long one, across the North Sea and the Atlantic Ocean, around South America, and

halfway across the Pacific Ocean. The Norwegian contract laborers suffered from stormy seas, tedium, and terrible food. *Beta* passengers found water scarce, and their diet consisted of bread "hard
as a brick and very dark," salt dried fish, barley, peas, flour, and a
little beef or pork served only "now and then." Nine children died
on the *Beta*, most of them from lack of nourishment. Conditions on
board the *Musca* were also harsh, and one of the passengers later
bitterly described the horror they experienced:

> We had not progressed further than the North Sea when we got bad
> meat; for a long while the food consisted of the following: Sundays,
> about 30 ounces of meat, 3 potatoes, 25 cubic inches soup pro per-
> sona. Mondays and Fridays mackerel and soup as above, which was
> cooked with salt fish. Tuesdays, pork and sourkrout [sic]. Wednes-
> days and Saturdays, herring and 3 potatoes pro persona. Thursdays,
> salt meat and bean soup; coffee we had every morning with boiled
> cracked wheat and the same at evenings, the bread was good and
> was served out twice a week—of water we got one quart pro persona
> every day at one o'clock, but if anyone came too late he had to go
> without water that day. All this had been well enough, if the water
> had been clean and fresh, but the most of it was damaged; the water
> was to that degree rotten that it stunk all over the deck when it came
> out of the hold; it had been filled in old, dirty casks, and it looked
> like a soup made of rye bread and beer (dark brown). With this nasty
> water the meat was cooked, and was thereby made very bad. But
> what could we do? Where was the fault? With the captain or the
> authorities in Drammen? If we made any complaint, the answer was
> "it was good enough for slaves—shut up; otherwise we will put you
> in irons and lock you up. . . ." Nobody was punished except one
> man, who was handcuffed and locked up, the others got their backs
> up about that, so we refused to work; our grub was then stopped for
> a day, and we were told that if we did not want to work and help the
> crew, we could go without food, and we were then forced on ac-
> count of weeping wives and small children to give in.[25]

The Norwegians sailing to Hawaii had not expected such abuse
and hardship and drew together for strength and comfort. On the
Beta some of the passengers formed a band and performed vocal
and instrumental music. One of the passengers, a preacher, held
religious services on Sundays. Young men and women developed
romantic relationships during the seemingly interminable trip and
passed away their time making plans for weddings in the islands.
Shortly after the *Beta* had finally reached its destination, the *Ha-*

waiian Gazette amusingly noted: "A long voyage together proved favorable to love-making and twelve or fourteen couples are reported as ready to be married. Preparations for a grand union wedding and reception are in progress, to come off soon."[26]

But wedding plans had to be postponed, for the Norwegians were under labor contracts and were given plantation assignments immediately after they had arrived in Hawaii. The *Beta* passengers were taken to Maalaea Landing on Maui where the planters divided them by lot. They were placed in a line and had numbers pinned on them; then the planters drew corresponding numbers from an urn and the Norwegians were accordingly assigned to plantations on Maui and Hawaii. One of the laborers later wrote about this degrading experience:

> On the 14 Februare' 1881, we arrived after much suffering, to the Sandwich Islands, to a place called Lahaina . . . on the island of Maui. On board came Chr. Lorange, the slave traders' mediator. . . . The same day we proceeded further, to a place . . . situated far from inhabited places. Here the trading should go on and so it did. The following day, our salesman, went ashore and returned with two natives, and six white planters. When they came on board, we were told that they were our owners. . . . In the evening the lottery of us helpless emigrants began, and went on for a day and a night. . . . The following day we were summoned up after namcleers [nomenclatures] and each received a thicket [sic], with different marks, applied to the breast. Some of us received no marks. These were informed that they should go to another island called Hawaii. . . . The following day, the discharge began, all who had the mark came ashore at Maui; but those who had no mark, should stay till the end of the week, when the steamer brought us to our destination.[27]

Theirs had been a long and difficult voyage to Hawaii. The Norwegian laborers had been told Hawaii was a land where the climate was like a perpetual "Norwegian summer" and where oranges, guavas, figs, and mangoes were abundant all year around. They had been assured they could work and save their money in Hawaii, even enter into small business ventures and become their own bosses. But they found the experience of the passage to the islands sobering and shocking, and the Norwegians anxiously wondered what would be in store for them on the plantations.[28]

Altogether only two shiploads of laborers came from Norway; after 1884, scores of ships would carry to Hawaii laborers from Japan.

Hawaii Netsu

The Japanese described it as "Hawaii Netsu"—the emigration "fever" sweeping through the southwestern prefectures of Yamaguchi, Fukuoka, Kumamoto, and Hiroshima in the 1880s. In small villages, recruiting agents for emigration companies depicted Hawaii as a land of eternal summer where people were "sincere and gentle by nature" and "very kind towards strangers." Everyone, it seemed, talked excitedly about going to the islands. Some of them must have had doubts and fears, for they remembered stories about the "Gannen Mono," the first 153 contract laborers who had been taken to Hawaii in 1868: how their ship, the *Scioto*, had encountered a fierce storm which frightened some of the passengers so much they cut off their topknots and threw them into the sea in thanks when the waters had calmed; and how they had suffered much abuse and ill treatment on the plantations. But many prospective emigrants hoped their experiences in Hawaii would be different. They imagined bold possibilities for themselves in Hawaii, the place where they would be able to fulfill dreams of making money and building bright new futures.[29]

Most of the Japanese emigrants were not poor. They were small farmers and tenant farmers, but they were experiencing mounting economic hardships. The southwestern prefectures were in economic difficulty in the late nineteenth century: Hiroshima and Yamaguchi had an average of only 381.895 yen and 489.005 yen per capita, respectively, compared to a national average of 505.755 yen. The farmers did not know these statistics, but they knew the economic crisis was serious. Many villagers were subsisting on tree barks and roots and others were starving to death; food was becoming scarce in the densely populated prefectures. While Oshima County in Yamaguchi Prefecture was an especially acute case, it seemed to highlight the problem of overpopulation: it had a population of 70,000 or an average of 7,000 people for one square *ri*, 2.4 miles, of land. "The depression of trade in Japan has increased month by month and year by year, showing no signs of abatement," editorialized the *Japan Weekly Mail* in December of 1884. "It seems to have come to a climax during the autumn of the present year, for the distress among the agricultural class has reached a point never before attained. Most of the farmers have been unable to pay their taxes, and . . . hundreds of families in one village alone . . . [have been] compelled to sell their property in order to liquidate their debts."[30]

The future in Japan seemed bleak for these farmers in the southwestern prefectures, and the Hawaii Netsu seized many of them. They saw Hawaii as an alternative to moving to the cities in Japan, where they would be inducted into factory labor and forced to live in congested urban housing. Financially distressed farmers saw the Hawaiian Islands as an opportunity to earn a livelihood. Hopefully, as *dekasegi*, laborers who would leave home temporarily to work in a foreign country, they might even succeed in saving one or two hundred dollars by working for three years in the sugar fields and build a nucleus of capital for future enterprise. Indeed, they might even be able to save enough money to purchase land in Japan and become farmers in their homeland once again. Three years of hard labor in faraway cane fields; three years of separation from friends, family, and village seemed to be a small sacrifice to make for the realization of such an ambitious dream.[31]

And so thousands of Japanese decided to become contract laborers and to work in Hawaii for three years for $9 a month, plus food, lodging, and medical care. Most of them were young men: Kasuke Okawa, for example, was only nineteen years old when he left Yamaguchi Prefecture in 1886. Their passage to Hawaii was to be paid by the sugar planters, and they agreed to have 25 percent of their wages deducted from their earnings and deposited in a savings fund for their return passage to Japan. They were told they would be able to save 400 yen in three years. The notion of accumulating so much money in a small span of time had an electrifying appeal to people who knew that a silk mill worker would be able to acquire such a sum only if she worked every day for ten years and saved all of her wages. Thus Hawaii symbolized a new beginning for many farmers, and when the government of Japan announced its intention to fill 600 emigrant slots for the first ship to Hawaii in 1884, it received 28,000 applications.[32]

On 20 January 1885, the initial group of immigrants boarded the *City of Tokyo* at Yokohama: 666 men, 158 women, 69 boys, and 48 girls. Accompanied by Consul Jiro Nakamura, they were divided into groups on the basis of their place of origin, and group leaders were appointed. After the ship had been quarantined for a week at Nagaura, it set sail on January 27. The vessel, reported Nakamura, "encountered no storms or rough weather," but "did not sail well due to the winter seas. There were some who suffered seasickness as well as from other chronic ailments. There were two doctors on board who diagnosed and treated the ill. Those who were too ill to be properly treated in the ship's steerage compartments were transferred to the ship's hospital. In addition to the customary Japanese dishes, special rations of milk, noodles, and rice cakes were served to the immigrants on their voyage across the ocean."[33]

On February 8 the *City of Tokyo* arrived at Honolulu, where the Japanese laborers and their families were taken to the immigration compound near Kakaako. There hula dancers entertained them and King Kalakaua welcomed them personally. The sports-loving king also invited some of them to his palace to demonstrate their fencing skills in a tournament and gave each participant a dollar. Allowed to go sightseeing in groups of tens and twenties, they playfully and curiously toured the city. A few of them put on western-style suits, while most of them wore their traditional attire. Generally the women were dressed in light kimonos and white short Japanese socks, and carried parasols to shade them from the sun. As the newcomers walked through the streets of Honolulu, they were approached by natives who offered gifts of hats and clothes. One group of immigrants stood in front of a huge mansion and peeked inside to look at its furnishings. Several of them were invited in and given a tour by the owner. Some of the immigrants also visited the Royal Hawaiian Hotel, where they "shed their wooden clogs, sandals, slippers, shoes, or whatever else they were wearing, arranged them in neat rows near the entrance, bowed low and went on a tour of the second and third floors, acting as if they were visiting a public hall."[34]

But the Japanese had been transported to Hawaii to labor, not to relax and sightsee, and were promptly made to sign labor contracts and assigned to the plantations. "The manpower shortage in this nation is such that all our people were assigned employment within a few days after arrival," reported Nakamura. "I have heard that many employers have been unable to have their requests filled and are anxiously awaiting the arrival of the next batch of emigrant laborers. . . ." The processing was done effi-

ARRIVAL OF JAPANESE LABORERS
Hawaii State Archives
"I have heard that many employers have been unable to have their
requests filled and are anxiously awaiting the arrival of the next batch
of emigrant laborers."

ciently and quickly, and by February 23 all of the immigrants had
left Honolulu, obligated by labor contract to three years of plantation labor. Meanwhile planters waited impatiently for the "next
batch" of Japanese laborers.[35]

Many more batches of laborers from Japan would arrive in the
islands, as the Hawaii Netsu evoked dreams and hopes among the
people of the southwestern prefectures and as the Sugar Kingdom
demanded more and more labor. After 1887 Japanese laborers paid
for their own passages to Hawaii—an expense of two hundred yen,
or about a hundred dollars. This meant one had to be at least a
member of the farming middle class to be able to afford to work in
Hawaii. Still they came. By 1924, forty years after the first group
had been enlisted as plantation laborers for passage on the *City
of Tokyo*, over two hundred thousand Japanese had migrated to
Hawaii. They had decided to go to a strange and foreign country.

> Huge dreams of fortune
> Go with me to foreign lands,
> Across the ocean.

Yet, as they boarded their ships to begin their courageous sojourn, they felt a loneliness and an emptiness that they had never before experienced.

> With tears in my eyes
> I turn back to my homeland,
> Taking one last look.[36]

Another group of laborers also cried as they left their homeland. But they did so for a different reason: they feared Japan would destroy the political independence of Korea.

Kaeguk Chinch Wi

"We have just received about fifty laborers and their families from Korea," wrote C. M. Cooke of the Hawaiian Sugar Planters' Association (HSPA) on 27 January 1903, shortly after the arrival of the first group of Korean immigrants. "As the people there are in a starving condition we hope that we shall be able to get a number of them as they seem to be just what our Plantations need." Within three years, over seven thousand Koreans—6,048 men, 637 women, and 541 children—made the crossing to the islands. They were farmers, common laborers in port cities, ex-soldiers of the Korean Army, government clerks, students, policemen, miners, domestic servants, and even Buddhist monks. Most of them were urban dwellers. As the Korean migrants sailed from from their homeland, many of them declared: "Kaeguk chinch wi" 'the country is open, go forward.'[37]

For the Korean immigrants, an open country meant a place free from Japanese expansion and domination. They had suffered from two wars—the Sino-Japanese and the Russo-Japanese wars. They fervently resented the repressive Japanese presence, which violated the integrity of their country and restricted their political and economic lives. Hawaii represented political refuge from Japanese imperialism. "There was little or no opportunity for my grandfather to find a job in Korea in those days," a Korean in Hawaii explained many years later. "The Japanese imperial government was controlling Korea at the time and the outlook toward the future was very poor. The Japanese were cruel oppressors and when it was found that the Japanese government was letting people out of the country to work in Hawaii, Mr. Lee was happy to volunteer." For many Koreans, to escape to Hawaii was not to abandon the old country but rather to struggle for Korean national independence in the islands. One of the immigrants later recalled: "When I saw my country fall into the hands of the Japanese aggressors, I was filled with sorrow, but, unable to do much to help, I applied for the status of an immigrant and came to Hawaii hoping to learn something in order to help my country." They saw the islands as a place where they could organize a strong independence movement, condemn Japanese control of Korea—even form militia units to fight for the liberation of their homeland.[38]

Many Koreans also migrated to Hawaii for religious purposes. American missionaries had been active in Korea, and many of the immigrants had been converted to Christianity before they had left the old country. "I was born in Korea," said one of them, "and was a Christian before I came to the United States. I was converted to Christianity by the American missionaries." Encouraged to emigrate to Hawaii by missionaries like the Reverend George Heber Jones of the Methodist Episcopal Church in Inchon, Koreans were told they would find both high-paying work and pleasant weather in Hawaii. More important they would be able to establish churches and help to spread the Christian gospel in the islands. A striking 40 percent of all Korean immigrants were Christians.[39]

But Hawaii's most compelling promise was freedom from poverty and hunger. Famine and drought had inflicted hard times on the Korean people. In 1901 King Kojong had to set up a relief office to feed the many starving Koreans. One American missionary described the situation: "We have never known such unrest among the Koreans due to the excitement of so many going to the Hawaiian Islands to work on sugar plantations, and the dreadful hardtimes. . . . We can't blame them for wanting to go to America." Kato Motoshiro, Japanese Consul in Inchon, reported that the applicants for this emigration came mainly from those districts where the harvests had been the poorest. Horace N. Allen, chief of the United States legation in Seoul, made a similar observation in a letter to Governor Sanford Dole of Hawaii: "The severe famine of the past winter made the matter [of emigrating to Hawaii] seem all the more attractive to the people." Many years later in Hawaii, one Korean woman recalled: "We left Korea because we were too poor." Unable to restrain tears, brought on by memories of suffering, she added: "We had nothing to eat. . . . There was absolutely no way we could survive." Another immigrant similarly described the plight of people in the old country: "There were no opportunities for work of any kind and . . . conditions were bad. It was then that we heard of a man who was talking a lot about the opportunities in Hawaii. He said that it was a land of opportunity where everybody was rich."[40]

Compared to the harsh reality surrounding people in Korea, Hawaii appeared to be attractive and bright, especially as it had been described by the labor recruiters. A massive advertising campaign had been organized by the East-West Development Company, which had been established in Korea by the Hawaiian sugar planters to recruit Korean workers. In cities such as Seoul, Inchon, Pusan, and Wonsan, people read newspaper advertisements and posters that announced employment opportunities in Hawaii. There, they were promised, they would receive as plantation laborers free housing, medical care, and $16 per month for a sixty-hour work week—a sum equal to about sixty-four *wun* (Korean dollars), a small fortune to many Koreans. In their imaginations, Hawaii was a "paradise" where "clothing . . . grew on trees, free to be picked," and where "gold dollars were blossoming on every bush." Lured toward the fantasy islands of Hawaii, Koreans secured "loans" from a bank in Korea financed by the HSPA to pay for passage to Hawaii. According to one of these immigrants, Yang Choo-en, they had their steamship fare for transportation to Hawaii paid by the Hawaiian plantation owners with the understanding that the total expense of $100 would be deducted from their monthly pay over a three year period. With this understanding, Koreans signed contracts and boarded steamships bound for Hawaii.[41]

The passage to Hawaii was a long, sometimes frightening, trip. One immigrant remembered how he had taken the train from Nam Dae Mun to Inchon, where he boarded a Korean steamship: "After boarding, when we got close to the Mokpo River, the turbulence was heavy. We felt the ship rocking and the people in the ship moved like a football and threw up. A voice shouted, 'every one will die.' I felt we could not live." As they crossed the ocean, Korean immigrants began to prepare themselves for life in the new land. Many men put on western suits and cut off their topknots. On board one of the ships, a group of Christian Koreans held prayer meetings in the steerage and became involved in evangelical work. By the time they had landed in Honolulu, they had converted thirty-two fellow passengers and organized themselves into a Methodist Episcopal Church.[42]

Landing in Honolulu was an exciting and anxious moment. Many of the newcomers were so apprehensive they were unable to sleep, wondering what would happen to them in this foreign country. They did not know how to speak English, and knew nothing about plantation work. But they had little time to worry. Upon arriving in Honolulu on 20 February 1903 Hyon Sun and his fellow Koreans were rushed to the quarantine station, where they were kept for two days; then they were transported by train to the Kahuku Sugar Plantation. There they were welcomed by Andrew Adams, the plantation manager, and entertained in a big dining hall. After they purchased the things they needed at the plantation store on credit, they were finally housed in a camp composed of twenty little cottages.

Uprooted by war and famine, seeking asylum from Japanese political tyranny, Koreans came to Hawaii. In numbers the Koreans would never "equal" the Japanese, as some planters had hoped; but soon a new group of migrants—the Filipinos—would succeed the Koreans and eventually even outnumber the Japanese on the plantations.

Kasla Glorya Ti Hawaii

"Why go to Hawaii?" Filipinos asked, and were told: "Kasla glorya ti Hawaii, Hawaii is like a land of glory." Many of them had gone there to work on the sugar plantations and returned as "Hawaiianos." They appeared "very showy" as they walked around with their "white high-heeled shoes, even in the dust," and wore "Amerikana" suits and stetson hats "even on hot days in town." Flashing gold watches hanging on glittering chains, they looked so rich with their "money to blow." These fancy men stirred in the minds of their countrymen dreams of a land where people could "pick up" money.[43]

The promise of Hawaii, which the Hawaiianos personified, attracted Filipino peasants. "Life was getting harder," one Filipino immigrant explained, and a man had to "reach farther and farther away to make ends meet." Peasant families were in debt, "sinking down into the toilet." Life had once been good on the farm: there had always been food to eat. "In the forest behind us," a Filipino plantation laborer recalled as he described his childhood in the Philippines, "we got so much to live on. I would go hunting there with a string trap once a month and you would have to call me clumsy if I brought down less than four wild chickens. We used to trap wild pigs there too and deer, but that wasn't too often. Usually, that was done for a big feast." But then "the rich people" from town came to hunt with guns. "Those lazy bastards would even come at night when the animals and birds were asleep and blind them with their flashlights. And boom! No miss. Boom! They fell like shaken mangoes to the ground." Soon the animals disappeared from the forests.[44]

Then the peasants lost their farms as well as the wildlife in the forests; increasingly "the rich rice lands were owned by men who never saw them." Each year the landlords demanded a larger share, until it became almost impossible for the peasants to live. The landlords also developed a system of "caciquism," or political bossism and corruption, to maintain their control and protect their expanding agricultural holdings. Many years later a Filipino immigrant described this process of dispossession: "There was a time when my ancestors owned almost the whole town of Bulac and the surrounding villages. But when the Americans came conditions changed. Little by little my father's lands were sold. My share was mortgaged finally to keep the family from starvation and I soon found myself tilling the soil as did the poor Filipino peasants." He was becoming entrapped in a system of virtual peonage. "Though I worked hard daily, half of what I made I gave to my master as every tenant had to do. Therefore, my financial affairs were discouraging and most disappointing."[45]

As conditions for the peasants deteriorated, class tensions sharpened and sometimes erupted into bristling personal encounters. A young Filipino boy never forgot one such incident. One day his mother and he had gone into town to sell beans. They noticed an elegantly dressed young woman walking down the street and were awed by her beautiful clothes. The woman, irritated by their stares, raised her silk umbrella and angrily asked: "What are you looking at, poor woman?" Suddenly the wealthy woman struck the basket of beans and scattered them on the pavement. Crawling on her knees, his mother scooped the beans into the basket. Her son was shocked and she tried to assure him: "It is all right. It is all right." But he knew it was not all right, as he knelt on the wet cement and picked out the dirt and pebbles from the beans.[46]

But there was, the peasants were told, a "land of glory" in Hawaii. There laborers were paid in gold and lived in houses made of lumber, a luxury only wealthy people enjoyed in the Philippines. There they could turn a little handle and water would flow from a pipe; they would no longer have to draw their water from a spring and carry heavy buckets to their homes. More important, in Hawaii, dispossessed Filipino peasants could satisfy their sole ambition—to save enough money to pay back the mortgages on their lands in the Philippines. "Everyone," said a Filipino immigrant, "became fascinated by the tales told of Hawaii."[47]

And so by the thousands, Filipinos signed labor contracts to be transported to Hawaii, where they would be bound to labor for three years at wages of $18 a month plus housing, water, fuel, and medical care. If they worked a total of 720 days, they would be given transportation back to their homeland. Most of the labor recruits, or *sakadas*, from the Philippines were men coming to Hawaii to work temporarily.

One Filipino immigrant vividly remembered the day he signed his contract:

> The agent was just coming down the steps when I halted my horse in front of the recruiter's office. He was a fellow Filipino, but a Hawaiian.
>
> "Where are you going?" he asked.
>
> "I would like to present myself for Hawaii, Apo," I answered as I came down from my horse.
>
> "Wait, I'll go see if I can place you on the next load," he said, and turned back up into the door.
>
> When he came out, he had a paper in his hand. "Come up, so we can fill in the forms," he waved; so I went in.
>
> "You write?" he asked.
>
> "No," I said; so he filled in for me.
>
> "Come back Monday for the doctor to check you up," he said, patting me on the back. "When you come back, bring *beinte cinco*,

twenty-five, and I'll make sure of your papers for a place," he said, shaking my hand.

It was like that. "Tip" is what we call it here. But that is our custom to *pasekeok*, slipsome, for a favor.[48]

As the immigrants prepared to board their ships in Manila, they were surrounded by friends and relatives. They showered them with wishes of good luck and told the sakadas to hurry back to the Philippines with money for big parties. Pretty girls came to the wharf and gave the young men those "remember me manong" smiles. Sometimes immigrants would hear other Filipinos returning on ships from Hawaii shout: "You're going to Hawaii, kompadre!" From the decks of the ships about to sail, hopeful men would shout back: "We're going to try and see how it is, kompadre!" But the returning Filipinos would respond: "Go back, brother. Hardship is Hawaii! *Narigat ti Hawaii!* Go on home."[49]

But the new immigrants were already on their way. Sailing out of the harbor, they felt waves of bewildering sensations as they gazed upon "the fading shores of Manila . . . the disappearing Philippines, the most beautiful sight in the world." They waved their hats in a final farewell and descended into the filthy holds below, where the steerage passengers were crowded together.[50]

There in the darkness they lay on their bunk beds, lonely and seasick, wondering what life would be like in the new land, wondering why they had ever left home. "It was crowded below deck," one of the passengers later recalled. "I think there were more than 300 of us [steerage passengers]; my husband was in a different section while the women and children were in another section. During the long voyage I would always sit on deck, holding my youngest child. . . . My husband and my other child, who was four, would often go and watch through the fence the first class passengers playing in the swimming pool." The smell of freight, oil, and machines filled the air below deck, and sometimes the Filipino passengers were locked in the holds and denied fresh air and sunshine. Food was served in great buckets, and many Filipinos were disappointed to find them filled with bread rather than rice, "food which every hardworking Filipino cannot do without, especially in the morning." Sometimes the seas were so rough that the passengers could not keep their food down. Occasionally epidemics threatened to sweep through the steerage, and young doctors

ARRIVAL OF FILIPINO LABORERS
Hawaii State Archives
"As we came down the gangplank . . . we shouted the
plantation of our destiny."

would go down "now and then to check the number of deaths and examine those about to die."[51]

Finally their ships reached Honolulu, and the Filipino passengers were marched down the gangplank, carrying their belongings. Some of them cradled fighting cocks in their arms. Describing the day of his arrival in Hawaii, one Filipino immigrant said: "At 8 A.M. we pulled into the immigration station of Honolulu. There was a band playing. We disembarked alphabetically and as we came down the gangplank, they [the immigration officials] asked us where we were going and we shouted the plantation of our destiny. 'Waialua Sugar Company!' 'Puunene Maui!' people shouted. I shouted, 'Naalehu, Hawaii.' "[52]

The tired travelers were in the land of glory, hopeful they would not be there very long, determined to return to the Philippines as "Hawaiianos." Peasant farmers, they had been imported to become plantation laborers. As they were assembled for assignment to the plantations, the newly arrived laborers heard their names called. They were ordered to step forward individually, and a plantation official then placed a *bango*, a metal tag with a number stamped on it, around the neck of each man, like a lei.

Strangers in the Islands

And so they came—from many different lands and different cultures—Chinese, Portuguese, Norwegians, Japanese, Koreans, and Filipinos. Others came too—Puerto Ricans, Spaniards, Germans, and Russians. The experiences of the various immigrant groups were different in important ways. While only a few hundred Norwegians migrated here, tens of thousands of Japanese arrived in the islands, becoming the largest ethnic community in Hawaiian society. While generally the Chinese and Japanese came as sojourners, the Portuguese emigrated to Hawaii as settlers. While the Japanese and Portuguese were worried about their economic futures in their homelands, many of the Koreans were driven by religious and political motives, seeking to carry Christianity to Hawaii and to establish an overseas base for the Korean nationalist struggle against Japanese imperialism. While the Chinese and Filipino migrants were overwhelmingly male, the German, Norwegian, Japanese, Portuguese, and Korean migrations included significant numbers of women.

Still, all of the migrants, regardless of their place of origin and nationality, shared many experiences. The future for them in the old countries seemed grim. Vast political, economic, and social changes undermined communities in Asia as well as Europe, uprooting millions of people and forcing them to seek new homes in distant lands. Over three hundred thousand men and women left everything they knew and loved—their farms, families, temples and churches, their villages—and migrated to Hawaii. By word of mouth and from notices and advertisements, they had learned about the sugar-growing islands in the Pacific and the possibilities for employment there. Many did not even know where Hawaii was. But this did not matter. Discontented and desperate, all of them felt they had to make a bold decision, to take drastic action. On opposite sides of the world, in Japan and Norway, prospective immigrant laborers heard recruiters, sent by sugar agencies like Castle and Cooke and H. Hackfeld and Company, describe Hawaii as a paradise, as a place where poor men could find work and a better life. They signed labor contracts. But most of them could not even read their contracts, and the very concept of a contract was new and unfamiliar to them.

Virtually everything ahead of them would be foreign and strange. Most of the laborers had lived in a world of the farm and the village. They found the port cities noisy, frenetic, and crowded. The next step in the journey was even more terrifying, for they had never been on a ship before. They boarded the huge vessels apprehensively, and were suddenly herded into dark and stifling steerages. Had they known how terrible the crossing would be—the poor food, the seasickness, the tedium, the diseases, and the deaths —they might have stayed home. When they arrived in Hawaii, they found themselves stripped of their names—names given to them by their parents, names that told them who they were, names that were important in the old village; they were tagged and assigned numbers. Reduced to commodities, they were placed in a labor market where planters inspected them and chose the ones they wanted, and where sugar agencies made selections and filled "orders" for the plantations.

Finally the laborers were on the plantations. Few of the newcomers, if any, thought they would stay there. Many workers hoped they would be able to save enough money to return to the old country, to begin again in their homeland, and to recover their names, their personhood. Others planned to stay permanently in the islands and open their own businesses or plow again their own fields in a foreign land. Whether they intended to be sojourners or settlers, a great many of them remained in Hawaii. Representing different languages, customs, and races, they would make Hawaii a uniquely multiethnic society. All of them carried in their hearts a fierce and tenacious hope, which was expressed in the language they used to describe the islands: "Tan Heung Shan," "Terra Nova," "Hawaii Netsu," "kaeguk chinch wi," and "kasla glorya ti Hawaii."

On the plantations, all of the migrants would find themselves in a new world of labor. Peasant farmers and craftsmen in the old country, they had labored to provide for their families and to fulfill feudal obligations. They had greater control of their time and activities, working in the fields with family members or in small craftsmaking shops. Traditions and ancient rules and understandings defined and regulated their work. But once in the islands, all of them would be thrust into a wage-earning system and the regimented life of modern agricultural labor. Their experiences as plantation laborers would radically transform their lives and the way they viewed Hawaii.

III

A New World of Labor: From Siren to Siren

The Five A.M. Whistle

In the early morning darkness, the rude screams of the plantation whistle suddenly announced the beginning of *hana* 'work', the moment of first stirring on the plantation:

> "Awake! stir your bones! Rouse up!"
>   Shrieks the Five o'Clock Whistle.
>   "Don't dream you can nestle
> For one more sweet nap.
> Or your ear-drums I'll rap
> With my steam-hammer tap
>   Till they burst.
> Br-r-row-aw-i-e-ur-ur-rup!
> Wake up! wake up! wake up! w-a-k-e-u-u-u-up!
>
>   Filipino and Japanee;
>   Porto Rican and Portugee;
>   Korean, Kanaka and Chinese;
>   Everybody whoever you be
>   On the whole plantation—
> Wake up! wake up! wake up! w-a-k-e-u-u-u-up!
> Br-r-ow-aw-i-e-ur-ur-rup!
>
>   Luna and book-keeper;
>   Sugar-boiler, store-keeper;
>   Time-keeper, chemist;
>   Clerk and machinist;
>   Boss and Boss' Missus;
>   I proclaim this is
>   The hour to get up,
>   And eat a rice cup;
>   For I boss the Boss,
>   Same as man, mule and hoss,

> And everything on the plantation,
> I, the Sugar Mill Whistle!
>
> Br-r-ow-aw-i-e-ur-ur-rup!
> Get up! get up! get up! get up!
> Mind the Five A.M. Whistle
> The signal to hustle!"

After the whistle had awakened the workers, company policemen went through the camps, shouting, "Get up, get up" and "Hana-hana, hana-hana." "You must wake up," explained Dorotio Allian-ic, and go to work or else a policeman would kick the door of your room and chase you out of bed. "I got one companion, he like lay off" one morning, Allianic added. "Oh, the policeman come, and my friend was so scared that he ran to work in his underpants." At five-thirty, after a quick breakfast, laborers gathered at a meeting place, and a boss or luna led them away in gangs of twenty to thirty workers. They marched or were transported in wagons or trains to the fields. At six o'clock, they began work, taking a half-hour break for lunch at eleven-thirty and finishing work at four-thirty in the afternoon.[1]

Work on the plantation involved a wide range of tasks and activities. Laborers were divided into gangs, and each gang was given a work assignment—planting, watering, hoeing, ploughing, cultivating, ditching, stripping off dead leaves from the cane stalks, cutting the cane, carting the cane, or loading the cane onto small tram cars. Each gang, a visitor noted, was watched by "a luna, or overseer, almost always a white man." The combination of ethnic backgrounds in each gang varied: some of them were composed of laborers of one nationality, while others were mixed. A missionary visiting a plantation observed that the Koreans worked "under white or Hawaiian bosses, either in gangs or by themselves or in mixed gangs alongside Japanese, Puerto Ricans, and Portuguese." One luna said he had workers of all races in his group—Hawaiians, Filipinos, Puerto Ricans, Chinese, Japanese, Portuguese, and Koreans.[2]

Plantation labor was highly routinized and regimented. One of the most tedious and backbreaking tasks was hoeing weeds. Work-ers had to "hoe hoe hoe . . . for four hours in a straight line and no talking," said a laborer. They stopped only to sharpen the blades and then walked to the next lot. "Hoe every weed along the way to your three rows. Hoe—chop chop chop, one chop for one small weed, two for all big ones." As they hoed, they were not permitted to stand up straight and ease the pain in their shoulders and backs. After a week of "hoe hana," many of the workers felt as if they had been "kicked and beaten all over," their bodies "tight" and their backs aching from stooping and working "at one thing for so long without a say or without fun mixed in."[3]

More demanding and more dangerous than hoe hana was *hole hole* (ho-li ho-li) work, the stripping of dry, withered leaves from the stalks of sugar cane. Down in the gulches, amidst the tall cane, workers pulled away dead leaves in the hot sun, often without "a breath of wind to cool the heated stagnant air." As they worked, many of them sang:

> *Kane* wa Kachiken
> Washa *horehore* yo
> Ase to namida no
> Tomokasegi
>
> My husband cuts the cane stalks
> And I trim their leaves
> With sweat and tears we both work
> For our means.

To protect themselves against the sharp, spiney needles of the cane leaves and the wasps or yellow jackets infesting the cane fields, laborers had to wear heavy clothing that covered their hands and faces. Still, they found that the leaves cut their hands so badly that they "could hardly stand it."[4]

When the cane was ripe and ready to be cut, the laborers were sent into the fields. Standing against green forests of twelve-foot tall cane, they resembled miniature soldiers; on command, they moved forward, swinging their machetes and cutting the juicy cane stalks close to the ground. They found the cane fighting back: "When you cutting the cane and you pulling the cane back, sometimes you get scratched with the leaves from the cane because they have a little edge just like a saw blade." As the workers advanced against the bristling cane, they became enveloped in reddish clouds of dust. They tried to breathe "the less dusty air in gasps," and tied the bottoms of their pants to keep out the dust. Frequently they were forced to stop and use their blue handkerchieves to clean their nostrils of "chocolate dust."[5]

"The sugar cane fields were endless and [the stalks were] twice the height of myself," a Korean worker said, recalling the long hours she had spent cutting the cane. "Now that I look back, I thank goodness for the height, for if I had seen how far the fields stretched, I probably would have fainted from knowing how much work was ahead. My waistline got slimmer and my back ached from bending over all the time to cut the sugar cane. Sometimes I wished I was a dwarf so that I would not have to bend down constantly." Describing the harvesting process, a visitor to a plantation near Hilo wrote: "Just beyond these Chinese huts were canefields, an intense yellow-green, the long, slender leaves tossing in the breeze like a maize-field before the harvest. There were great bands of Japanese at work in the field." In the heat and dust of the canefields, they worked "with incredible rapidity, the line of men crossing a field, levelling the cane." Returning, they collected the cane stalks and tied them into bundles, which they loaded onto the cars of a narrow-gauge railway, a temporary, movable line laid between the mills and the fields and shifted as occasion required.[6]

The cut cane was then transported to the mill, where it was crushed and its juices boiled into molasses and sugar. The mill, standing in the midst of verdant fields of cane, was a factory, a machine in the garden; plantation laborers assigned to the mill were factory operatives, machine attendants. Under the supervision of engineers and technicians, they operated engines, presses, furnaces, boilers, vacuum pans, centrifugal drums, and other machines. Inside the mill, workers felt like they were in the "hold of a steamer," its thundering machinery deafening and its heat terrible. "It was so hot with steam in the mill," Baishiro Tamashiro recalled, "that I became just like pupule [crazy]." After electric lights were installed in the mills, laborers worked in shifts, night and day during the grinding season.[7]

Plantation Paternalism

Although they knew that the plantation was in reality a factory in the fields and a capitalistic enterprise designed to earn profits, many managers viewed it as a social community, and they saw themselves as guardians responsible for the welfare of the workers. Planters claimed they treated their employees with "consideration and humanity," seeking in "every possible way to advance their

CUTTING CANE

Hawaii State Archives

"The sugar cane fields were endless and [the stalks were] twice the height of myself."

Sugar cane on wagons being hauled to the mill by oxen on the Grove Farm Plantation in 1887. *Hawaii State Archives*

They loaded the cane onto the cars of a narrow gauge railway, a temporary, movable line laid between the mills and the fields. *Hawaii State Archives*

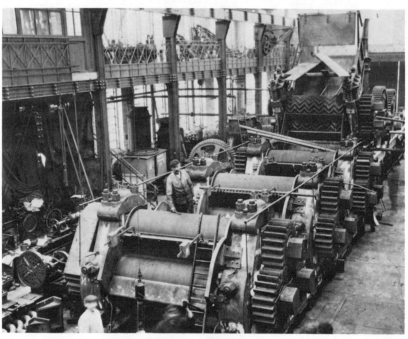

INSIDE THE MILL (NAALEHU, 1910)
Bishop Museum

comfort and make them contented and happy." They described their hands as "thoroughly satisfied with their pay, hours of labor, and general treatment," as working "cheerfuly and uncomplainingly." In their efforts to build bonds of respect, planters cherished expressions of loyalty from the laborers. When D. D. Baldwin, manager of the Kohala Plantation, retired in 1872, he was honored at a farewell feast where he was pleased to receive a gold watch from his workers. Reporting on the event, a writer for the *Pacific Commercial Advertiser* commented on the meaning of the gift: "The deep and sincere attachment which evidently exists between . . . Mr. D. D. Baldwin and the employees, both foreigners and natives . . . is highly creditable to both parties. . . . It shows what unbounded influence a manager acquainted with Hawaiian character can acquire over his men without in the least degree relaxing discipline or tolerating laziness." But many years later, in 1911, a mainland journalist concluded wryly after he had investigated management-labor relations in Hawaii: "I never knew a more complete nor more benevolent example of feudalism than this; and never more respectable and less democratic conditions."[8]

"The comfort and happiness of the people of the plantation," a worker stated, "depends largely on the kind of manager that rules over them. Whether he takes a lively interest in seeing his subjects enjoy life as much as possible in so far as he could afford to better their living conditions . . . or whether he refuses to do all these things, is all left up to his discretion." In his report to the HSPA in 1916, Montague Lord criticized a few of the managers for neglecting the welfare of their laborers, but commended most of them for their benevolent supervision. The manager of the Waiakea Plantation, Lord noted, was able to walk through the camps and call "most of the men by name." During his visit to the Onomea Sugar Company, Lord asked the workers about plantation conditions, and they "all referred to the manager in the highest terms." Some of them, unable to speak English, told Lord they were studying English at night in order to "understand and work better" for the plantation manager.[9]

Planters sometimes took great personal interest in particular workers. Yonematsu Sakuma, a Gannen Mono, received special support from his plantation manager. In an interview in 1917, Sakuma said: "My entire family is grateful to my master for his generosity. Now that I am aged and can no longer work, he built us this comfortable home and is giving us a generous pension of $25 a month. He put my oldest son through college and my daughter through normal school. He is also paying for the education of all my other children." Another laborer, Kiyomatsu Takaki, was also given special consideration. He had accidentally injured his right hand while working in the mill; the manager, noticing the injury had not healed satisfactorily after three weeks, released Takaki from his contract and advised him to return to Japan for proper medical care. He also canceled Takaki's debt of $135 and gave him $30. In Honolulu, Takaki received successful medical treatment and decided to return to the plantation. Pleased to see his worker again, the manager raised Takaki's wage rate from $15 (the amount usually paid to contract laborers) to $25 a month.[10]

The paternalism of plantation managers, while it sometimes sprang from a sincere concern for their workers, played an important role in plantation production and profit-making. Managers took an "intelligent interest" in their laborers in order to secure more work from them and increase production. On the Laupahoehoe Plantation, an investigator for the HSPA found that the manager was able to generate work from his men by cultivating loyalty and self-discipline: "In passing a fluming cane field, we went in alone seeing the men without the manager being present. They were cutting, carrying and fluming, and all said their condition was fine but would not stop work to talk long. There seems to be a large percentage of Tagalogs on this place which goes to show what can be done with even the despised Tagalogs where there is a little understanding of these people."[11]

Seeking to maximize production, plantation managers regulated many personal areas of their workers' lives, including their eating habits. Theo. H. Davies and Company, for example, urged the manager of the Laupahoehoe Plantation to give his Puerto Rican laborers closer supervision and make certain they had regular schedules for their meals: "We understand that it has been the experience at some of the plantations that these people do not know how to look after themselves. They do not take food before going to work, as they have never been used to taking their meals regularly, and therefore, should you find the people sent you do not take their food as they should, we would suggest that you give the matter your attention, as it is, of course, necessary for a man to eat to enable him to put in a good day's work." The vice president of

H. Hackfeld and Company sent George N. Wilcox of the Grove Farm Plantation a circular that warned planters that the Filipino was "very incapable of caring for himself." Left entirely to his own resources, the Filipino was likely to spend his money for "fancy groceries" and consequently be "insufficiently nourished." The vice president advised planters to have Filipino laborers "looked after" and have them fed by Japanese or Chinese camp cooks. David Bowman, director of the Industrial Service Bureau of the HSPA, recommended that planters place their Filipino laborers in boarding houses on the plantation, for it was "good business" to have them "properly fed." It "paid" to make such boarding arrangements, "the results being a well-fed, contented lot of laborers."[12]

Plantation paternalism was designed not only to extract a good day's work from the laborers but also to weaken the power of workers to organize and strike. John M. Horner, manager of the Kukaiau Plantation, bluntly told the Labor Commission in 1895 that paternalism was an effective tactic to avoid strikes: "Let me say here, if some plantation managers will look more closely after their lunas and prevent their unwise and unjust dealings with their laborers, we would hear of fewer strikes and less trouble on some plantations. All men, though these be shipped [contract] laborers, are capable of comprehending the difference between kind words, kind acts, kind wages generally and ruffian roughness and abuse." During the 1909 strike the trustees of the HSPA urged planters to promote paternalism as a strategy to pacify labor unrest: "We should avail to get our house in order before a storm breaks. It will come without doubt unless radical and immediate steps are taken to thwart it. Once the great majority of the laboring classes are busy under conditions which breed contentment and eliminate grievances, then can we expect a gradual and effectual diminution in the power of the agitating element." In *The Sugar Industry of Hawaii and the Labor Shortage*, published shortly after the 1920 strike, the HSPA summed up the essential purpose of plantation paternalism: "That the plantations have a humanitarian interest in their employees is self-evident. Money and time have been spent liberally by the plantations to cater to the physical, mental and moral welfare of the laborers. The planters find that humanity in industry pays."[13]

But plantation paternalism not only paid: it also functioned as an ideology to maintain the caste/class reality of plantation society. While planters did draw white laborers from Germany, Norway, and Portugal, they brought only a limited number of them to Hawaii and located them in a stratified system based on class. Planters recruited most of their laborers first from the local population and then from Asia, and placed them in a racial, as well as class, structure. Consistently nonwhites constituted the overwhelming majority of all plantation laborers: 94 percent in 1872, 87 percent in 1902, and 88 percent in 1920. In this racial and class hierarchy, white planters expressed concern for the welfare of their nonwhite laborers and assumed a "parental" role. Planters thought Koreans were "childlike" and Filipinos were "by nature" always "more or less like children." "Where there is a drop of the Anglo Saxon blood, it is sure to rule," planters declared. Acknowledging that the laborer had a soul and feeling and thus was entitled to some humane treatment, they identified themselves as members of "a stronger race" and urged their fellow planters to show "mercy" to their workers. They proudly claimed they had spread "Caucasian civilization" to Hawaii. In the sugar kingdom, planters argued, white men had to be the directors, the paternalistic supervisors of nonwhite laborers. From the perspective of the HSPA, Caucasians were "constitutionally and tempermentally unfitted for labor" in a tropical climate, while Asians and "brown" men were "peculiarly adapted to the exactions of tropical labor," and could serve as satisfactory and "permanent" field workers.[14]

The Strong Hand of Authority

While planters governed their workers paternalistically, they also required strict obedience. Their philosophy of firm management was succinctly stated in an editorial of the *Pacific Commercial Advertiser:* Offer the "plantation coolie" a compromise and "he regards it as a sign of fear; yield to his demands and he thinks he is the master and makes new demands; use the strong hand and he recognizes the power to which, from immemorial times, he has abjectly bowed. There is one word which holds the lower classes of every nation in check and that is Authority."[15]

In the exercise of their "strong hand," planters devised an intricate system of rules and regulations for their laborers. The manager of the Waihee Plantation, for example, developed a formidable list of rules designed to govern plantation life and labor:

1. Laborers are expected to be industrious and docile and obedient to their overseers.

2. Any cause of complaint against the overseers, of injustice or ill treatment, shall be heard by the manager through the interpreter, but in no case shall any laborer be permitted to raise his hand or any weapon in an aggressive manner or cabal with his associates or incite them to acts of insubordination.

3. The working hours shall be ten each day, or more, if by mutual consent, in which case they shall have extra pay, but when work is not pressing, laborers will be allowed to stop on Saturdays at 4 o'clock.

4. When laborers desire to have a stint for the day's work, the overseer shall be the judge of the amount required, then laborers shall have their choice, to accept or to work their usual ten hours; on this subject there shall be no appeal.

5. Laborers are expected to be regular and cleanly in their personal habits, to retire, to rest and rise at the appointed hours, to keep their persons, beds, clothing, rooms, enclosures, and offices clean, and are strictly forbidden to enter that part of the cook house set apart for plantation cooking arrangements. A fire place will be provided for the latter purpose and permission given to cut indigo for firewood.

6. Rooms will be set apart for married laborers, and a separate bed will be provided for each male unmarried laborer, which they are expected to occupy except in case of continued illness—no two men shall be permitted to occupy the same bed.

7. No fires will be allowed after 6 1/2 P.M. and no lights after 8 1/2 P.M.; every laborer is required to be in bed at 8 1/2 P.M. and to rise at 5 A.M., the hours before breakfast being devoted to habits of cleanliness and order about their persons and premises. During the hours appointed for rest no talking permitted or any noise calculated to disturb those wishing to sleep.

8. A separate lodging house will be provided for those whose sickness or inability to labor shall last over 24 hours and all persons on the sick or disabled list are required to submit to such treatment and obey such directions as are given by the medical attendant and manager.

9. It is required that laborers sick or unable to work shall immediately report themselves through the interpreter to their overseer or to the manager as any person absent from work without permission shall be considered and punished as a deserter.

10. Each laborer shall be held responsible for any sickness or inability to work which shall result from breaking the laws of this land or the sanitary rules of this plantation.

11. Gambling, fast riding, and leaving the plantation without permission are strictly forbidden.

Planters had rules for virtually every aspect of their laborers' lives, and had devised a system of military discipline. The bulletin of the Ewa Plantation, for example, explicitly drew an analogy between the army and the plantation work force:

> To gain a picture of the plantation organization, as it directly affects irrigation, one may compare it roughly to a military organization, as follows:
> Plantation Manager . . . . .The General
> Department of Agriculture:
> Control and Research,
> acting in advisory capacity . . . . .The Staff
> Plantation Head
> Overseer . . . . .Lieutenant General Head
> Irrigation Overseer. . . . . .Major Section
> Overseers. . . . . .Captains
> Reservoir Men . . . . .Supply Sergeants
> Ditchmen . . . . .Corporals
> Irrigation Men . . . . .The Troops[16]

But planters did more than simply issue long lists of detailed rules and organize their workers using a military model: they also developed a wide range of strategies designed to extract efficiency and obedience from the labor force through both persuasion and punishment.

In their efforts to control their workers, planters saw that nationalistic consciousness and a strong sense of ethnicity could be used to induce the laborers to be more disciplined and willing workers. As early as the 1850s, the Royal Hawaiian Agricultural Society advised planters to procure as many "coolies" as possible and use them to set an "example" for the natives. The Society argued that the Chinese would have "a stimulating effect" on the Hawaiians, for the native laborers were "naturally jealous" of the Chinese and "ambitious" to outdo them. Indeed, planters were pleased to find that the "coolies" worked harder than the natives and condescendingly called them *wahine! wahine!* 'women! women!'[17]

This practice of promoting competition between different groups of laborers continued as planters expanded the ethnic diversity of their work force, and it became a policy of the HSPA.

For example, in 1917 the association sent a circular to plantation managers in which it showed that nearly 20 percent of the time of the average laborer was "unavailable" to the plantations. Calling this loss of time "enormous," the association then described the "race pride" program (introduced on the Hilo Sugar Company Plantation), designed to stimulate interethnic rivalry to reduce absenteeism: "At the place where the section luna meets his men in the morning, is a board on which the timekeeper places each morning the daily attendance of the previous day. This is listed by nationalities, the idea being to bring up the attendance of Filipinos and Spaniards to that of the Japanese. This appeal to race pride has, we understand, produced good results in the few months the plan has been in operation." Lunas also made direct appeals to the Filipinos' sense of nationalism: "Work hard and be thrifty and don't get into trouble. Don't show laziness—that would look bad on us Filipinos. The plantation bosses know Filipinos are good workers. That's why they chose to bring us here. It pleases them to see us work hard. Remember that! It is our flag!" One Filipino luna, giving instructions in Ilocano, said to his gang: "We are all Filipinos, brothers. We all know how to hoe. So, let's do a good job and show the people of other nations what we can do. Let us not shame our skin!"[18]

To exert greater influence over their laborers, planters worked closely with the representatives of the home governments of the workers. They saw that such representatives, able to speak to the laborers in their own languages and personify traditional authority, could appeal to their national pride and persuade them to perform their tasks obediently. Planters welcomed Acting Korean Foreign Minister Baron Yun during his visit to Hawaii and invited him to their plantations. There Baron Yun instructed his fellow Koreans to "1) Act kindly to the plantation managers and win their hearts; 2) Stay on one plantation calmly and do your best for your work by studying how to grow sugar; and 3) Save all you can and come back to your fatherland." On the Kekaha Plantation, Baron Yun learned from the manager that the Korean workers there would drink liquor excessively and then damage plantation property. Displeased with this behavior, he admonished them to be industrious in their work and temperate in their habits, and sternly stated that Koreans who were found drunk again should be drowned "in the name of Korea."[19]

Planters exploited even more systematically the assistance of

Japanese representatives, particularly the Japanese Consul General and the Central Japanese League. Organized in 1903 by the consul general, the League worked to instill into the laborers an attachment to their plantations, and to promote a feeling of mutual obligation and regard between employer and employee. Aware they had reason to be generous to the League, planters helped the League finance Japanese language schools and the Japanese Red Cross. On 21 May 1904 H. Hackfeld and Company wrote to George N. Wilcox of the Grove Farm Plantation: "We would recommend that you address a letter to the representative of the Japanese League on your plantation, handing him a draft for the sum of $50.00, in favor of Mrs. Miki Saito, and requesting him to forward the same to the Japanese Consul in Honolulu, as a donation to the Japanese Red Cross." A few weeks later on June 29, H. Hackfeld and Company sent Wilcox a copy of a letter written by Miki Saito, president of the Central Japanese League, in which he instructed Japanese workers not to engage in strikes to settle labor disputes. "Strikes . . . are, in their nature, like the doings of unruly children or like the acts of barbarians," Saito chided his countrymen. "We are absolutely opposed to them." He advised that should labor difficulties arise on the plantations, branches of the League should ascertain the grievances of the laborers and then "acquaint the employers only with the reasonable grievances." The main objective should be to secure "a peaceful solution" to labor problems.[20]

Four months later, the Japanese League participated in tense negotiations between management and Japanese laborers on the Laupahoehoe Plantation. Angrily charging that luna Charles Kramer had raped a Japanese woman, laborers threatened to strike. But the officers of the Japanese League advised them that striking was "not a good way to settle the trouble," and would not recognize the strike. After they had promised to inform the management of the laborers' demand for the luna's dismissal, the officers persuaded the workers to return to work. On 13 October 1904, the director of Theo. H. Davies and Company thanked Miki Saito and the League for preventing a strike on the Laupahoehoe Plantation.[21]

But planters did not rely entirely on persuasion to control their workers: they also used coercion. The most widely used form of punishment was the fine, or docking system. Planters developed an elaborate system of fines, which specified a charge for virtually every kind of misconduct. On one plantation, for example, workers were fined for

> breaking wagon through negligence—$5.00
> refusal to do work as ordered—$.25
> trespass—$.50
> cutting harness—$2.00
> insubordination—$1.00
> neglect of duty—$.50
> drunkenness—$.50
> drunken brawling—$5.00
> gambling in Japanese or Chinese camps—$5.00

The purpose of the system was to force workers to be punctual and productive. The Gannen Mono of 1868 were penalized for tardiness: they had a fourth of a day's wage deducted from their pay if they were ten to fifteen minutes late for work. If they were absent from work, they had two days of wages deducted for each day of absence. Norwegian laborers also found themselves deprived of their wages through fines. "If any one comes five or ten minutes too late," one of them stated, "he is immediately imposed with a fine of half a dollar." A German contract laborer felt he had been unfairly docked: "On one occasion I had not finished my assigned number of rows, not because I was lazy, but because I always took enough time to do my work carefully. At the end of the month my overseer refused to pay me a full wage for that day's work." The Makaweli Plantation had the *poho* 'out of luck' system. When they did not work efficiently, one of the workers explained, they would be told by the luna: "You poho." The luna would subtract fifty cents from the wages for each poho. Chinese workers on the Olowalu Plantation complained their wages were constantly being docked. While investigating their complaint, Wray Taylor of the Bureau of Immigration examined one of the plantation time books, records of the Chinese laborers' work time and pay for each month from March 1896 to April 1897. "The book speaks for itself," Taylor concluded, "and proves on every page that the men's complaint is not without foundation. The manager admitted he docked the men for working slow; it was the law, and he would do it. He is too severe, and if this docking habit of his is not checked there will always be trouble with laborers at Olowalu."[22]

Police power in Hawaii supported plantation discipline and authority. Asked how he would punish a contract laborer for idleness, a planter replied: "We dock him; we give him only one-half or three-quarters of a day; and if he keeps it up we resort to the law and have him arrested for refusing to work." One of the essential functions of the police in Hawaii was to maintain law and order on the plantations. The director of Theo. H. Davies and Company, for example, assured the manager of the Laupahoehoe Plantation that certain Puerto Rican laborers would work steadily. "If they do not," he added sternly, "the Sheriff of your district will have instructions to arrest them for vagrancy and employ them as prisoners on the roads." Planters also used policemen to watch for "tramps, loafers and gamblers," and to keep such "breeders of discontent and turbulence" away from the camps. During the contract labor period, planters constantly depended on the police to capture and arrest deserters—workers who had broken their contracts and run away.[23]

Due to the law enforcement needs of the plantations, expenditures for the maintenance of large police forces soared. Marshal Charles B. Wilson said in 1892: "I am of the opinion that the Government is put to considerable expense for the benefit of the employers of labor; and, were no warrants of arrests allowed to be issued by law for contract laborers, the police force could be considerably reduced without lessening its present efficiency." If the police did not have to track down and arrest deserters, Sheriff E. G. Hitchcock of the Big Island calculated, it "might be very easily reduced to two-thirds of its present number and cost."[24]

Funding appropriations for law enforcement agencies in the islands revealed the relationship between police budgets and the need for policemen to function as special security officers for the plantations. The appropriations in 1903, for example, were:

Island	Population	Appropriation
Hawaii	46,843	$105,000
Maui	24,794	$ 57,000
Oahu	58,000	$170,000
Kauai	20,000	$ 40,000
Molokai	3,123	$ 1,600

Hawaii, Maui, Oahu, and Kauai had sugar plantations and plantation laborers to police; they also received proportionately much larger appropriations than Molokai, which had no sugar plantations. The per capita allocation for police forces on the sugar producing islands was $2.00 and more; for Molokai, it was only $.51. In effect, the people of Hawaii were taxed to finance the policing of plantation workers.[25]

Though plantation laborers were taxed, most of them were not able to vote and hence influence the policies of law enforcement institutions. The Hawaiian Constitution of 1887 limited suffrage to male residents of "Hawaiian, American, or European birth or descent." When the planters seized control of the government and established the Republic seven years later, they wrote a new constitution which continued the disfranchisement of immigrant plantation workers: it required that the voter be a citizen of Hawaii and able to read and write either the English or Hawaiian language. Annexation of Hawaii to the United States did not open the political process to Asian immigrants in the islands, for the United States Naturalization Law of 1790, which was extended to Hawaii, limited naturalized citizenship to "whites" only. In 1911, in his explanation of "how King Sugar ruled," Ray Stannard Baker described the political powerlessness of plantation laborers:

> Control is made easier in Hawaii, as it was in the old South, by the presence of a very large population of non-voting workmen. This not only includes that half of the population which is made up of Chinese and Japanese, but of thousands of ignorant Portuguese, Spanish, Russians, and others, who are not yet naturalized. Fully three-quarters of the population of Hawaii have no more to say about the government under which they are living than the old slaves. The total registered voters in the islands, indeed, is only 14,442 (in 1910). Of these, nearly 10,000 are native Hawaiians, and only 1,763 are American born. The remainder is made up of naturalized Portuguese, British, German and other whites, and 396 Chinese and 234 Japanese. Of the 234 registered Japanese, the highest number who ever voted in an election is thirteen.

Thus, with plantation laborers effectively disfranchised, planters were able to utilize the police power of the state to protect their vested interests.[26]

As a more direct method of discipline, planters sometimes resorted to physical violence. "The bare knowledge on their [the laborers'] part, of the fact that their master was at liberty to give them a sound flogging, say a dozen lashes well laid on," observed a planter in 1866, "would . . . exert a more healthy influence toward good discipline than all the laws our state affords at present." In 1895 the manager of the Paauhau Plantation frankly stated to the Labor Commission that he had doubts about the effectiveness of incarceration and preferred instead the whipping of disobedient "Japs." "This class of people," he argued, "have no feelings except through the hide."[27]

Planters could not legally whip their workers, however: corporal punishment had been declared by law to be "an actionable offense" in the Hawaiian kingdom. "The coolie and the Hawaiian laborer," the editor of the *Hawaiian Gazette* wrote in 1867, "are alike under the protection of the law." But the law did not reflect reality; it did not actually protect workers on the plantations. Even the editor of the *Pacific Commercial Advertiser*, a supporter of plantation interests, conceded in 1868: "It is well known that many are the stripes inflicted and borne because the sufferer is ignorant of the law, or if he knows it, knows also that it is next to useless to seek redress."[28]

For many workers, the black snake whip, carried by the luna or overseer, was a symbol of plantation authority. In a letter to his agent William G. Irwin dated 22 August 1879, George Dole of the Makee Plantation on Kauai inquired about a "black snake whip" he had ordered for one of his overseers. "If you have received it," the plantation manager wrote, "please forward it." Korean laborer Kim Hyung-soon bitterly recalled the use of physical punishment to enforce harsh plantation rules: Korean workers were "treated no better than cows or horses. . . . Every worker was called by number, never by name. During working hours, nobody was allowed to talk, smoke, or even stretch his back. A foreman kept his eyes on his workers at all times. When he found anyone violating working regulations, he whipped the violator without mercy." An old Korean woman told an interviewer: "I'll never forget the foreman. . . . He said we worked like 'lazy.' He wanted us to work faster. . . . He would gallop around on horseback and crack and snap his whip." On the Ewa Plantation in 1906, according to a Japanese worker, "the luna carried a whip and rode a horse. Up until our time, if we talked too much the man swung the whip. He did not actually whip us but just swung his whip so that we would work harder." Hashiji Kakazu recalled that laborers on the Puunene Plantation on Maui feared the camp policeman because he would use his whip to make them go to work. Puerto Rican workers at Ookala Plantation on the island of Hawaii went out on strike in 1901 to protest against physical abuse. "Some of the men," the *Hawaii Herald* reported, "bear marks which they say were made with a whip."[29]

Physical punishment was used on some plantations as a way to intimidate workers—to keep them in line and to make them more efficient and productive. Chinese laborers on the Lihue Plantation, according to Goo Kim in 1897, were allowed five minutes for lunch, at times fifteen, depending on how far they had to go for their meal. But if they were not ready when their allotted time had expired, they were told to "get out" and were "kicked" if they did not hurry. Laborers on the Olowalu Plantation complained to the Secretary of the Bureau of Immigration in 1897 that they had been kicked by the plantation manager. The manager denied their statements, but admitted that he had "pulled the men out of their quarters for various reasons and pushed them around." Lee Hong-ki, a Korean worker who had come to Hawaii in 1903, described his German luna as very strict. "If anyone violated his orders," Lee said, "he was punished, usually with a slap on the face. . . ." Other Korean laborers told Baron Yun that the luna's methods of making them work were harsh, and that they had been "too roughly treated." When they were apprehended and brought back to the plantation, Japanese deserters were sometimes physically punished. According to Yasutaro Soga in his book *Reflections on Fifty Years in Hawaii*, captured deserter Masaji Watanabe was placed in one of the plantation offices and the manager, "a man of colossal physique, alone, gripping a thick leather lash, entered the room. After a time Watanabe, his shirt and 'āhina (denim) pants torn to ribbons, his back covered with blood, crawled out." Such incidents led a United States Labor Commission investigating labor conditions in Hawaii in 1910 to conclude that some lunas were "brutal and overbearing" and "prone" to use "physical violence."[30]

The Plantation Occupational Structure

Plantation authority was reinforced by an occupational structure that stratified plantation employment according to race. On 18 November 1904 the HSPA trustees adopted a resolution that in effect made racial discrimination a formal policy. While the resolution itself did not specify race or racial groups, it did state that all skilled positions should be filled by "American citizens, or those eligible for citizenship." The restriction had a racial function, for it excluded from skilled occupations Asians or immigrants regarded as not "white" according to federal law and hence ineligible to become naturalized citizens. Thus, the Naturalization Law of 1790, enacted long before the entrance of Asians into the United States or Hawaii, became a basis for employment discrimination in the sugar industry. Seven years later the association made its discriminatory policy more explicit and direct by approving another resolution, which instructed plantation managers to reserve skilled and semiskilled positions for Hawaiians and whites.[31]

Actually planters had been developing a pattern of occupational stratification based on race long before it had become a policy of the HSPA. As planters imported workers to meet their labor needs in the nineteenth century, they created a racially stratified labor structure based on an ideology of white supremacy. In 1882 the editor of the *Planters' Monthly*, a journal representing the views of the planter class, declared that it was too well known that "different characteristics" of laborers of different races qualified them for "different positions" in plantation employment: "the regular plodding manner of the Chinaman" and "his aptness for imitating or learning from example" fitted him "peculiarly" for "the routine of hand field work."[32]

Whether or not they were peculiarly fitted for unskilled and routine labor, most of the Chinese plantation laborers were assigned to unskilled positions in the field or mill in 1882. Not all unskilled laborers were Asian or Hawaiian or nonwhite: among them could be found Norwegians, Germans, and Portuguese. But skilled positions, such as sugar boilers, engineers, and lunas or foremen, were held mainly by whites. Of the total number of lunas and clerks 88 percent were white, while 28.5 percent of the laborers were Hawaiian and 48.3 percent were Chinese. None of the lunas were Chinese.[33]

In 1915, thirty-three years later, the basic structure of occupational stratification by race persisted. Japanese workers were mostly field hands and mill laborers. There were only 1 Japanese, 1 Hawaiian, and 3 part-Hawaiian mill engineers; the remaining 41 mill engineers (89 percent) were of European descent. A racial division was particularly evident in supervisory positions: of the 377 overseers, only 2 were Chinese and 17 Japanese; 313 of all overseers (83 percent) were white. Field and mill laborers, predominantly Asians, took orders from lunas or overseers, usually white men.[34]

Asian laborers were very aware of the plantations' hierarchy and the limited possibilities of occupational advancement for them. "Lunas were all Portuguese," observed Minoru Hayashida of the Puunene Plantation on Maui. "Above that was Caucasian field boss called o luna, the big foreman." Another Japanese worker, knowing he would never be able to get ahead on the plantation, expressed his frustration. Told by an interviewer that he would be promoted, become a "big shot" if he had "the stuff," the laborer retorted: "Don't kid me. You know yourself I haven't got a chance. You can't go very high up and get big money unless your skin is white. You can work here all your life and yet a haole who doesn't know a thing about the work can be ahead of you in no time."[35]

Even when workers of different nationalities were employed to do the same tasks, they were paid at different wage rates. Filipino cane cutters, for example, were paid only $.69 in average wages per day in 1910, as compared to $.99 for Japanese cane cutters. "American" or white carpenters earned $4.36 in average wages per day, while Japanese carpenters made only $1.28. The wage differential between "American" overseers and Japanese overseers was enormous—$3.01 to $1.25. The wage differentials between workers of different nationalities assigned to similar occupations reinforced divisions within the work force and also maintained the racial and social hierarchy of the plantation.[36]

The plantation labor force included a small but significant number of women. According to Dora Isenberg of Kauai, during the 1860s Hawaiian women assisted in mill operations. "When the mill was grinding, ox-carts wound slowly up the hill to this old trash yard, bringing the damp fibrous cane refuse from the rollers in the mill. In sunny weather Hawaiian women stood tossing it on the ground outside the sheds to dry it, and piling it up to be carted down the hill and used for fuel in the mill furnace." Portuguese, Norwegian, and German women as well as a small handful of Chinese women were also employed as plantation laborers. As Japanese women increasingly entered the plantation work force after 1885, they boosted the number of women involved in plantation operations. In 1894, for example, 1,618 women were employed as plantation laborers, representing about 7 percent of the entire

WOMEN PLANTATION LABORERS OF MANY NATIONALITIES
Hawaii State Archives

work force; in 1920, 14 percent of all Oahu plantation laborers were women. The preponderance of women workers—over 80 percent of them—were Japanese. Japanese women were concentrated in field operations, such as hoe hana, hole hole work, cane cutting, and even cane loading—a strenuous and backbreaking activity. In 1915, Japanese women constituted 38 percent of all Japanese cane loaders. Though women were given many of the same work assignments as men, they were paid less than their male counterparts. Japanese female field hands, for example, received an average wage of only $.55 per day in 1915, as compared to the $.78 Japanese male field hands received.[37]

While many women were employed directly in plantation production, others performed important support functions on the plantation: they serviced the domestic needs of single men. German women washed laundry and did housecleaning for the laborers; they also took in boarders. A Portuguese immigrant said his mother "washed and served for the 'single man' folks. She get about $10 one month, and with this money she buy our clothes and some things for the house." A Korean woman told an interviewer: "I made custom shirts with hand-bound button holes for 25 cents—of course, customers brought their own fabric. My mother and sister-in-law took in laundry. They scrubbed, ironed and mended shirts for a nickel a piece. It was pitiful! Their knuck-

HAPAI KŌ: JAPANESE WOMAN LOADING CANE
Hawaii State Archives

WOMEN WORKERS SEWING CLOTHES FOR LABORERS
Hawaii State Archives

les became swollen and raw from using the harsh yellow soap."
Japanese women operated bath and boarding houses where bachelor workers could wash off the red dirt covering their bodies and eat homecooked Japanese dinners. On the Hawi Plantation, Katsu Okawa fed her husband, eight children, and fifteen men every night. As the operator of a boarding house on a plantation at Honokaa, Mrs. Tai Yoo Kim prepared meals for her husband and twenty bachelors. Every morning at five o'clock, she fed them a breakfast of rice, broth, and kim chee. For six days each week, she "packed twenty-one lunch tins with rice and dried salt fish. Dinner consisted of soup, rice, and either a soy seasoned dish of vegetables, meat, or fish, or a dish of corned beef and onions." She also did the laundry for each man for one dollar a month. Using a wood fire to heat the water in her galvanized tub filled with denim work pants and shirts, Mrs. Kim boiled the clothes to remove the red dirt and sweat. After scrubbing the clothes on a washboard, rinsing them, and drying them on a clothesline, she starched them with flour and water and then ironed them with a charcoal-heated iron. Thus everywhere on the plantation—in the fields, mills, boarding house, camps—women contributed directly and indirectly to the process of production.[38]

Finally, children were also employed and served as blacksmiths' helpers, camp cleaners, cane cutters, carriers, loaders, store clerks, field hands, hospital servants, and mill laborers. The children's school hours were scheduled around their working hours. In 1895 the HSPA asked the Hawaii Board of Education to schedule school hours from seven o'clock in the morning to noon in order to allow children to work in the afternoons and supplement their parents' income. Many years later, in 1919, C. S. Childs noted the continued employment of children in his "Report on Welfare Investigation: Grove Farm Plantation": "The children go to work at the same hour as the adults, 6 A.M., and stop work at the same hour in the afternoon, 4:30 P.M. They are used for cutting back, hoeing, planting, cutting seed and irrigating newly planted seed. As many children as can be obtained are used during vacation time, but no children are employed during school months. They are given fifteen minutes for breakfast and half hour for lunch." A year later, 305 boys and 59 girls worked on Oahu plantations, representing 3 percent of the entire labor force.[39]

William Rego of the Waialua Plantation was one of those boys

HOE HANA BOYS (MAUI, 1911)
Bishop Museum

in 1920. Born in 1909, he became a *hapai ko* 'carry cane' man at age eleven. "My first job was loading cane, carrying cane, sugar cane on the back," he said years later. "We built up a bundle about fifty to seventy-five pounds weight and we carry that cane up the ladder into the cane cars. . . . We had lots of young boys at our age, little older than I was, working also for the plantation because plantation needed labor in those days." On Maui, fifteen-year-old Tokusuke Oshiro carried lunch boxes to the workers in the fields. As an old man of seventy-eight years looking back at those early days, he chuckled: "My salary was 50 cents a day which my father took. But I was still mischievous then." The Portuguese and Spanish boys and I "took the bottles out from the lunch boxes and lined them up on the side of the road. We used them as targets and broke them all."[40]

Wages: The Carrot and the Stick

On Saturdays, twice a month, plantation workers assembled in lines in front of the manager's office to receive their pay. Workers carried, usually on a chain, their bangos—small brass or aluminum disks with their identification numbers stamped on them. They were required to remember their bango numbers and carry their tags during working hours. The laborers' accounts were kept under their bango numbers. The use of the bango system, a director of the HSPA explained to the manager of the Grove Farm Plantation, gave management "a big saving both in time and worry due to writing difficult names." As they entered the office, workers showed their bangos to plantation police; they were then handed pay envelopes with their bango numbers, as well as accountings of deductions for purchases made at the plantation store. As they left the office with their pay envelopes, workers were quickly surrounded by crowds of creditors: local storekeepers, fish and vegetable peddlers, boarding housekeepers, laundry women, and merchants, all of them anxious to collect payments for their bimonthly bills.[41]

After satisfying their creditors, many workers found they had a little money left to repay banks that had made loans to them for transportation to Hawaii. "Since I owed 100 yen to the bank," Ko Shigeta said, "I could not afford to rest. The boarding fee was $7 or $8 a month, and the wives cooked for us. I worked hard, and in two years I was able to pay the bank the 100 yen." But other plantation laborers found it difficult to make financial ends meet. "I worked in the sugar cane fields in Maui ten hours per day," explained Kanichi Tsukamaki. "I thought I could earn enough money in three months, but I soon realized that I had made a great mistake. Except Sundays, I worked all day without resting even for one hour, and yet I was only paid $16 a month. Furthermore, they charged me $7 for meals and additional fees for bathing, haircuts and so on. To save money I tolerated my unkempt hair and had it cut only one-third as often as formerly." During his visit to the islands in 1915, an editor of a Japanese newspaper commented: "No, the Japanese here, the thousands who labor on your plantations, are not contented. They feel that . . . the process of saving money from their wages . . . is very slow."[42]

One of the planters' chief concerns was the need to control wages. In 1882 they organized the Planters' Labor and Supply Company to fix the rate of wages for plantation laborers, as well as to provide labor and protect the contract labor system. In a memo sent to all plantation managers in 1883, E. P. Adams, secretary of the company, warned that Chinese leaders in Honolulu would try to distribute Chinese immigrants to plantations in Hawaii "with the view of keeping up the present and unreliable system of day

labor." Fearful such an effort would force wages upward as planters competed for day or unbound workers supplied by Chinese
labor companies, the secretary urged planters to break up the day
labor system by refusing to employ Chinese as day laborers. Planters were told they should hire Chinese only as contract laborers and offer them wages of $10 per month, plus board and
lodging.[43]

Twelve years later, the planters founded an even more formidable and powerful organization—the Hawaiian Sugar Planters' Association. Designed to centralize management information and
decision-making and to do agricultural research, the HSPA became the primary mechanism for the regulation of wages. After
federal law had terminated the contract labor system in 1900, the
HSPA quickly instituted new measures for the control of the newly
freed laborers. In a "Confidential Letter" to plantation managers
dated 24 July 1901, the HSPA stated that the high rates of wages
caused "grave concern and much alarm," and called for island
conventions at which managers would meet to form wage-fixing
agreements. "The deliberations of Island conventions at which
manager would meet should be behind closed doors," the association advised, "as it would be embarrassing to have such proceedings published." The association organized a central labor bureau
to coordinate all employment of Asian laborers and to force them
to be paid wage rates set by the HSPA. The association also introduced a passbook system in which all Asian laborers would be
issued passbooks containing the worker's name, nationality, pass-
port number, date of employment, date of discharge (voluntary or
involuntary), record of work days, and a plantation stamp.[44]

In 1901 the Board of Trustees of the HSPA passed a resolution
that fixed the maximum rate or wages for all laborers. The resolution, which was sent to all plantation managers, specified the rates
for each island, even for particular regions and plantations:

Hawaii: Hilo Plantation—$18 per mo.
         Hamakua & Kohala—$20 per mo.
         Kau & Kona, Puna—$19 per mo.

Maui: Hana—$20 per mo.
         Kihei—$24 per mo.
         South Spreckelsville—$22 per mo.
         All Others—$19 per mo.

Oahu: All Plantations—$20 per mo.

Kauai: Waimea & Kekaha—$23 per mo.
Kilauea—$21 per mo.
All others—$20 per mo.

The wages were to become effective 1 September 1901. Though the HSPA allowed the wage rates to vary from plantation to plantation, it warned laborers that they should not try to leave their plantations to seek more attractive wages at other plantations. Laborers were told that if they did leave, they would not be hired by other plantations unless they could show a certificate of discharge. The association also developed a centralized interisland system of information to monitor movements of laborers trying to bargain for higher wages. When the HSPA learned that sixty Filipino laborers at the Olaa Sugar Company had refused to work under the terms of the labor agreement and left the plantation, it immediately instructed all managers to offer them only the same terms.[45]

After 1900 planters increasingly began to pay their workers on the basis of short- and long-term contracts. Under a short-term contract, workers were employed at piecework rates. They were paid at a specified rate for the completion of an assigned unit of work, such as cane cutting, cane loading, weeding, irrigating, bagging of sugar, or cleaning boilers. Under a long-term contract, workers were organized into small groups and allotted areas of land. They were furnished with seed cane, water, fertilizer, and tools, and were responsible for cultivating the cane. Under a headman, they weeded, irrigated, fertilized the fields, stripped the cane, harvested, and transported the crop to the mills, where it was weighed and the workers were paid for the cane at the rate stipulated in the contract. The entire process usually took two years, and during this time laborers were provided with housing, gardens, and fuel. Their work time was recorded by the plantation timekeeper, and they were allowed advances for subsistence based on the amount of work done. The advances were deducted from the amount of money owed to the workers for the harvested cane, and the remainder—the *kompang* 'share'—constituted what the workers called the "big pay." But the pay in the end was seldom big. Describing his experience under the long-term contract, one worker said: "In 1909, the manager gave me 12 acres of land between the school and the sea. I got five men. I was the head and we worked hard. In 1911, we cut the first crop and the cane was good, but the scale man at the mill was a robber and he cheated us. We hardly made any money."[46]

The purpose of the long-term contract, however, was not to cheat the workers but to control them. Concerned about the movement of Japanese laborers to the mainland, planters sought to keep them in Hawaii, to "induce them to stay by means of cane growing contracts." They also used the contract arrangement as an incentive system, a way to instill in laborers "a direct interest" in the total output of their field and to extract from them "more and better work than on a day-wage basis." If all hands were "interested parties" and the plantation's output were reduced to dollars and cents, planters reasoned, "a concentration of effort" would be "a matter of course." Every worker would "expect" his fellow laborer to do his duty," and "loafers and laggards" would "not be tolerated" by the workers themselves.[47]

More important, the long-term contract offered planters a weapon against organized labor. At a meeting held 24 March 1909, the HSPA trustees decided that the long-term contract system should be more generally adopted on the plantations in order to "offset" the "agitation" of the Japanese Higher Wages Association. In a letter sent to all plantation managers on April 9, the trustees warned: "We have an agitation on foot. The Higher Wages Association is out for business, and the business it has in hand is . . . to increase wages all along the line." Although they admitted an increase of two dollars a month in wages would be "an easy matter" to concede to the workers, the trustees stated that they feared such a raise would be a "stimulus" for the Laborers' Association to make more demands for higher wages and to become a "permanent institution," a "formidable adversary" and an "embryo tyrant" whose "bidding" would become an "order." Convinced they had to "devise some way to control the situation" and "put the agitators out of the game," the trustees argued: "The only way to cut them out of the situation . . . is by some covered deal with the laborers direct, and the only method so far conceived is by means of contracts with the laborers." Contract laborers would have greater incentive to increase crop production, and thus the "agitator for higher wages"—"a mischief maker and leech"— would find his "point of attack closed." The whole question of workers' earnings would be rendered elusive, for the rates on contracts would be immensely more difficult to assess and criticize than wage rates. "Contract rates in different districts would vary to such an extent that inside information as to its detail would not be generally public or readily obtained, contrasting markedly with the present notoriously public knowledge based on the '$18.00 per month' hue and cry."[48]

In addition to the long-term contract, planters instituted a complex "bonus" system. As early as 1899 the trustees of the HSPA recommended that the plantations "act together" to raise wages in the form of a bonus, payable at the termination of the contract. Nine years later the HSPA developed a sliding scale for the bonus based on the average number of work days per month: laborers who averaged twenty work days per month annually would be paid a bonus at the end of the year. In 1912 the HSPA converted the bonus system into a so-called "profit sharing" program. Under this new arrangement, laborers who worked an average of twenty days per month for a year and who received $24 a month or less in wages were paid a share of the plantation's profits. They received a bonus of 1 percent of their annual earnings for every dollar increase over $70 for the average price of a ton of sugar. Thus if the price of sugar were $80 a ton, workers who qualified for a bonus were paid 10 percent of their annual earnings on their regular pay day in November or December for the year ending October 31.[49]

The bonus system was designed to help planters solve the problem of labor shortage and lost labor time. Laborers had not been performing a full month's work each month; time sheets showed planters that the average number of days worked by each laborer was less than eighteen days per month. The bonus program, planters calculated, would reduce the number of days workers wasted in "laying off," and hence would appreciably increase the supply of labor without the importation of more laborers. It would add from 10 to 20 percent labor to the work force of the plantation, and the amount of money necessary for bonus payments would be less than the cost of importing the three to six thousand workers needed to realize an equivalent increase in labor. In addition, the cost of maintaining camps and housing for laborers would be less with a smaller force working full time than with a larger force working only part of the time.[50]

The bonus system was more than a plan to increase the supply of labor and cut camp costs: it also served as a means for planters to exercise greater control over their workers—as a "carrot and stick" strategy of incentive as well as intimidation. In a circular issued to all plantations on 22 August 1910, the HSPA explained: "The whole intention of the bonus is that it shall be an annual payment based on a whole year's faithful work. . . ." And eleven years later, in its pamphlet on *The Sugar Industry of Hawaii and the Labor Shortage*, the HSPA again stated: "The Hawaiian sugar plantations . . . are actuated in granting a bonus by the principle of desiring to compensate their employees for loyal labor. It is a reward for faithful service and a spur to productivity. And the bonus payments actually amount to profit sharing with the laborers." But the bonus system was also intended to compel workers to labor at least twenty days a month for one year and keep them from leaving the plantation. In a letter to George N. Wilcox of the Grove Farm Plantation, the vice president of H. Hackfeld and Company noted that the bonus for the year paid on October 31 would "prevent a large exodus of laborers after the settlement is made. We find that the Japanese leave in large numbers between March and October. The bonus is paid yearly. If the laborers leave before the end of the year, they forfeit it." In a letter to C. Brewer and Company, the manager of the Hawaiian Agricultural Company Plantation stated frankly: "I wanted to have a string on them by their being on the annual bonus list."[51]

The Eight P.M. Whistle

At four-thirty in the afternoon, the workers again heard the blast of the plantation whistle. They had begun work early in the morning and had labored all day under the blazing sun. They felt they had been worked "like horses, moving mechanically under the whipping hands of the luna." "We worked like machines," a laborer recalled. "For 200 of us workers, there were seven or eight lunas and above them was a field boss on a horse. We were watched constantly." Another worker described the strict supervision even more graphically: "Really, life on the plantation is one of restrictions, unwritten rules and regulations imposed upon the inhabitants by the manager . . . who is assisted by his various ranks of overseers and lunas to see to it that the people obey these regulations and do the amount and nature of the work that is expected of

CARRYING CANE
Hawaii State Archives

them. . . . In conclusion I say that life on a plantation is much like life in a prison."

> Hawaii, Hawaii
> But when I came
> What I saw
> Was hell
> The boss was Satan
> The lunas
> His helpers.[52]

But finally, after a long day of labor, it was pau hana time—time to stop working and return to camp. Everywhere, from Koloa to Waialua to Lahaina to Kau, plantation laborers scrambled from the fields.

> In the rush at pau hana
> I get caught in cane leaves
> When I stumble and fall
> They prickle, they jab.

In their camps, the workers comforted their weary and dust-covered bodies in the *furos* 'hot baths'. "The bath was communal," Tokusuke Oshiro said. "We all took a bath together. If, however, you got in last, it would be very dirty. So you wanted to get in first. For that reason I'd come running even if I were two or three miles away. It would make about 20 minutes difference. By the time everyone got back I'd already taken a bath." Then the laborers ate their dinners, the families in their cottages and the single men in boarding houses. After dinner, some of them read letters from home.

> Today's work
> Was not so hard
> Because last night
> A letter from home
> Came from Japan.

Sitting around fires, workers nursed their sore hands. "We suffered from blisters on our hands all the time," Choki Oshiro said. "Because we did not have any medicine, we tried to cure them by burning them over the fire, at night, while we prepared for the next day's work."[53]

Mostly the laborers sat on rocks and porches and "talked story." They noted how work was so different in Hawaii: "In Japan we could say, 'It's okay to take the day off today,' since it was our own work. We were free to do what we wanted. We didn't have that freedom on the plantation. We had to work ten hours every day." Their new surroundings seemed so dreary: "Here you couldn't see anything, no view, no landscape, just fields and hills. Ah, such a place. Is Hawaii a place like this?" Slapping at the buzzing and bothersome mosquitoes, laborers also complained about the heat in the fields, the stinging yellow jackets, their bruised muscles, and the mean lunas. "It burns us up to have an ignorant *luna* stand around and holler and swear at us all the time for not working fast enough. Every so often, just to show how good he is, he'll come up and grab a hoe or whatever we are working with and work like _____ for about two minutes and then say sarcastically, 'Why you no work like that?' He knows and we know he couldn't work for ten minutes at that pace." The workers also grumbled about the lunas calling them by their bangos: "They never call a man by his name. Always by the bango, 7209 or 6508 in that manner." "And that was the thing I objected to. I wanted my name, not the number." They were not willing to suffer such abuse forever, they insist-

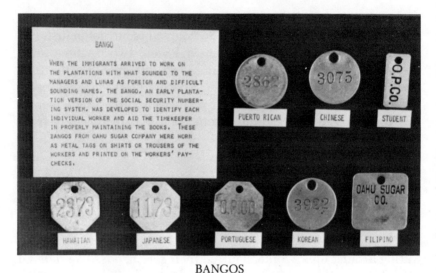

BANGOS
Waipahu Cultural Garden Park Collection

"They never call a man by his name. Always by the bango, 7209 or 6508 in that manner." "And that was the thing I objected to. I wanted my name, not the number."

ed, and they discussed their "big plans" to leave the plantation as soon as they had some money: to open a grocery store in town, move to the mainland, or return home to become rich and secure landowners.

> The only reason I'm doing
> This tough and painful holehole work
> Is for the sake of my wife and children
> Who live back home.

Feeling homesick, they shared stories and news about the old country. A Portuguese laborer remembered how his family and neighbors gathered together in the camp after dinner and "talked and talked." "My father folks," he said, "they talk about Azores and they wonder what so and so is doing now."[54]

At eight o'clock, the plantation siren sounded again, to signal it was time for bed. All lights were turned out at eight-thirty; talking was not permitted, and every laborer had to be in bed. "After work," a Filipino laborer stated, "all I wanted to do was go to sleep, exhausted as I was from the hard work in the cane fields." But in their sleep, many found themselves struggling against repressed fears and worries. "At night, instead of a sweet dream of my wife and child left in Okinawa," a laborer said, "I was wakened up frightened by the nightmare of being whipped by the luna." And even when they did not have nightmares, they slept restlessly, their tense bodies waiting for the blast of the five A.M. whistle. "For the first two and a half years here," a Filipino plantation worker recounted, "I lived pretty much the same. Six days a week I worked from siren to siren."[55]

IV

Plantation Camps: Community and Culture

The Plantation Pyramid

The plantation resembled a "pyramid," explained Milton Mura-yama in *All I Asking For Is My Body*. At the top of the slope was the big house, the home of the manager; below were the "nicer-looking" homes of the Portuguese, Spanish, and Japanese lunas; then the "identical wooden frame houses of Japanese Camp"; and finally the "more run-down Filipino Camp." Moreover, the organization of the housing hierarchy was "planned and built around its sewage system." The concrete ditches that serviced the toilets and outhouses ran from the manager's house on the highest slope down to the Filipino Camp on the lowest perimeter of the plantation. The tiered housing pattern and sewage system seemed emblematic: "Shit too was organized according to the plantation pyramid."[1]

Indeed the physical organization of plantation housing reflected, as well as reinforced, a social hierarchy. The manager lived in a mansion with spacious verandas and white columns overlooking the plantation; his foremen and the technical employees were housed in "handsome bungalow cottages." Surrounded by well-kept lawns and flower gardens, these homes reminded one visitor of the attractive houses he had seen in Manoa and Kaimuki. A Korean worker said that his three haole bosses lived in "big houses" quite a distance away from the camps. In 1900 Wray Taylor found that the kind of housing varied with the class of labor: European laborers (either a family or two single men) were assigned two rooms in a four-room cottage, while Chinese workers were placed in barracks with from six to forty men in a room.[2]

Workers of different nationalities were usually housed in separate buildings or camps. A Korean laborer recalled how all of the workers, living in "one big camp," were "segregated racially—the

Japanese occupying one building, the Chinese another, etc." In his investigation of plantation conditions, R. A. Duckworth-Ford reported that residential districts on the plantation were "subdivided into racial sections" for Filipinos, Portuguese, Japanese, Koreans, and Puerto Ricans. The formation of separate ethnic camps reflected the wave pattern of labor recruitment and immigration. As planters recruited groups of laborers from different countries, they constructed new camps for them. The laborers themselves preferred camps of their own, so they could practice the customs and traditions of their respective homelands and speak their native languages. A Filipino worker, describing the development of separate camps for different nationalities on the Ewa Plantation, said: "At that time nearly everyone who worked at all in this plantation lived in one camp. There were Puerto Ricans, Spanish, a handful of Portuguese, Chinese, a few Japanese and a few Koreans. Each nationality group more or less constituted an exclusive group of its own; no group seemed to mingle with any other. . . . Every year there were many Filipino immigrants who joined our camp. There were so many Filipinos that a separate camp was given to them. The other nationalities soon had a camp of their own too, a thing which pleased everyone, as not only work was thought of but also parties among the laborers could be held."[3]

While the organization of camps into different nationalities may not have sprung from a consciously designed planter policy of residential segregation, it did support the planters' strategy of dividing and thus controlling their work force. Assigned to separate camps, workers of different nationalities were urged to compete against each other not only in the fields but also in the camps. Visiting the McBryde Plantation on Kauai, an official of the HSPA found the Filipino camp was filthy. He called the men together and told them he was "very much ashamed" of their camp, "especially after passing a clean Jap camp." Subsequently the Filipinos quickly tidied their camp, and the next morning, one of them assured the pleased official: "We are all going to keep it clean. Now you will not find it like this [dirty] again."[4]

But not all plantations had separate ethnic camps and a few planters even deliberately assigned their workers to integrated camps. The manager of the Waialua Plantation, for example, placed Korean workers in a "detached camp" after they arrived in 1903 in order to avoid the "danger of race troubles of any kind with Japanese, Chinese or Portuguese." This arrangement, however, was intended to be only temporary. "Should Korean immigration . . . be finally established," he wrote to the HSPA, "I would consider it better to give them houses to themselves . . . in the regular plantation camps where they will be subject to the same rules . . . and thereby lose their identity as Koreans and be merged into the plantation community as a whole." In his *Plantation Sketches*, Jared G. Smith described the integrated camps of the Hawaiian Commercial and Sugar Company in Wailuku on Maui: "None of the camps are given over to one race exclusively, and equal treatment is given to all. The result of this mixing of all races in one village has been the disappearance of racial antagonisms and jealousies and the development of mutual respect."[5]

Housing conditions for workers varied from plantation to plantation. In 1899 Dr. Charles A. Peterson of the Bureau of Immigration found model camps where every house was weather-proof and where the surrounding space was clean and well drained. But he also visited camps that were "decrepit and dilapidated rookeries with roofs leaking and danger and disease threatening the occupants, with masses of filth blocking the drains and decaying refuse all about and beneath the houses." Seventeen years later, another investigator, Montague Lord of the HSPA, also noted a wide range of housing conditions. Some plantations, like Laupahoehoe and Waialua, had "splendid camps," which were "satisfactory," "very clean," and "well-planted [with flowers]." But he reported that other plantations, like Pepeekeo and that of the Hawaiian Sugar Company, had very dirty camps with houses in "a rotten condition."[6]

Generally plantation laborers lived in crowded and unsanitary camps. According to the editor of a Japanese newspaper published in Honolulu, workers were housed in dwellings resembling "pig sties [rather than] human habitations." Several hundred laborers "swarmed together" in one-storied, white-washed "tenements." A laborer on the Aiea Plantation in 1903, Ko Shigeta recalled: "Fifty of us, both bachelors and married couples, lived together in a humble shed—a long ten-foot-wide hallway made of wattle and lined along the sides with a slightly raised floor covered with a grass rug, and two *tatami* mats to be shared among us." A Japanese worker on the Makaweli Plantation said that the men would line up and sleep "like sardines" in a can. Norwegian laborers

EARLY PLANTATION CAMP
Bishop Museum

complained that a worker with a wife and children was furnished
with only a small six-by-eight-foot room. Cramped together in barracks, single men slept on "blankets spread over hay, on tiers of
bunks, like silkworms" or on wood floors with one blanket for each
worker. Chinese laborers on the Paia Plantation were crowded
into "big warehouses filled with bunks stacked four or five high,
steamer style. Two or three hundred [of them] lived in a building."
Visiting the camps of Korean laborers, Hyun Soon found his compatriots living in tenements: "The married men each occupy one
room, but single ones are put in compartments in groups of five or
six people. The filth and uncleanliness of their living quarters are
beyond description." According to Montague Lord's report ad-
dressed to the HSPA's Labor Committee in 1916, housing for Filipino workers on the Hawaiian Sugar Company Plantation was
congested. In many instances, Lord wrote, six men occupied a
small eight-by-twelve-foot room and two families had to share a
single room. Several workers told Lord that they "were going to
send their families home . . . on account of being overcrowded."[7]

Due to the lack of privacy and space, workers often became
tense and nervous. "Ten of us shared a small house and in such a

cramped space we were constantly brushing against each other," a Filipino worker said. "We were often irritated at each other. Small annoyances led to quarrels. Endless arguments arose as to whose turn it was to prepare supper, wash dishes or buy the food. An innocent remark or comment, interpreted wrongly, might result in a fight." Conflicts sometimes erupted between single men and families. On one plantation, for example, some Japanese single men sharing houses with families were kept awake at night by a crying baby. Tired and angry, the men worried they would not be able to maintain the demanding pace of work set by the luna, and they insisted the mother take her baby and leave the house. After camping in the cane field for several nights, the distraught mother appealed to the manager for help but was told: "No pilikia me go kaukau" 'Don't bother me; I'm going to dinner'.[8]

After Hawaii became a territory of the United States, planters increasingly admitted the existence of congested and squalid conditions in plantation camps and made systematic efforts to improve housing for their workers. In September 1910, the HSPA advised planters to award cash prizes to workers who had the best kept yards and gardens around their homes. "An attractive camp," the association stated, "is something which always attracts visitors, and which always gives them a favorable impression of the treatment of laborers by the plantations. When taking visitors around we always show them camps that are well kept in preference to those that are barren. . . . The plantations should also see to it that trees are furnished to laborers and that they are encouraged to plant and care for them."[9]

As planters increasingly employed men with families rather than single men, they began to abandon the barrack system and provided cottages for families. In a letter to the manager of the Hawaiian Agricultural Company Plantation in 1916, C. Brewer and Company wrote that "dependable married men" were "preferred" as workers and authorized the building of cottages for married laborers. In 1920 the HSPA promoted the development of family housing units for workers. "Housing conditions on the plantations have changed greatly during the past few years, lately on account of the change in labor from single to married men," stated Donald S. Bowman, director of the HSPA's Industrial Service Bureau. "We recommend that all future construction of laborers' and semi-skilled married men's quarters be of the one-family single house type, with not less than two bedrooms, situated on a lot of approximately 5,000 square feet, with the necessary wash, bath house, and other sanitary arrangements on the premises."[10]

Planters had self-interested reasons for their camp improvement program. They wanted to "stimulate" the "home feeling" in the camps in order to make workers happier and more productive. "Pleasant surroundings, with some of the modern comforts and conveniences," explained an HSPA director, "go a long way to make the worker healthier and more efficient in his work."[11]

The laborers also had their reasons for beautifying their camps. Japanese workers developed artistic gardens around their plantation cottages, and a mainland visitor observed that the flowers and "miniature gardens with little rocky pools and goldfish" suggested "a corner of Japan." Determined to have their traditional hot baths, Japanese workers also built furos in the camps. The manager of the Hawaiian Agricultural Company Plantation observed in a letter to C. Brewer and Company that the Japanese camp at Pahala had separate bathhouses for men and women. "But we find that both men and women are still making use of both tubs," he added. "It will be difficult to break the Japs of this time worn custom." A Japanese laborer recalled how men and women shared bathing facilities on the Ewa Planation, and how he washed himself with the wives of other men stepping over him matter-of-factly as if he were "a dog or cat in their path," "the cold drops from the ends of their hair" falling on his back.[12]

Workers also cultivated vegetable gardens on plots assigned to them by the plantation manager. Located adjacent to or near the camp, these gardens enabled workers and their families to grow their own fruit and vegetables. They also used their plots of land to raise chickens, rabbits, ducks, and pigs. During his investigation of welfare conditions on the Grove Farm Plantation, C. S. Childs found an extensive system of vegetable gardens. "At the Puhi camp," he reported, "each house is provided with a small amount of ground immediately around it, on which quite a large tract of land has been set aside a little distance from the camp on the other side of the road. Each family is given a plot in this division and given water for the purpose of irrigation. These gardens have been very successful and supply a large part of the vegetable need of the

The Hawi Plantation where Catherine Okawa was born. *Hawaii State Archives*

families." A Japanese laborer recalled how he cultivated his garden even after ten hours of hard work in the cane fields: "After we came home from the field, it was dark especially in the winter months but we tilled our little vegetable garden with the help of the kerosene lamp light to raise the vegetables we ate."[13]

Gradually, over the years, the workers transformed the camps into communities as cottages for families replaced barracks for single men. As the workers themselves landscaped their yards and planted vegetable gardens, they developed the "home feeling" in their camps. People began to know and care for each other. "There were other Portuguese people in Paia from previous shipments," an immigrant laborer stated, "and they were all very good in helping the newcomers with clothes, food and especially bread. . . . Just about every family was provided with a plot of land big enough to grow vegetables. . . . Most families had a milk cow." "There was another thing I'd come to like about the camp," remarked Kiyoshi in Murayama's novel about plantation life. "The hundred Japanese families were like one big family. Everybody knew everybody else, everybody was friendly." In the camps, immigrant laborers created working class communities for themselves—places to raise families, play, worship, and transplant their cultures from the old country to Hawaii.[14]

Medical Care

The plantation was a complete community, providing hospital care as well as housing. Workers found that medical service varied widely from plantation to plantation, from "a daily constant attendance and comfortable, well-equipped hospital . . . to fortnightly visits and no provision for care other than the camp barracks . . . helped out by the mercies of fellow workers." But whether they had available the facilities of a modern hospital or only camp barracks, laborers learned that plantation medical care had its limits.[15]

Language and cultural barriers between doctor and patient rendered medical care difficult to administer, sometimes even hazardous. According to Dr. Charles A. Davis of the Ewa Plantation, even prescribing medicine was not always a simple matter, for many patients had never seen a pill before in their lives. Given pills to swallow, many of them would hesitate, uncertain what to do with them until "instructed by their better informed friends." But occasionally their friends were not as explicit as they should have been, and some patients would "chew the pills before swallowing as they would a piece of bread, and apparently with as much relish." But the problem of communication was sometimes more serious. Recalling the frustration he and his fellow Korean laborers felt because they were unable to speak English and explain their bodily afflictions to the doctor, Yang Choo-en said bitterly: "I saw with my eyes some of my good friends die in the plantation camps. In fact, one of them died in my lap with an unknown illness after he got back from his doctor."[16]

Some plantation doctors were simply incompetent. Dr. Davis admitted that he knew of plantation doctors who had such confidence in their own power of diagnosing disease that they would ignore a patient's descriptions of his ailment and would refuse to give medicine if they did not find pathological symptoms. Consequently sick laborers would sometimes be sent back to their bunks or would even be ordered to return to the fields. "The failure of the doctor's diagnostic acumen in one case," Dr. Davis added, "proved fatal." When Ko Shigeta, a laborer on the Aiea Plantation, came down with pleurisy due to over-exertion and lack of rest, he asked for help from the plantation doctor. "The white doctor at the farm came," he complained, "but merely looked into the shed through the window and didn't give me decent treatment."[17]

But the plantation physician was more than a dispenser of medicine: he also functioned as a disciplinarian. Laborers were not permitted to evaluate their own physical condition and decide whether or not they were able to work; only the doctor had the power to determine whether they were ill and to excuse them from work. "Even if one were sick," said Taro Yoshitake of the Waipahu Plantation, "he could not stay in his bunk without a doctor's certificate. If one were discovered in camp, in bed without this certificate, the Portuguese foreman came with a long whip and drove him out." Yasutaro Soga, who served as an interpreter between the plantation doctor and Japanese laborers of the same plantation, charged that medical service seemed designed to discipline rather than care for workers: "Those laborers who were ill and wished to rest from work . . . applied for permission, and the doctor examined them and decided whether to grant the request. The medical examination was perfunctory. Most illnesses went unheeded, the applicant being sent to the fields. Within the camp, police . . . made the rounds and drove the truants to work one after another. . . . One time a man from Yamaguchi prefecture, who suffered from a high fever, in spite of his and my protests, was sent against his will to the fields. And it happened that while working in the fields he died." When plantation worker João Fereira complained to the Portuguese consul general that he was sick and not given food for his family, the manager of the Hutchinson Plantation replied to the Portuguese official: "The man may be sick, though the Doctor hardly sees reason for excusing him from work." A Norwegian laborer angrily complained: "The doctor sticks up for the planter and declares the sick to be well."[18]

In administering medical care to plantation laborers, the doctor was expected to ferret out and punish malingerers. He could declare that a worker claiming to be ill was fit and fine him $3 for the first offense and $9 for subsequent offenses. He could also use his hospital as a "jail." In his investigation of the Olowalu Plantation in 1897, Wray Taylor of the Bureau of Immigration found that the treatment of sick laborers practically amounted to "cruelty." Describing the punitive purpose of the hospital, he wrote: "Near the beach, a good distance from the men's quarters, is a room about 12 by 12 used as a hospital. The laborers call it jail. I found in it at the time of my visit five Chinese and four Japanese laborers, all sick. The room was in a filthy condition. These sick men have to leave their quarters early in the morning, when the whistle blows, and go to the hospital, remaining there all day until the evening whistle blows when they are allowed to return to their quarters. Is this humane treatment? I hardly think so."[19]

Plantation physicians had been placed in a frustrating and difficult situation. "I administer medicine and otherwise treat, on the average, one hundred and eighty persons every day of the year," wrote Dr. Davis. "There are some who are quite sick, many indifferently sick and others malingering; all of whom however report themselves 'too much sick.' " "There were," conceded Yasutaro Soga, "some good-for-nothing, lazy fellows who deliberately drank such things as soy bean sauce and pretended to be ill." The problem, however, was that the plantation doctor was not always able to discern whether or not a worker was shamming his sickness. A doctor on the Laupahoehoe Plantation, for example, examined a laborer claiming he had a "Chinese sickness." "Sometimes this means 'loafing,' " the director of Theo. H. Davies and Company commented, "but sometimes weakness." Unable to discern the true condition of many patients, the doctor often felt compelled to order them back to work. A government physician explained the predicament plantation doctors faced: "The early symptoms of many diseases are masked. The man's tongue and pulse may appear normal, and yet he may feel very sick indeed. . . . Some cases that leave the doctor's presence, go into the fields to die."[20]

Little wonder many laborers lacked confidence in the plantation doctor. In 1896 Japanese workers on the Lihue Plantation went out on strike to demand medical treatment by Japanese doctors. Many Korean plantation laborers used traditional medicines purchased from Chinese herb shops in nearby towns, or turned to fellow workers trained in acupuncture. "We used to drink our own medicine that we kept at home," explained Jitsuo Fujimura of the Waialua Plantation. "People used to carry around those things and bring it and leave it in your house. In a big package. Fever medicine or diarrhea medicine. . . . They were all from Japan." Self-care and reliance on medical cures and practices carried to Hawaii from the old country seemed to offer them more dependable, even safer medical care than that of many western-trained doctors employed by the plantation management.[21]

Recreation

To escape from the drab and routine existence of plantation life, laborers found ways to entertain themselves. Many of them went fishing. "One good thing," said a Portuguese worker, "you could go out fishing one hour on Sunday and come home with a flour sack full of fish." A Filipino worker recollected that he "went with friends to the rocky edge of the ocean" to "throw net" on Sundays. "After *pau hana* . . . we caught small shrimp for fish bait," a Japanese plantation laborer told an interviewer. "There were a lot of fish there. We could catch as many *papio* as we wanted in those days."[22]

Lonely, far away from families they had left behind in their homelands, workers sought solace and entertainment in card playing and gambling. "Here and there gambling was in favor," reported Yasutaro Soga of the Waipahu Plantation. "On the Saturday evening following pay day, questionable women and professional gamblers from Honolulu came on business to the camp. Some profiteers rented their rooms to such creatures. And the visitors wrung from the workers the fruits of their painstaking toil." Chinese gamblers traveled from plantation to plantation, and gambling in the Chinese quarters was so intense it sometimes interfered with the work schedule. On 2 September 1881 the manager of the Paauhau Plantation on the Big Island angrily scribbled into his diary: "There are only a few Chinamen carrying cane. O. Otto—a foreman went to the China house and drove the gambler outsiders out and told those who did not come to get their money and leave." According to the Japanese Consul in 1888, gambling among Japanese workers had reached a point where "all night sessions" were "common." On the Kilauea Plantation, Baishiro Tamashiro became so involved in gambling that he stopped working. "When I won," he recalled, "I would pay for my cook charge first of all. If not, I had to borrow money. I spent about half a year on gambling." Cockfight gambling was popular among Filipino laborers. One of them said: "On Sundays . . . I just sat around playing Sakura [Japanese card game] and talking stories. But mostly, I watched the cockfights. It felt good to see blood spilled regularly." Many workers spent their weekends and nights gambling to help them forget their isolation, hoping to win big—perhaps even enough money to return rich to their homeland. Usually they lost, and in the fields the next day, they would sing:

> The thirty-five cents
> That I earned and saved
> Is gone by night
> From gambling.[23]

Many Filipino laborers also found their wages gone by the end of the evening, spent at taxi dance halls. On paydays, Filipino string bands, traveling from plantation to plantation, played music at crowded dances. Craving the company of women, Filipino men eagerly purchased tickets that offered them a momentary escape, three minutes to touch, hold, and dance with a woman. "Some guys, they spend $50, $30, one man. One night," recalled Dorotio Allianic, the organizer of a string band on Kauai, "go for broke, the men."[24]

After the 1909 strike, planters recognized the need to develop recreational programs for their workers. In 1910 the HSPA urged managers to provide amusements on the plantations. Sports, especially baseball, should be promoted: "A baseball ground well laid out and grassed, could be afforded by every plantation, and to encourage this sport, which every nationality of laborers is keen for, prizes could be offered to winning teams." Musical activities should also be supported: "Every plantation could afford to encourage a band or a stringed orchestra; instruments could be provided by the plantation, and concerts and dances would become a feature of plantation life." Films and movies should also be shown regularly on the plantation: "A moving picture show is something all nationalities enjoy. . . . Carefully selected films which would give the most satisfaction could be shown on every plantation." Such a "welfare program" of athletics, music, and movie entertainment, explained the vice president of H. Hackfeld and Company, would offer plantation managers "magnificent results," "not only in holding the laborer on the plantation, but in preventing strikes." He added: "Leaving out of consideration the humanitarian side of any such welfare work, we believe it would be to the financial benefit of the plantation to endeavor to cultivate a spirit of contentment among the laborers."[25]

Six years later, the HSPA sent Montague Lord to investigate

conditions on the plantations. In his report, he noted the presence of recreational programs on several plantations. The Hutchinson Plantation on the Big Island had "racially mixed" baseball teams of Japanese and Filipino workers. The Pioneer Mill Company of Maui had a club and baseball team, and the Waialua Plantation on Oahu allowed workers to own a fish trap on the beach where they had a shack and dining room for Sunday picnics. In the conclusion of his report, Lord underscored the relationship between the recruitment and control of Filipino laborers and the need to establish recreational programs and facilities on the plantations: "The Philippines is about the only source from which we can recruit at the present time. The difficulties of recruiting are constantly increasing and it seems the plantation should endeavor to find out the best methods of handling this labor and making it contented on the plantation. The Filipino is something of an overgrown boy. He requires a certain amount of looking after. A little interest taken by the overseer in charge of his amusements, camp life, etc., will work wonders."[26]

Aware of growing labor discontent and the need to accelerate the development of recreational programs, plantation managers hired welfare workers to organize sports activities in order to give their laborers "something to do in the evenings" and render them "contented." In February of 1919, for example, a plantation manager hired Miss R. Miner as a social worker to oversee the "amusements" provided for the men and their families. According to an announcement published in the *Pacific Commercial Advertiser*, Miss Miner had come to the islands recently from New York, where she had been "in charge of a farm home for wayward girls." Two months later, the manager of another plantation wrote to the HSPA: "Every Sunday we have baseball games between the Filipino laborers and our young Japanese and Portuguese boys in which our timekeepers and some of our overseers join. . . . In looking around at the almost universal unrest amongst labor and thinking of the absence of it upon these Islands, we feel that an unremitting endeavor should be made to keep our laborers contented and happy." Shortly before the massive 1920 strike, the Social Welfare Committee of the HSPA warned that the sugar industry of Hawaii would be "fortunate" if it "escaped" from the "world-wide unrest of labor," and urged planters to expand their recreational and welfare programs. Calling for the employment of more social welfare workers and the provision of more amusements, the committee declared: "Social welfare work should be considered good business and not philanthropy."[27]

Camp Religion

A mainland visitor to a Maui plantation was surprised to find macadamized streets lined with trees and "flanked with pleasant cottages," as well as a park, library, clubhouse, amusement hall, and a church. Most plantations had places of worship and planters encouraged their workers to participate in religious activities.[28]

During the nineteenth century, Christian missionaries were permitted by the planters to engage in evangelical work on the plantations. They distributed Chinese translations of Bibles and religious publications to Chinese plantation laborers. In 1867 the Hawaiian Board of Missions made an effort to give a Chinese translation of the New Testament, a "very neat little volume, beautifully printed," to every "Chinaman" on the plantations. In 1882 the Hawaiian Evangelical Association declared that planters had a responsibility to care for the moral and spiritual welfare of the Chinese workers. The Chinese were not "mere chattels," the Association said; rather they possessed "rational and immortal souls" and had the same "natural rights" as all others.[29]

In order to advance their evangelical effort, missionaries held church services and organized congregations on plantations throughout the islands. In Paia, missionary Frank Damon was pleased to report in 1882: "A most suitable and commodious church has recently been erected here, which is used by . . . the natives in the morning and the Chinese in the afternoon." In Kohala, Luke Aseu became a layreader at St. Paul's Episcopal Church, where he continued his mission work until 1898, and Kong Tet Yin served the Chinese members of the Congregational Church under the direction of the Reverend Elias Bond. Many of the Chinese workers in Kohala had been converted to Christianity in China. In a letter to her daughter dated 5 January 1877, Mrs. Paul Isenberg wrote from Honolulu: "Did I tell you that quite a company of Christian Chinese have come recently. . . ? They have a teacher, and went in company to Kohala. That heathen China is sending us Christians has been one of my greatest joys."[30]

The most energetic evangelist to the Chinese plantation laborers was S. P. Aheong. According to the Reverend Bond, Aheong was "a young man, not much beyond 30, able to speak twelve Chinese dialects, a good singer and player of the melodeon, perfectly at home in what interested our Hawaiian Zion and speaking . . . with intelligence and unaffected Christian attachment to our work." Educated in China, Aheong was the son of a school superintendent in Kwangtung Province. He was separated from his family during the turmoil of the Taiping Rebellion and was forced to seek employment at one of the seaports, where he signed a labor contract and was shipped to Hawaii in 1854. While working on the Makawao Plantation on Maui, he was converted to Christianity by the Reverend Jonathan Green. He completed his labor contract in 1859, then moved to Lahaina, where he married Naukana Hikiau and became a prosperous merchant, as well as an active member of the Wainee Church. In 1868 the Hawaiian Evangelical Association appointed Aheong to be a colporteur and asked him to distribute religious literature to Chinese plantation laborers and share the Christian message with them. Shortly after Aheong's appointment, the *Pacific Commercial Advertiser* announced: "Agreeable to present arrangements, Aheong will close up his business, and about the 1st of November enter upon his labors among his countrymen on a salary of $800 per annum. . . . We have thus stated these facts in order to introduce Aheong to the island community, but especially to those planters and others who may have Chinese laborers in their employ."[31]

Aheong plunged into a whirlpool of evangelical activity, visiting plantations and holding religious meetings for his countrymen. In his reports for ten months of religious work, he listed seventy-five sermons delivered in Chinese, fifty-eight in Hawaiian, and even a few sermons in Japanese. On 18 August 1868 he wrote to the Reverend L. H. Gulick from Lahaina: "My work was commenced the same day which you pointed out and I hold a Chinese meeting here at last Sabbath. Five out of 13 Chinamen came. I gave them some books to read which know how to read. One of them says how can a man say that China's idol are not the God because if a man say a bad word to the idol, then he shall have pain in the whole body. I say to him that he has by all mistaking, for I am since the great many years refuse the idol; and speak bad word to them but I do not pain my body at all, and I told him good deal about our heavenly father is the true God." Several weeks later

Aheong was in Hilo, carrying the word of Christ to Chinese plantation workers. "I am here this few week with Rev. T. Coan and family," he wrote to the Reverend S. C. Damon, "and try to do my work so hard as I could among my countrymen and native also. I preach in Chinese and in native both every week since I commence to work. . . . I am glad to tell you about the Hilo Chinamen. Some of them been in this country more than 40 or 30 years, and never been to church since they been in these Islands, until I came here."[32]

Aheong soon felt the need to spread the gospel among his countrymen back home. On 25 May 1870 he told a group meeting in weekly prayer at Bethel Church: "Perhaps this will be the last time I shall speak to you. I expect a ship from California to take me to China. I came sixteen years ago as one of the lower class of laborers. I was a heathen man, but I learned about God, and the Savior. Now I go back to see my father and mother, grand-parents and brothers and sisters. They all heathen, and know nothing about God and our Savior. I want to tell them about our Savior. . . . Perhaps I come back. God knows; I don't know." Two days later, Aheong sailed to China with his family, determined to be an evangelist to millions of his countrymen in his homeland.[33]

As a colporteur in Hawaii, Aheong had preached in Hawaiian, Chinese, and Japanese; had he remained in Hawaii he would have found himself delivering sermons in Korean as well. Koreans, probably more than the Chinese, gave Christianity a visible presence on the plantations. And like the Chinese, they received support from the planters for their evangelical activities. Visiting plantations in 1905, missionary Homer Hulbert reported the construction of seven plantation chapels for Koreans: "The Koreans themselves subscribed generously toward the erection of these edifices. A good part of the money was subscribed by the plantation proprietors who are keen to encourage all agencies looking toward peace and order and morality." Planters also provided financial support for the salaries of Korean ministers. One of them, Hyun Soon, sent to Kauai by the Methodist Mission in Honolulu to serve Korean plantation laborers, received monetary assistance from Kauai planters Hans Isenberg and George Wilcox. With the hope that Soon could help them improve relations between the planters and Korean laborers, they provided him with a house and paid for some of the traveling expenses he incurred while preaching the gospel to Koreans. The manager of the Hawaiian Agricultural Company Plantation on the Big Island also made financial contributions to a Korean minister. In a letter to C. Brewer and Company dated 12 October 1915, he explained what he expected in return: "We are at present paying $10.00 towards the Korean pastor's pay. . . . We have quite a gang of Koreans here at present (about 40 men in all) but they are rather an uncertain bunch, and sometimes we may not have more than 15. Now I am going to ask you to give me authority, to try out the idea of regulating the pastor's pay, according as the gang holds up. Say $5.00 per month when they dwindle to 15 men and up to $10.00 per month, should the gang hold up to 50 to 60."[34]

The first Korean Christian church was founded in Hawaii within six months after the arrival of the first group of Korean laborers in 1903. Christianity spread rapidly among them and in 1906 a visiting missionary was delighted to find "little congregations" of Koreans everywhere in the islands. "In the evening," he reported, "the sound of their hymns can be heard in most camps." He calculated that one third of all the Koreans in Hawaii were Christians, and commended them for the moral influence they had on the camp community: "They dominate the life in the camps on the islands of Oahu, Kauai, and Maui where they are stamping out gambling and intoxication."[35]

While planters supported Christian missionary activities for Chinese and Koreans, they allowed Japanese workers to bring Buddhism with them to Hawaii and establish temples on the plantations. Planters viewed Buddhism as a stabilizing influence on their workers; consequently they donated lands for temples and subsidized Buddhist programs and priests. The Waipahu and Kahuku plantations financially supported Buddhist temples and schools; the Ewa, Aiea, Waialua, Waianae, and Waimanalo plantations on Oahu and many plantations on the other islands also provided grants of rent-free lands and monetary subsidies to Buddhist temples. In a letter to the manager of the Laupahoehoe Plantation dated 10 February 1902, the director of Theo. H. Davies and Company encouraged planters to give financial support to Japanese Buddhist schools and added: "The Directors are quite in sympathy with any movement on the part of the Japanese which should have a good influence amongst them."[36]

Management support for the development of Buddhist temples

and programs on the plantations was reinforced during the 1904 strike on the Waipahu Plantation. Demanding the dismissal of a vicious luna, Japanese laborers struck, and forty-six policemen were summoned to quell a riot. Finally the plantation manager asked Bishop Yemyō Imamura of the Honpa Honwanji Temple of Honolulu to help the plantation restore order. Bishop Imamura advised the striking workers to place their trust in Amida Buddha, the source of "boundless love," and persuaded them to return to work. Years later, in his *History of the Hongwanji Mission in Hawaii*, Bishop Imamura proudly claimed credit for building a cooperative relationship between the Buddhist temples and the plantations: "I shall not be accused of pretentiousness if I say that our mission has done its humble share of duty in realizing this much-hoped for state of stable and steady pursuit of work and happiness in the plantation. Managers of the plantations were not slow in their appreciation of our honest efforts, and soon after the strike agitation in Waipahu Plantation in 1904 was amicably settled owing to the intercession of our mission, our activities in the plantation enjoyed the hearty co-operation of the plantation officials in various ways."[37]

Christian churches and Buddhist temples were important and visible institutions on the plantations. Managers understood the value of evangelists like Aheong and priests like Imamura and their messages of cooperation and respect for order; in turn, religious leaders realized that they could secure planter support and financial assistance for their religious activities. Meanwhile, the laborers themselves built places of worship to satisfy deep spiritual needs and to experience again a feeling of home and re-connect themselves to old traditions and customs.

Traditions and Customs in the Camps

Though they were separated from their homelands, laborers retained a strong sense of national identity, and plantation camps became multinational and multicultural communities. When the Norwegian immigrants of the *Beta* completed their three year contracts on Maui, they held a feast to celebrate their freedom and unfurled the flag of Norway at the center of the plantation. German laborers subscribed to German newspapers and magazines like *Hannoversches Sonntagsblatt*, *Die Harke*, *Die Woche*, *Dahein*, and *Die Garenlaube*. They also drank to the Kaiser's health, and on the Lihue Plantation, they celebrated German victories in Europe during World War I. Japanese laborers nurtured an even more intense nationalism. Immediately after Japan won the Sino-Japanese War in 1895, Japanese immigrants rejoiced all over the islands. In Honolulu they hoisted national flags in the streets, and "a triumphal arch 20 feet high, colorfully decorated with tropical flowers, foliage, lights, and flags stood in front of the consulate building." Huge signs above and beside the arch expressed the nationalistic passions of the Japanese in Hawaii: "Emperor Banzai," "Army Banzai," "Navy Banzai." Feeling powerful ties to Japan, issei parents registered their Hawaii-born nisei children as Japanese citizens. Korean plantation workers felt a unique and fierce nationalism. After their country had been declared a protectorate in 1905 and annexed by Japan in 1910, Koreans in Hawaii viewed themselves as political refugees. Unable to return to their homeland, they transformed their communities in Hawaii into a base where they could continue the struggle for Korean national independence. In 1905 Koreans on the Ewa Plantation organized the Ewha Chi'n mok-hoe, the Friendship Society of Ewa Plantation, to launch a movement to boycott Japanese goods. Two years later, representatives from twenty-four Korean organizations on Oahu, Hawaii, Maui, and Kauai met in Honolulu to form the Korean Consolidated Association, which published the *United Korean News* and worked for the "restoration of the sovereignty" of the Korean "fatherland."[38]

The nationalism of immigrant plantation laborers also led them to celebrate traditional festivals in the camps and to recreate in Hawaii familiar scenes of their homelands.

"The explosion of crackers throughout the day," reported the *Hawaiian Gazette* in 1867, "demonstrated that the great day of the Chinese year was being properly remembered." On their New Year's day, Chinese plantation laborers took off from work; the manager of the Paauhau Plantation recorded in his diary on 17 February 1882: "No work on account of the Chinese New Year." To celebrate the important event, the Chinese trimmed the roofs of their joss houses with "long lines of small flags of every hue," and hung colored lanterns on the verandas of their barracks and cottages. Then they exchanged cards or slips of pink paper to wish each other good luck, and set off chains of noisy firecrackers. Some of them strummed Chinese musical instruments that resembled "a cross between a banjo and a guitar." Minnie Grant, a visitor to a plantation in 1888, recorded a description of the Chinese New Year's festival: "Ah See, was, apparently, something of a fire-wor-shipper, as one morning, when a Chinese feast was in progress on the plantation, we heard a tremendous cracking and fizzing, and on going out . . . we found he had lighted two bundles or fire-crackers, which were going off in every direction, and Ah See, with his hands up to his forehead, was bowing and grimacing to the crackers, as though they were so many spirits, and muttering what I suppose were charms against evil." On the Kohala Plantation during festival time, two rival Chinese benevolent societies within view of each other across the Kapaau Gulch competed to see which one could burn the longest or loudest string of firecrackers.[39]

Portuguese laborers also brought their share of colorful tradi-tions and new sounds to the plantation. During Christmas, they wore white costumes and immense animal heads made of paper on their shoulders, and danced around the May Pole with its bright ribbons. On New Year's Eve, they strolled through the camps dressed in masks and comic costumes, serenading their friends with their stringed musical instruments such as the guitar and the *bregina*, from which the Hawaiian ukulele was later developed. Portuguese workers considered the Friday before Easter a reli-gious holiday. On 7 April 1882 the manager of the Paauhau Plan-tation wrote in his diary: "Good Friday. The Portuguese do not work today on account of the holy day."[40]

Meanwhile German laborers introduced the Christmas tree to plantation society. They had carried Christmas tree decorations in their baggage to Hawaii; unable to find evergreen trees to cele-brate Christmas in 1881, they used papaya trees as their *tannen-baum*. On Christmas eve, everyone sang Christmas carols, and "der Weinhnachtsmann" or "Knecht Rupprecht" or "Santa Claus" visited the camps, giving presents to the children.[41]

During the midsummer, Japanese plantation laborers held their traditional *bon* festival. Dressed in kimonos, they danced in circles to the beat of *taiko* drums in celebration of the cycles of life and the seasons and in rememberance of the dead. In early November they observed the Mikado's birthday as a holiday and interrupted plantation production schedules. Irritated plantation managers found they had no choice but to let their Japanese workers have

Immigrant workers brought their musical intruments to Hawaii.
Hawaii State Archives

their way on this important day for them. "There is an old custom
here among the Japs of observing the 3rd of November as a holiday, but we shall endeavor to have them postpone this for a week,"
reported a plantation manager to C. Brewer and Company on 17
October 1911. Two weeks later, he wrote again: "We have been
unable to arrange with the Japs to postpone the celebration of the
Mikado's Birthday. However, they have agreed to work on Sunday
the 12th of November." "The Emperor's Birthday was celebrated
everywhere," Tokusuke Oshiro recalled. "Mainly there was *sumo*.
. . . Several young men, usually the good ones, got together at a
camp and had Japanese-style *sumo* matches." Seichin Nagayama
stated that on the emperor's birthday or "Tenchosetsu," the "Okinawans would rest from work and order *bento* from the *meshiya*
(eating place). At night the Okinawans would play *shamisens*
(three stringed musical instruments) made out of *tengara* (tin cans)
on which they put strings. So we had music with the *tengara
shamisen*—'*jara-jara, jan-jan, chan-chan*'—and we danced Okinawan dances."[42]

The most important celebration for Filipino plantation workers
was Rizal Day. On plantations everywhere, they held a holiday on

December 30, the day the Spanish had executed the famous Filipino revolutionary leader Jose Rizal in 1896. The director of the Bureau of Labor of the HSPA instructed plantation managers to make allowances for their Filipino laborers on this significant occasion: "In line with the established policy of making our laborers as satisfied as possible and joining in with all the things that tend to increase in its morale, it is suggested that each plantation management take an interest in such festivities or ceremonies as the Filipinos desire to have on this day, and that the day be considered a holiday, absence from work not being counted against the bonus requirements." To honor Rizal, the George Washington of the Philippines, Filipino plantation bands played mandolins and guitars to entertain Filipino laborers. On the Union Mill Plantation in 1910, laborer Ysidore Enriques created a bust of Rizal, which was unveiled during the celebration. According to the *Kohala Midget*, Enriques had sculpted the bust "from a photograph, by his own unaided native genius as a modeler. Those who had seen the photograph pronounced the lifelike statue, full of expression and wonderfully artistic for untrained hands. . . . It was admired by the sixty Filipinos of Union Mill, and numbers of Japanese and other nationalities, including several whites, who were struck with wonder at the artistic excellence of the work." As the Filipino laborers remembered Rizal, they told each other tales of his heroic deeds. "The Kastilas could not kill him, because the bullets bounced off his chest," a worker would boast. And a compatriot would "tell it up one notch" and quickly add, "He caught them with his bare hands!" Filipino laborers repeatedly told the story about how the revolutionary leader actually did not die: "After he was buried, his wife poured his love potion on his freshly filled grave, and in the night—he rose, Apo Rizal rose from the grave." Flying on a "winged white horse that grazed on the yellow green leaves of bamboo tips . . . Apo Rizal appeared during the Guerra, war, with Espanya."[43]

Recruited from all over the world, plantation laborers introduced to camp society a wide variety of ethnic foods. The Chinese ate rice and dried, salted, and preserved food imported from their own country. Duck was one of their favorite dishes, and tea was a "never-failing beverage." Germans made potato salad and German sausage. Portuguese laborers grew peppers and garlic and used them to make Portuguese sausage and blood sausage; they

PORTUGUESE WOMEN BAKING BREAD IN OUTDOOR OVEN
Hawaii State Archives

also baked Portuguese bread in a traditional brick oven which was
"rounded like an igloo and mortared on the outside." On special
occasions such as Christmas, Portuguese women baked their delicious sweetbread. Korean women planted vegetables and red peppers to pickle *kimchee*, which they served with every meal, including breakfast. The Japanese retained their taste for foods from the
home country, and plantation managers found themselves order-
ing from their agents in Honolulu what they thought were strange
foods—*somen, kamaboko, miso, shoyu, umiboshi,* and *daikon.*
Tofu was in great demand on the plantations. "My wife and I
made the tofu and I would go out and sell it [in the camps]," Toku-
sake Oshiro stated. "The farthest I went to sell was Olaa's Juyonri
—the camp at the 14 mile marker in Olaa. I had regular customers
who knew the days that I would come. So when I honked my horn,
people would come out with container in hand." Japanese families
made *mochi* 'rice cakes', especially on New Year's Day. For their
bento, Japanese laborers ate *musubi* 'rice balls' with *ume* 'pickled
red plums' in the center, and Filipinos spread *bagoong* 'salted fish'
over their rice.[44]

KAUKAU TIME IN THE FIELDS
Bishop Museum
"We get in a group, and we spread our lunch cans on the ground
and eat together."

As laborers and their families mingled together on the plantations, they began to exchange and enjoy the different ethnic dishes
of their friends and co-workers. The daughter of a Portuguese
laborer recalled how her mother would make gifts of her bread
and "little buns for the children in the camp. The Japanese families gave us sushis and the Hawaiians would give us fish." "Everybody took their own lunches" to school, Lucy Robello of the Waialua Plantation said. "And like the Japanese used to take their little
riceballs with an ume inside and little daikon. . . . And us Portuguese, we used to take bread with butter and jelly or bread with
cheese inside." Then, at noon time, Japanese and Portuguese children would trade their *kaukaus* 'lunches' with each other. Meanwhile in the fields, their parents were also sharing lunches. "We get
in a group and we spread our lunch cans on the ground and eat
together," William Rego told an interviewer. "We pick from this
guy's lunch and that guy'll pick from my lunch and so forth."
Crossing ethnic lines, workers would taste each other's foods and
exclaim: "Ono, ono!" 'Tasty, tasty!'[45]

Immigrant laborers brought not only their foods but also their traditional social organizations to the plantation. The Japanese organized themselves into Buddhist associations, chapters of the Japanese League, and *kenjinkais*, prefectural associations. Japanese laborers also put together *tanomoshis*, or credit-rotating systems. Several workers would contribute money to a common fund, and individuals would be able to take out a loan at a certain interest rate. The Chinese established a *wui-goon*, a meeting hall or fraternal lodge responsible for the care of the elderly, burials, and the settling of disputes. They also gathered themselves into family societies, as well as village and district associations. By 1910 seventy-five Chinese organizations existed in Hawaii, including the Chee Ying Society of Hamakua, the Hung Wo Society of Kohala, and the Fuk Sing Tong of Wailuku.

Two of the most elaborate organizations were developed by Korean plantation laborers: the sworn brotherhood and the village council. The sworn brotherhood was composed of fifty or sixty Koreans, each tatooed for membership and identification. All brothers were pledged to help a member in time of need: to give him financial assistance and moral or emotional support and to defend him during quarrels or conflicts with outsiders. The village council, or self-governing organization called the Dong-hoi, was another mutual aid society. At the annual assembly of the Dong-hoi, all the Korean men of a plantation met to elect the Dong-chang, council head respected for his age, wisdom, education, and honesty. Assisted by the Sachal (sergeant-at-arms) and the Kyung-chal (police), the Dong-chang functioned as the governor of the Korean plantation community. He served as the judge in all disputes, the spokesman of the Korean laborers and their families, and the administrator of the council's laws and regulations. The tenets of the Dong-hoi included love for fellow Korean immigrants, respect for and protection of Korean women, and prohibition of gambling and drinking of alcohol. Punishments for violations of the rules ranged from fines of one and two dollars to flogging and expulsion from camp. The money collected from the fines was used to provide financial support for the education of Korean children, the care of the sick, and for holiday celebrations.

In their holidays, festivals, foods, and social organizations, immigrant laborers had recreated the traditions and customs of their homelands. Everywhere in the plantation camps of Hawaii emerged ethnic working class communities which formed the basis for the cultural richness and diversity of modern Hawaii.

Plantation Pidgin—Not the "English of Shakespeare"

The recruitment of laborers from all over the world also led to the formation of a multilingual plantation community. The presence of a variety of languages on the plantation impressed a mainland visitor in 1888. "Amongst the many dialects and languages which assailed one's ear on a walk through the plantation," wrote Minnie Grant, were "English, Portuguese, German, Native, Japanese, Norwegian, Chinese. . . ."[46]

For these plantation workers of different nationalities, the languages of their home countries provided an essential basis for their particular identities and cultures. Languages gave each ethnic group a sense of community within the plantation camps, by enabling its members to maintain ties with each other as they shared memories of their distant homeland and stories of their experiences in the new country. Describing the closely-knit Korean community on the plantation, the daughter of a Korean laborer recalled that Korean laborers and their families "were inclined to stay together; so, of the original group, it was not uncommon for them not to learn English."[47]

To preserve their language and culture, many plantation workers sent their children to language schools. German families in Lihue enrolled their children in both the German language school and the English-speaking public school. In 1888 eighty-one out of the eighty-six German children in the public school also attended the German language school. Similarly, Japanese parents determined to have their children learn the language of the old country organized Japanese language schools on the plantations. In 1920, 98 percent of the Japanese students enrolled in public schools were also attending Japanese language schools. Visiting the camps of Korean laborers in 1906, a missionary observed: "In the larger settlements like Ewa, a school in Korean . . . taught by a Korean schoolmaster, is maintained by the Koreans themselves." Koreans in Hawaii were determined to raise their children as Koreans, teaching them Korean history, culture, and language, and keeping "a Korean spirit" alive in the minds of the next generation. Due to the Japanese annexation of Korea, they felt an urgent sense of mis-

sion and a special need for Korean language schools on the plantations. "Every Korean overseas thought that Japan would destroy
the Korean history and culture, so that we Koreans in America
thought we should preserve our culture and urged Koreans to
support the Korean school financially," explained Yang Choo-en.
Through the schools, Korean communities in Hawaii could become sanctuaries for Korean nationalism and culture.[48]

Although laborers of different nationalities wished to maintain
their native languages, they found that working together on the
plantation required cross-ethnic communication. Bosses and workers had to have a common language. At first Chinese laborers
under the supervision of Hawaiian lunas learned to take orders
and instructions in the Hawaiian language. The Reverend William
Spear noted in 1856 the facility of the Chinese to speak Hawaiian,
even to each other: "One of the amusing sights I have seen on the
islands has been 'Canton' men and 'Amoy' men resorting to the
dialect of the Hawaiians as the only medium of ready communication with each other."[49]

But soon English became the "language of command" on the
plantations, and gradually there developed a plantation dialect
called "pidgin English." According to language specialist John
Reinecke, pidgin English was based on the mixed speech of the
ports and contained elements found in other English jargons of the
Pacific and many Hawaiian words. On the plantation, a foreman
was able to address an ethnically diverse group of laborers in a
pidgin language and communicate to all of them at once, and
workers were able to respond in a pidgin that incorporated peculiarly Japanese, Portuguese, Chinese, or other elements in their
speech.[50]

Plantation managers recognized the need to teach immigrant
laborers a functional spoken English or "a working knowledge of
the English language." "By this," explained the manager of the
Hawaiian Agricultural Company Plantation to the HSPA, "we do
not mean the English of Shakespeare but the terms used in every-
day plantation life. A great many of the small troubles arise from
the imperfect understanding between overseers and laborers."[51]

Isolated on the plantations, workers sometimes came to think
pidgin was the English language. This impression sometimes created confusion for both the boss and his laborers. For example, a
field boss was angrily trying to explain to a gang of Chinese work-

men that the cane should be cut close to the ground and the tops
lopped off and thrown between the furrows for fertilizer. Educated
at an English university and a recent arrival in Hawaii, he issued
his instructions in "pure English." Noticing that the men did not
seem to understand the boss, a bystander then gave them a translation of the instructions in pidgin: "*Luna*, big boss speak, all men
down below cutch; suppose too much *mauka* (uphill, high) cutch,
too mucha sugar *poho* (wasted)—*keiki* (shoots) no use. Savvy? All
men *opala* (trash) cutch, one side t'row—byenby mule men come,
lepo (dirt) too mucha guru (good). Savvy?" "Savvy," replied the
Chinese, adding disgustingly: "Huy! wasamalla dis *Haole*—he no
can taok *haole!*"[52]

As pidgin English became the common language of plantation
laborers and their families, it enabled people from different countries to communicate with each other and helped to create a new
island identity for them. "The language we used had to be either
pidgin English or broken English," explained Faustino Baysa of
the Waialua Plantation. "And when we don't understand each
other, we had to add some other words that would help to explain
ourselves. That's how this pidgin English comes out beautiful." A
Korean mother recalled how she noticed her children were growing up as "Hawaiians," for they spoke "Hawaiian English" much
more fluently than their native tongue. Speaking Hawaiian English or pidgin, the immigrants and their children were no longer
only Korean, Japanese, Chinese, Filipino, Puerto Rican, or Portuguese. On the plantations, pidgin English began to give its users a
working class as well as a Hawaiian or "local" identity, which
transcended their particular ethnic identity.[53]

No Can Go Home: Families on the Plantation

Plantation camps were predominantly communities of single men.
Planters wanted a "cheap" labor force: single men could exist on
wages lower than that of married men with families, and housing
costs were less for single men in barracks than for families in cottages. In a memo to C. Brewer and Company, the manager of the
Hawaiian Agricultural Company Plantation stated that he "preferred" "single Filipinos." But such a preference was not the only
reason why most Asian men went to Hawaii without women:
many, probably most, viewed themselves as sojourners rather than

The Hana Plantation where Kasuke Okawa first worked as a contract laborer. *Hawaii State Archives*

settlers. They had traveled to Hawaii to labor and earn money rather than to stay and raise families. Thus between 1852 and 1887, 26,000 Chinese arrived in the islands and 10,000 returned to China; similarly, between 1886 and 1924, 199,564 Japanese entered Hawaii and 113,362 went back to their homeland.[54]

The preponderance of men in the plantation camps may be seen in the male/female ratios for different nationalities in Hawaii. In 1853 Chinese women constituted only 5.5 percent of the Chinese population; nearly forty years later, in 1890, they still represented only 8.5 percent. Between 1885 and 1892, most of the Japanese migrants to Hawaii were male; only 20 percent of the migrants were women. Even by 1910, 69 percent of the Japanese population in the islands was male. "Camp life," observed Yasutaro Soga of the Waipahu Plantation, "was dull in the extreme. There were about five men to every woman." Only 10 percent of the Korean population in Hawaii was female in 1905. The Filipino migration was even more unbalanced in terms of sex ratios: by 1920, of the 52,672 Filipinos in Hawaii, 9 out of 10 were men.[55]

The presence of a large, single male Chinese population on the plantations led the editor of the *Pacific Commercial Advertiser* in 1864 to recommend the importation of Chinese women. "To throw in these islands, hundreds or thousands of laborers without their wives, to encourage their importation without that controlling and softening influence which women, by God's will, exercise over man, would be to encourage vice and urge on the fearful evils originated by dissolute habits." In 1877, as planters expanded sugar cultivation and recruited increasing nunbers of Chinese laborers, the editor of the *Pacific Commercial Advertiser* again expressed his concern for the influx of so many Chinese men in "the prime of life" and "full of the animal instincts natural [to youth]." "No Chinaman," he concluded, "should be allowed henceforth to come here . . . unless they are accompanied by their women." Missionaries also worried about this population of Chinese male laborers "without women and children" living like "animals" and working like "machines" on the plantation. In his appeal to the planters to bring Chinese women to Hawaii, missionary Frank Damon declared: "No surer safeguard can be erected against the thousand possible ills which may arise from the indiscriminate herding together of thousands of men! Let the sweet and gentle influence of the mother, the wife, the sister, the daughter be brought to bear upon the large and yearly increasing company of Chinese in our midst, and we shall soon see a change wrought, such as police regulations cannot produce."[56]

Gradually planters themselves realized women could serve an important function in the process of production: they could be used to control laborers, possibly even more effectively than police regulations. In a letter to Damon, planter H. M. Whitney wrote in 1881: "With Chinese families established on every plantation . . . there would be much less fear of riotous disturbances. . . . The influence of families especially *where settlers locate in a foreign country*—has always been a peaceful influence." Five years later, shortly after planters had shifted from China to Japan as their primary source of labor, Inspector-General of Immigration A. S. Cleghorn reported that Japanese men did much better work and were more satisfied on plantations where they had their wives. "Several of the planters," he commented, "are desirous that each man should have his wife."[57]

In 1900 the abolition of the contract labor system released workers from their legal obligation to labor for a specified period of time, and it became necessary to entice men to stay on the plantation. Planters realized that men with families were not as likely to leave the plantation as single men. In their orders sent to their business agents in Honolulu, many planters requested "men with families." The manager of the Hutchinson Sugar Plantation, for example, wrote to William G. Irwin and Company: "Will you be kind enough to send us as soon as you are able to do so, forty Japanese married couples. We want them for the Hilea section of the Plantation where we have always had more or less trouble in keeping Japanese laborers, and believe that by having married couples only the laborers would remain."[58]

In addition, planters became convinced that men with families were steadier workers than single men. A study conducted in 1916 by the HSPA clearly demonstrated the "influence of family responsibility": Japanese men, many of them married, worked an average of 21.9 days a month (84 percent of full time), while Filipino men, mostly young and single, worked only 18 days a month (69 percent). To encourage Filipino men to have families on the plantation and thus become more responsible workers, the HSPA approved a plan for the importation of women from the Philippines. In a letter to H. Hackfeld and Company in 1916, R. D. Mead of the association announced a new plan to "start an active campaign among the Filipinos on the plantations to induce them to secure wives from the Philippine Islands." The plan was, in effect, a picture bride arrangement. "If these men will furnish us with letters to their wives or prospective wives, photographs of themselves and letters from the managers and from some Filipino women in the camps recommending the men as being desirable husbands," Mead stated, "we will endeavor to induce the wives or prospective wives to come to Hawaii, and will see that they reach the men who send for them."[59]

By then Japanese and Korean families had begun to establish themselves on the plantations. This important social development was reflected in the increasing numbers of Japanese and Korean females. Where females had constituted only 19 percent of the total Japanese population in Hawaii (2,391 out of 12,610) in 1890, they represented 46 percent (46,630 out of 109,274) in 1920. Korean females numbered only 13 percent of the Korean population in Hawaii (602) in 1910, and ten years later they composed nearly 30 percent. Many of the Japanese and Korean women came as picture brides. There were 14,276 Japanese picture brides who emigrated to Hawaii between 1907 and 1923; during the same time, 951 picture brides arrived from Korea.

Marriage in the home country had been traditionally arranged by the families; out of context in Hawaii, however, the arranged marriage became a distressing experience for many picture brides. One of them, Anna Choi, later recalled:

> I came to Hawaii as a picture bride not due to the fact that my family was poor but because I had heard so many times about an uncle on my mother's side who was doing quite well for himself in Hawaii. . . . In 1915, I decided to go to Hawaii and asked my mother whether I could be a picture bride, since my uncle's family in Korea knew of a man there looking for a wife. My mother thought I was crazy and tried to persuade me to abandon such a notion, but in vain. So, when I was fifteen, equipped with an introduction and a photograph, I boarded a ship at Pusan port with five other girls. . . . We boarded another ship in Yokohama after physical examinations, and three long months later we finally arrived at our destination.
>
> When I first saw my fiance, I could not believe my eyes. His hair was grey and I could not see any resemblance to the picture I had. He was a lot older than I had imagined. . . . He was forty-six years old. . . . I definitely looked upon him more as my father than my husband. We were meant to work, I believe, rather than to enjoy our life together.

Most of the picture brides were much younger than their husbands-to-be. Surprised and shocked to find older men waiting for them on the dock in Honolulu, many of them cried, "Aigo omani" 'Oh dear me, what shall I do?' One of these disconcerted picture brides was Woo Hong Pong Yun. At the age of twenty-three, she traveled to Hawaii to marry Woo Chong Cho, a plantation worker on Kauai. Years later, she told one of her grandchildren how startled she was when she first met her future husband and saw a thirty-six year old man: "When I see him, he skinny and black. I no like. No look like picture. But no can go home."[60]

Increasingly plantation workers were also saying, "No can go home." Many single men, particularly Chinese and Filipinos, found themselves staying here. They had failed to realize their dreams of wealth, or they had allowed the years to pass and had awakened one morning to see the wrinkled faces of old grey-haired bachelors greeting them in bathroom mirrors. Or they had felt uprooted, afraid they would not be able to feel at home again in the old country.

Meanwhile other laborers were developing new roots here. They were settling in the islands, and Hawaii was becoming home. Chinese men were marrying Hawaiian women and raising families in "Tan Heung Shan"; as early as 1871, 11 percent of the Chinese men were living with native women. Most of the Germans recruited as plantation laborers came as married couples, and many of them settled in the islands. The Portuguese emigrated to "Terra Nova" as families: of the 11,000 Portuguese who arrived in Hawaii between 1877 and 1898, 31 percent were men, 23 percent were women, and 46 percent were children. In 1907 the Gentlemen's Agreement restricted immigration of Japanese laborers to the United States, including Hawaii; afraid they would not be able to return to Hawaii if they went back to the old country, Japanese plantation workers summoned their kin *(yobiyose)* to the islands and increasingly viewed Hawaii as their new home. In 1910 Japan annexed Korea, cutting off Korean plantation laborers from their land of "Morning Calm." While they were determined to restore Korean national independence, many of them quietly began to make a new future for themselves in Hawaii. Immigrant plantation laborers were raising families, and the cries and laughter of children could be heard in the camps. By 1920 a new generation was taking root in Hawaii: minors constituted 59 percent of the Portuguese population, 29 of the Filipino, 41 of the Chinese, 32 of the Korean, 56 of the Puerto Rican, and 46 of the Japanese. In the public schools there were 5,304 Portuguese, 941 Filipino, 3,721 Chinese, 508 Korean, 1,068 Puerto Rican, and 17,541 Japanese students.[61]

The transformation of immigrant plantation laborers from sojourners to settlers occurred gradually, probably unknowingly at first. Originally they thought they would save their earnings for three years and then return home; but then they extended their stay to five years, then ten years and longer. Meanwhile they married and had children and found they were no longer temporary migratory immigrants. In his autobiographical novel, *Hawaii: End of the Rainbow*, Kazuo Miyamoto described the process that led Seikichi Arata to stay in the new land: "With the passage of the years, he came to love Kauai as a place to live and possibly raise a family. The carefree atmosphere of this new country, not tied

down by century-old traditions and taboos, and an immense opportunity that existed for those that could settle and seek their
fortune, changed Seikichi's original intention of returning to his
homeland at the expiration of the three year contract." Similarly
a second-generation Korean, born on the Kahuku Plantation in
1905, explained: "My parents . . . left Korea in the early part of
1903 and came to the Hawaiian Islands. Their intention was to
return to their land as soon as they had saved money. In this hope
they were disappointed, for they soon found out that it was not so
easy to save money as they thought it would be. However, they
became so used to the climate, freedom and advantages of this
land that they no longer desired to leave this land permanently."[62]

Slowly, the immigrants began to feel at home in Hawaii. Earlier
many of them were confused and asked in quiet moments of reflec-
tion:

> Should I return to Japan?
> I'm lost in thoughts
> Here in Hawaii.

But they wondered whether they should stay:

> When the term of my contract is over
> Shall I get my wife from Japan,
> And go to Hamakua
> On Hawaii?

Still they found themselves anxious, uncertain, for they feared to
stay too long.

> Two contract periods
> Have gone by
> Those who do not return
> Will end up as fertilizer
> For the cane.

But, over the years, their feelings changed. As the immigrants
transplanted many of their old customs and traditions and foods to
the new land, built new churches and temples near their cottages
and gardens, gathered in clubhouses and on baseball fields, became acquainted with fellow laborers from other countries, and
spoke pidgin English to each other, they developed a unique work-
ing-class culture and community in the camps. As they gazed at

morning rainbows brilliantly arching over the Koolaus and other mountain ranges, took walks into misty valleys like Iao and Wai-mea, and fished and picked 'opihi at secret beaches, they also began to feel an attachment to the islands. Perhaps they belonged here, they thought. And as they watched their children grow up and play in the camps—children born far away from Kwangtung, Kumamoto, the Azores, Pusan, Luzon, and other places familiar only to the first generation—they began to think of themselves as people of Hawaii.[63]

V

Contested Terrain: Patterns of Resistance

Violence

The plantation was, to borrow a term from Richard Edwards, a "contested terrain"—a place where planters tried to extract from laborers as much work as possible and where laborers struggled to acquire greater control over their work and a greater share of plantation earnings. It was also a place where bosses and workers sometimes engaged in violent confrontations.[1]

One day a luna had mistaken Chinzen Kinjo for someone else and whipped him. "I was really mad," Kinjo bitterly recalled, "and all the anger which had hitherto been suppressed in me exploded and I challenged him with karate." The luna was a big man, six feet tall, but Kinjo threw him to the ground. The crowd of laborers surrounding the two men cheered their fellow worker, waving their cane knives and roaring: "Kinjo, go ahead, go ahead! Beat him up; finish him!" Rage and an impulse to destroy, to kill seized Kinjo's entire body. Suddenly the head luna arrived and stopped the fight, restraining the furious worker from delivering the fatal blow. "I was at the point of jumping him, risking my whole life in that one blow," Kinjo said. "I wanted revenge even to the point of committing suicide."[2]

Most day-to-day acts of physical confrontation and resistance went unrecorded, but the evidence available reveals that workers did resort to violence as a way of protesting against harsh and unfair treatment. In 1866 a gang of Chinese laborers on the Koloa Plantation refused to obey the orders of their overseer; armed with knives, they rushed him and stopped only when the overseer fired his gun and wounded one of them. In the same year, a luna on the Lihue Plantation was not so lucky and was killed with a hoe by a laborer named Kapahukoa. A Chinese worker, wielding a hatchet, nearly murdered James Wood, manager of the Nuuanu Plantation.

Another Chinese laborer on the Waianae Plantation struck his boss with a hoe, breaking his arm and two ribs. On a Maui plantation in 1903 a gang of Chinese laborers attacked an Irish luna because he had hit one of them. They buried the luna under a ten-foot pile of cane stalks; he was later dug out by his friends. The foreman was so frightened by the experience that he quit his job. On the Papaaloa Plantation in 1900, striking Japanese workers armed with hoes fought lunas trying to evict them from their camps. In 1904 on the Waipahu Plantation, two hundred Korean laborers mobbed the plantation physician, claiming he had killed a Korean patient with a kick in the abdomen. A year later, after they had been told that a plantation peace officer had killed a compatriot, Korean workers at Makaweli assaulted the officer with their hoes. In 1915 after he had been threatened with dismissal for working too slowly, a Filipino laborer on the Paauilo Plantation fractured the skull of a luna with a hoe. Worker violence directed against plantation authority led planters to issue a rule: "In no case shall any laborer be permitted to raise his hand or any weapon in an aggressive manner or cabal with his associates or incite them to acts of insubordination."[3]

Laborers occasionally vented their anger against the bosses by committing acts of arson. Several Chinese laborers were arrested in 1865 for attempting to burn a building on the Princeville Plantation on Kauai. After a fire had gutted a sugar mill in Kaneohe in 1866, the editor of the *Pacific Commercial Advertiser* commented: "The risking of a building worth from twenty to fifty thousand dollars, wholly unprotected, and liable to be destroyed by accident or through the evil designs of some employee is too great for any one to incur." He advised planters to organize patrols to guard their mills at night. But fires continued to destroy plantation property—the sugar mill in Koolau in 1867 and Makawao Plantation sugar mill three years later. Dry cane fields were easy targets of arsonists. After the police had broken up a demonstration by protesting Chinese laborers on the Waianae Plantation in 1899, a fire swept through its cane fields. In its report on the incident, the *Pacific Commercial Advertiser* stated: "The trouble with the Chinese laborers at Waianae Plantation which had been brewing since Monday last, culminated last evening at about 6:45 in an attempt to fire the cane fields. It is believed by some of the men on the scene that this was undertaken by a fugitive Chinaman—one of the five

ringleaders of Tuesday's demonstration, and who is still at large."
Takashi Masuda, president of a Japanese labor recruiting company, recorded in his diary a fire incident involving workers from
Kumamoto: "I told [Robert] Irwin that people from Higo Kumamoto work very hard, but they are quick tempered and unless they
are handled with care, they may make some trouble. My predic-
tion unfortunately proved correct later. Immigrants from Higo set
fire to a sugar plantation." On the Big Island in 1904 a Japanese
field hand was arrested for arson. According to correspondence
from the manager of the Hutchinson Sugar Plantation to William
G. Irwin and Company, a worker named Takinada was charged
with incendiarism for a cane field fire at Honuapo and had been
sent to Honolulu as a "prisoner." On the Makaweli Plantation in
1915 three Filipino workers, discharged because of their involve-
ment in a strike, were arrested and charged with the "malicious
burning" of a cane field.[4]

In their acts of violence against the bosses and plantation property, workers were protesting exploitation and mistreatment. After
a Chinese laborers' riot on the Lihue Plantation, Wray Taylor of
the Bureau of Immigration visited the plantation and found that
labor aggression was the result of widespread discontent. Workers
were "arrested for not working quick enough," and they earned
very little each month due to persistent docking of their pay for
various and unexplained reasons. Finding their boss "always deaf
to any of their complaints," they felt it was futile to discuss their
dissatisfactions. Frustrated and angry, disgruntled workers turned
to violence to express their grievances.[5]

Recalcitrance

But workers also developed methods of resistance that were more
subtle and sometimes more vexatious than violence. Though they
did not control the process or the conditions of production, they
could minimize their labor every day. In the fields and mills, many
workers engaged in work slowdowns and were intentionally lazy
and inefficient. In their work songs, they described the changing
weather and their constant absence from the fields:

> When it rains I sleep;
> When it's sunny I stay away from work;

And, when cloudy, I spend the day
In drinking wine.

A writer for the *Pacific Commercial Advertiser* in 1880 observed
how the Chinese plantation laborers traveled to the cane fields like
"snails" but returned to the camps like "racehorses." They did not,
he commented, have the "least desire or intention of faithfully
serving any white employer." A few years later, the Japanese Consul reported to his government that Japanese plantation workers
did not work continuously. Though they were "full of competitive
spirit" and hard workers, they took "breaks during working hours
to have a leisurely smoke" and "indulged in gossip with their co-
workers."[6]

Actually plantation laborers did not flaunt their recalcitrance
often. They usually smoked and talked story secretly, away from
the surveillance of their bosses. Skillful practitioners of deception,
they presented an appearance of energetic activity. Hawaiian
plantation workers amused themselves in the cane fields by feigning labor. Describing this game of deception, a visitor wrote in
1853: "No beast of prey watches his victim with a closer scrutiny
than the kanaka watches his employer. In his presence he makes
every effort to appear active and useful; but the very minute he disappears it is a signal for a general cessation of work, and one keeps
a 'look-out' while the group indulges in a every variety of gossip.
On the reappearance of their master, the sentinel gives the alarm,
and every man is found to be at work as though he meant never to
lay down his tools. The owner may have watched them through a
clump of foliage; but they will swear him out of the use of his eyes,
and insist on it he was altogether mistaken." Japanese laborers
used similar tactics to avoid work. On a Kohala plantation, hoe
hana women became experts in the art of deception and supervis-
ing them was, a luna discovered, a frustrating task: "Hoeing was
more pleasant and would have been all right except for the fact
that the gangs on this work were largely composed of Japanese
wahines," luna Jack Hall complained in his diary, "and it always
seemed impossible to keep them together, especially if the fields
were not level. The consequence was that these damsels were usually scattered all over the place and as many as possible were out
of sight in the gulches or dips in the field where they could not be

seen, where they would calmly sit and smoke their little metal pipes until the luna appeared on the skyline, when they would be busy as bees."[7]

If laborers pretended to be busy, they also feigned illness in order to secure medical excuses from plantation doctors. They became adept actors, falsely feigning sickness, or pleading a death in the family or some other domestic calamity. To deceive the doctor, some Japanese laborers even resorted to drinking shoyu to raise their body temperatures. An English visitor to a plantation near Hilo noticed the prevalence of various ailments among the laborers and remarked: "It reminds me very much of plantation life in Georgia in the old days of slavery. I never elsewhere heard of so many headaches, sore hands, and other trifling ailments. It is very amusing to see the attempts which the would-be-invalids make to lengthen their brief smiling faces into lugubriousness, and the sudden relaxation into naturalness when they are allowed a holiday."[8]

But even when plantation laborers were at work and under the direct supervision of the lunas, they made efforts not to exert themselves. Their failure to conform to the regimentation and disciplined pace of plantation work exasperated their bosses. The manager of the Paauhau Plantation was driven into utter frustration by his workers. In his diary, he recorded his daily struggle against worker recalcitrance and absenteeism:

August 7, 1880: The men at the cane carrier, mostly Kanakas, work too bad, too slow altogether. . . . [T]hey don't listen to us and work their old lazy way.

August 19, 1880: Today we did not contract with the men so they worked along again their old lazy way.

August 30, 1880: Four men did not come this morning. As John Bull, the Kanaka, had absented himself very often without permission, we sent for the Sheriff and took out a warrant for this arrest.

September 19, 1880: We tried to make them work 4 more clarifiers and promised each of them 50 cents extra, but they would not do it.

September 30, 1881: The Chinamen worked very slow in the forenoon, making only 9 clarifiers up to noon. In the afternoon they worked so much quicker being threatened with dismissal.

December 24, 1881: No work. No steam. No cane on account of Christmas which is observed today, the 25th falling on a Sunday. People here take advantage of every chance they can to make a holiday.

March 24, 1882: Commenced early but only 7 Chinamen being at the carrier, work went on very slow.

August 17, 1883: There were a few less men loading cane today and they were loading slowly.

Spanish laborers on the plantation of the Hawaiian Agricultural Company were even more defiant. Once, the manager had taken a gang of them into the field to harvest cane. "Just 15 minutes after they had reached the field and commenced to cut cane," he reported, "six of them left their furrows and lit their pipes. I rode over where they were and told them we could not have them take up so much time with smoking at such an early hour of the day. Most of them returned to work—but one young fellow—Joan Carvonero Trego—spoke rather nasty and stood right in front of me with a large pipe in his mouth."[9]

Planters had recalcitrant and insubordinate workers arrested and punished in court. A Japanese work song told laborers what they should take with them to jail:

> Tomorrow's court sentence
> Will be three days
> So I'd better
> Bring my red blanket
> With me to jail.[10]

Nepenthe: Opium and Alcohol

To avoid or escape from work and daily drudgery, to slide numbly into recalcitrance, many plantation laborers resorted to drugs—opium and alcohol. While it would be impossible to know for certain the full and actual extent of drug usage on the plantation, there is evidence that many laborers smoked opium and drank liquor during weekends, evenings, and even during their lunch-breaks.

Visiting a Hilo plantation in 1873, Isabella Bird noted that the Chinese laborers smoked opium. Fifteen years later, during her travels through the islands, Minnie Grant also reported the availability of opium on the plantations: "Opium is the great curse of the Chinese—they lose their health, are unable to attend to their work or business, but still the drug has such a fascination for them that they cannot give it up." In a poem written on the Honokaa Plantation in 1885, Portuguese laborer Jose Tavares de Teves told in verse a story about how a judge had freed a Chinese thief who had stolen chickens from the Portuguese camp. But: "If it were for smoking opium, / He would pay about 100 dollars." Chinese plantation laborers on Maui visited opium dens in Kula and Keokea. Describing his childhood on Maui, Peter Chong said: "In Keokea there were opium dens. . . . People used to go up there to Keokea and smoke. Like this fellow Jong Ngee. He had a pipe of his own and we used to go and watch him when we were kids." A Chinese plantation worker recalled how the cook for his gang would bring their hot lunches to the field: "In the top of the bucket [lunch pail] was a little paper or envelope with the dope in it. All the men . . . took their dope that way with their dinner."[11]

Alcohol was even more extensively consumed on the plantation. Visiting the Wailuku Plantation in 1872, a correspondent for the *Pacific Commercial Advertiser* reported that an *awa* shop, which sold an alcoholic drink made from a root, was patronized by the natives frequently. Plantation laborers did not have to depend on an awa shop for their supply of alcohol—they were able to make it themselves on the plantation. On the Paauhau Plantation, for example, the workers brewed their own beer. "Had some trouble this week with the Kanakas," the manager anxiously wrote in his diary on 24 August 1880. "They made some beer out of syrup and got drunk on it. We give them no more syrup but they get liquor somewhere on the plantation." Heavy drinking was a favorite pastime of workers of other nationalities. On Saturdays, during pau hana time in the Japanese camps, "drinking bouts began everywhere" and "an uproar was made with drinking and singing" until quite late at night. Korean laborers were fond of liquor and had "a lively time after pay day." A Filipino worker recalled that "drinks were readily available because just about everyone knew how to make 'swipe wine.' You just ferment molasses with water and yeast and in a week it's ready. And if you distilled that, you got clear liquor ten times stronger than any gin you can buy from the store."[12]

Managers and lunas complained that the use of drugs made it "impossible" to get from their laborers "anything like a fair day's work." After saturating themselves with opium or alcohol on Sunday, laborers were "unfit for work" on Monday and even part of Tuesday. Plantation managers inspected the camps on Monday and sometimes found one third of their men "dead drunk." They argued that excessive drinking among the workers actually taxed the sugar industry, for it "robbed" the managers of a part of the labor for which they had paid. In his diary entry dated 25 September 1880, the manager of the Paauhau Plantation wrote: "This morning several men were absent having had again a drunken row up on the plantation." Another distressed planter anxiously found that even rules and penalties were ineffective in preventing laborers from "being out nights—sometimes all night," and from using opium excessively. The *Kohala Midget* voiced the frustrations of many plantation managers when it declared in 1911: "No employees can drink booze and do six honest days' work in a week. They are not 'up to the scratch,' even if they can keep awake. . . . Their brains are muddled by booze."[13]

Drugs eased, perhaps made more bearable, the emptiness plantation laborers felt on the weekends, as well as the painfulness of their meaningless work during the week. "There was very little to do when work was over," said a Chinese laborer, "and the other fellows who were having a good time smoking asked me to join them, so that in order to be a good sport I took up opium smoking, not realizing that I would probably have to die with it." Momentarily at least, drugs enabled workers to escape plantation reality and enter a dream world where they could hear again the voices of fathers, mothers, and other loved ones. Laborers smoked opium and drank on weekends to "get their feelings up." But they sometimes needed the nepenthe to get through the work week too. "Drinking killed time and made the work day seem to go faster," a Filipino plantation hand explained. "At least, it helped feeling like everything was together. So swipe wine was our coffee in the mornings. And swipe was our milk for lunch. Swipe was our evening juice. And swipe was for sleeping. And the next morning again, swipe was for work. Woozy with swipe was the only way I could stay down with patience for work."[14]

But laborers knew that drugs could give them only a temporary euphoria, and thus they found themselves seeking a more permanent form of escape from plantation drudgery.

Haʻalele Hana

"Chinaman Disappears," announced the *Pacific Commercial Advertiser* in a brief notice published on 4 January 1897. "A sick Chinaman was brought down on the *W. G. Hall* from Lihue Plantation very early Sunday morning," the newspaper stated. "He was carried ashore by two of the native sailors and placed in front of the Inter-Island wharf. About 5 o'clock he disappeared, and nothing has been seen of him since. Where he went is a mystery." What he had done, however, was hardly mysterious: he had broken his labor contract and deserted the plantation. Until Hawaii became a territory of the United States in 1900, the contract labor system was legal in the islands and plantation laborers under contract were obligated to serve three- to five-year terms. Most of the immigrant plantation workers were recruited as contract laborers, and many of them fled from their assigned plantations before the completion of their contracts. *Haʻalele hana*, desertion from service, was commonplace in plantation Hawaii during the era of contract labor.[15]

"On the island of Maui," the *Pacific Commercial Advertiser* noted in 1880, "scarcely a day passes which does not bring along some member of the police force in search of absconding Chinese plantation laborers, who are making quite a business of shipping, drawing large advances, then 'clearing out' causing their employers much inconvenience and expense." A year later the *Hawaiian Gazette* complained about Norwegian deserters: "Three Norwegians who were under contract to the Haiku Sugar Co. left on the *Kate Sudden* for San Francisco. . . . The Norwegians do not seem to be a very satisfactory kind of laborer; these sudden departures are becoming too frequent. It was only a short time before that two of the same class of laborers ran away from the Baldwin plantation." The problem of desertion was pervasive. Between 1880 and 1882 the police arrested 3,454 laborers for desertion. Ten years later Marshall Charles B. Wilson calculated that approximately one person out of five in the kingdom had been arrested between 1890 and 1892, and that one third of the arrests or 5,706 were for desertion.[16]

Haʻalele hana was a constant worry for plantation managers, and references to runaway contract laborers filled many pages of their diaries. On page four of his diary, Anton Cropp of the Koloa Plantation wrote: "On Saturday and Monday (December 12 and 14, 1891) Mr. Kahl-Cannu went as far as Mana on for Jap. Deserters, and found Yosida 17 and Yosiwa 22. Before the District Judge in Koloa, they were found guilty and sent to jail." On page twelve, manager Cropp listed the "Deserters Japanese":

#5	Nakajin recaught & redeserted
#8	Kaneki
#12	Murohisa recaught & redeserted
#16	Kako
#17	Toshida recaught
#19	Iwamoto
#21	Yamamoto Furokishi
#24	Murakami
#323	Asahare recaught
#326	Hayashi
#400	Imatzu
#418	Saito recaught
#409	Uyeda
#416	Murakami recaught
#655	Nakane
#685	Fukushima Kaisaku recaught
#619	Seto
#621	Kuba recaught Honolulu

On the next page of his diary, manager Cropp recorded the action of a Japanese woman who had abandoned both her boss and her husband: "Ura, wife of Fujinaka #700 deserted on January 1892. Ura was under contract with the K. S. C. to work for 3 years commencing in May 1891 and therefore was bound to work until May 1894. Having worked on 2/3rd of a year the K. S. C. charges Fujinaka #700 for passage and expenses for balance of term of Ura:

$$
\begin{array}{rr}
\text{passage} & \$15 \\
& 2 \text{ to plantation} \\
\text{pro-rata exp} & \underline{2} \\
\text{total} & 19 \\
\text{Interest percent of} & \\
\text{same for 2 1/3 years} & \underline{3} \\
& \$22
\end{array}
$$

of this 2 1/3 part of 3 to be charged to F.
charged payday—March 7, 1892."

Thus Fujinaka lost not only his wife but was forced to reimburse the Koloa Sugar Company for her desertion.[17]

To control the problem of haʻalele hana, planters formed surveillance networks and an informal system of mutual assistance for the capture of deserters. On 21 October 1889 H. Horner of the Kukaiau Plantation sent H. Center of the Hutchinson Sugar Plantation a description of two deserters: "About two months ago two Japanese ran away from the Kukaiau Plt. and the bearer W. Kaimi says they are at your place. . . . One is very cross eyed and the other has very large round eyes." Three days later, another plantation manager wrote to Center to request help: "Two of my runaway Japs are supposed to have gone to Hilo." Capturing deserters was very expensive: on 6 August 1889, J. A. Scott of the Hilo Sugar Company attached a bill to his letter to C. McLennan of the Laupahoehoe Plantation. "I enclose you a letter I received today from Mr. Center of Kau showing the expenses of the Japs' capture," he wrote. "By reference to it you will see that your share will be 2/3 of $94.10 for your two Japs." Managers found that deserters could be shrewd in their efforts to evade capture. H. Center of the Hutchinson Sugar Plantation, for example, sent a luna to Waiakea to search for "Jap runaways." In a letter from J. A. Scott dated 13 February 1890, Center learned that the luna had found the deserters but was given money as a bribe and told to go away and not disturb them. Tracking down runaways proved to be dangerous at times. A tracker sent by the manager of the Hutchinson Sugar Plantation to look for "runaway Jap #13" in Hookena, was found murdered. Sugar agencies in Honolulu helped coordinate efforts to capture deserters and kept plantation managers informed about police arrests of runaways. On 22 June 1894 Theo. H. Davies and Company wrote to C. McLennan of the Laupahoehoe Plantation: "The police have arrested 2 of your Mexican deserters—Salvador Lopez and William Pinto. The third deserter is still missing—Ignacio Sarabia."[18]

Planters offered rewards for the capture of runaways as "incentives" for everyone to be on the lookout for deserters and to report suspicious individuals or "wandering laborers" to the authorities. On 18 June 1894, for example, C. McLennan of the Laupahoehoe Plantation notified Theo. H. Davies and Company that three Mexican contract laborers had left the plantation, and instructed the agency to announce a reward of ten dollars for the capture of each

Mexican. Planters paid rewards regularly to policemen and sheriffs for the arrest and return of runaways. J. A. Scott of the Hilo Sugar Company sent H. Center of the Hutchinson Sugar Plantation "a draft for $29.00 being $20 reward for capture of 1 Jap and $9 endorsed on his warrant as expenses for Deputy Sheriff at Waiohuiu and which is to be handed to him." In a letter to H. Center of the Hutchinson Sugar Plantation dated 14 November 1890, William G. Irwin and Company enclosed the contract of a runaway Japanese laborer. "We have paid on his acct.," the agency wrote, "Jap Constable's bill for reward and expenses $15.75."[19]

To facilitate their search for deserters, some planters had contract laborers photographed in order to be able to send pictures of deserters to the police. On 25 March 1898 Theo. H. Davies and Company informed C. McLennan of the Laupahoehoe Plantation: "We are having all Japanese photographed now, and in case of any desertions we can supply you with copies of the photos free of cost if you will advise us of the numbers of the deserters." C. A. Chapin, manager of the Kohala Sugar Company, decided to photograph a newly imported group of ninety Chinese contract laborers. When the men arrived at the plantation, they were marched into the office one-by-one. In order to avoid arousing suspicion, Chapin had each laborer stand on a scale platform to be weighed and measured for height, and then quickly snapped a photograph. After he had processed all of the men, the manager gleefully remarked that he had them "just where he wanted them." But as he placed his camera in its case, Chapin realized that he had forgotten to change the plates after each exposure and had photographed all ninety Chinese on a single negative.[20]

The need for an identification system became acute as Japanese contract laborers completed their service and became free laborers. Planters found themselves facing a vexing problem: how to know whether men seeking employment on the plantation were actually free laborers and not deserters. To help solve this problem, planters issued laborers honorable discharge papers or certificates which stated they had fulfilled the terms of their contracts and were "free laborers." Plantation managers agreed they would not hire workers unless they were able to produce these papers. Planters also tried to institute a registration system for plantation laborers that would have rendered it virtually impossible for deserters to find employment as plantation laborers anywhere in the islands.

The scheme was not fully effective, however, for it required all free laborers to be registered in order for it to work. On 8 September 1894 the secretary of the Planters' Labor and Supply Company admitted to G. C. Hewitt of the Hutchinson Sugar Plantation: "Of the seventeen thousand Japanese *free* laborers in these Islands only eight thousand have applied for certificate books."[21]

By the late 1890s planters were demanding from labor recruiters and emigration companies guarantees for their contract laborers that provided refunds for deserters. In a letter to all planters dated 21 July 1896, the L. Chong Company specified the terms of its guarantee: "If you wish to be guaranteed against desertion of all or of any Laborers furnished by us, we are prepared to give you such guarantee in writing, upon your payment of an additional $5.00 per Laborer, and whenever you show us that any of the insured Laborers have deserted we shall refund you your expenses at the rate of $1.39 per month for each unexpired month of each such Laborer's time." Other emigration companies promised to give a refund or replace the deserter with another laborer. Planters repeatedly submitted claims for reimbursement. G. C. Hewitt of the Hutchinson Sugar Plantation, for example, instructed William G. Irwin and Company on 5 June 1896: "Please notify the Japanese Emigration Co. of Hiroshima that the Japanese laborer #778 Tsukemoto Itaro . . . has run away from his contract duties . . . ask for a reimbursement." In a letter to the manager of the Hutchinson Sugar Plantation dated 29 May 1899, William G. Irwin wrote: "We beg to advise you that we have credited your account with the following amounts refunded by the Kumamoto Emigration Co. for laborers supplied by them, and who deserted your plantation's service, viz:"

Number	Name	Date of Desertion	Amount Refunded[22]
491	Nakamitsu Nijiro	Feb. 6, 1899	$16.60
497	Nakano Sentaro	Feb. 6, 1899	$16.60

Unwilling to tolerate the regimentation, low wages, and harsh working conditions of plantation labor, thousands of men and women—Chinese, Norwegian, Portuguese, Mexican, and Japanese —walked away from their contracts and bosses. In their work songs, Japanese laborers expressed their dissatisfaction and their desire for freedom from the plantation:

I hate 'hole hole' work
Let's finish cutting cane
And go to Honolulu.[23]

Exodus

In 1859 the editor of the *Polynesian* called attention to the movement of Chinese workers from the plantations to Honolulu: "In
February next the last of the Coolie contracts expires, and we may
then expect a still further increase of liberated laborers from the
plantations on the other islands, to swell the crowd of Chinamen
now already prowling about Honolulu without any apparent
means of livelihood." On 11 January 1882 the manager of a plantation wrote in his diary: "Most of our Chinamen gave notice
today that they will leave after the end of this month." By 1882
only one-third of the Chinese population of 15,000 were employed
on the plantations. Between 1897 and 1902 more than 50 percent
of the 8,114 Chinese in the sugar industry left plantation employment. Many Japanese laborers also fled the plantation, seeking
employment in urban areas. The editor of the *Maui News* thought
a "traveling mania" had seized Japanese plantation workers.
"Very many of the Japanese," he nervously noted in 1900, were
"leaving the plantation by every steamer for Honolulu."[24]

This loss of labor led planters to develop ways to restrict their
workers to plantation employment. In 1890 the president of the
Board of Immigration warned planters: "There is no reason to
believe that all the laborers now on the plantations will remain
there during the next two years. On the contrary, there is a cer-
tainty that as large a number will leave as did during the last two
years, and probably more. . . ." In order to help planters keep their
Chinese laborers on the plantations, the Hawaiian legislature enacted a law designed to exclude Chinese from certain nonagricul-
tural occupations. Thirteen years later, the Territorial Legislature
passed a law stating that Asiatic labor should not be employed on
public works in the territory because the workers were needed on
the plantations.[25]

As the plantation experience dissipated their hopeful dreams of
a new and better life in Hawaii, thousands of laborers decided to
leave not only the plantation but also the islands. Many laborers
broke their contracts and remigrated to the United States; other

laborers waited until their contracts had expired and then took passage for the West Coast. After annexation and the prohibition of contract labor in the Territory of Hawaii, laborers were no longer bound to the plantations and tens of thousands of them boarded ships destined for the continent.

Most Chinese left the plantation as soon as they could, and many of them went to California, where they found employment in railroad construction, as well as industrial and agricultural production. German contract laborers followed a similar pattern: at the expiration of their contracts, many of them departed for the United States. In 1888 one hundred forty-three Germans sailed to the West Coast; most of them had been brought to the islands only a few years earlier as contract laborers. A Portuguese laborer on the Waipahu Plantation remembered how one hundred fifty Portuguese workers left for the mainland as soon as they had earned enough money to go. "The gold mine they thought they'd find wasn't here, so they left," he said. The departure of Spanish families disturbed plantation managers. After two of his "best" Spanish families had moved to California, the manager of the Hawaiian Agricultural Company wrote to C. Brewer and Company: "These people have always seemed contented here and up to a few days ago we had no intimation that they had any idea of leaving." Koreans also flocked to the mainland: between 1905 and 1907 one thousand Korean laborers—one-seventh of the entire Korean population in Hawaii—migrated to California. The exodus of Japanese plantation workers was the most dramatic in terms of sheer numbers. In 1902 one thousand Japanese laborers and their families remigrated to the continent; six thousand more of them followed in 1904, and nearly ten thousand a year later. By 1907 forty thousand Japanese had left Hawaii for the West Coast.[26]

On plantations everywhere Japanese workers read circulars and advertisements that enticed them to move to the mainland, where labor was in demand and wages higher than in Hawaii. An advertisement which appeared in the *Hawaiian Japanese Chronicle* on 22 March 1905 announced: "Through an arrangement made with Yasuzawa of San Francisco, we are able to recruit laborers to the mainland, and offer them work. The laborers will be subjected to no delay upon arriving in San Francisco, but can get work immediately through Yasuzawa. Employment offered in picking strawberries and tomatoes, planting beets, mining, and domestic service. Now is the time to go! Wages $1.50 a day." A year later the *Hawaiian Star* reported: "The 'American fever,' as it is called among the Japs, appears to be causing a lot of agitation among them, especially in Honolulu. Local Japanese papers contain the advertisement of Hasagawa, who recently got a license to solicit laborers, calling for 2,000 Japanese to go to the coast at once. The advertisement . . . offers wages of from $1.35 per day up, stating that men who are good can make from $2 to $4 per day under contracts." In a letter to the manager of the Grove Farm Plantation dated 5 February 1906, S. Sheba of the Committee of Japanese Businessmen of Kauai called the advertisements and efforts of labor recruiters a "scheme to depopulate Hawaii of Japanese."[27]

The massive migration of Japanese from Hawaii to the mainland alarmed planters. In an "uneasy and apprehensive state of mind," they worried about what they described as "the matter of the Japs going to California." They calculated that they were not importing sufficient numbers of Japanese laborers into Hawaii to "balance" the loss of laborers due to the remigration fever. Moreover they feared that the possible restriction of immigration from Japan would severely curtail both their production schedules and their power to control the wages of laborers.[28]

Planters readily acknowledged that labor was paid more in California than in Hawaii and recognized the need to offer Japanese laborers monetary inducements to remain on the plantation. In a letter to the manager of the Laupahoehoe Plantation dated 25 October 1904, Theo. H. Davies and Company anxiously predicted that laborers would continue to leave the islands as long as employers in California gave them more favorable wages, and the company advised him to increase the wages of his workers by $1 per month. Six months later the trustees of the HSPA authorized plantation managers to boost wages even higher—from $16 to $18 per month. But the manager of the Hutchinson Sugar Plantation questioned the wisdom of the trustees' decision and argued that the raise would actually promote the remigration of laborers. This raise of $2 a month would actually give workers the extra money they needed to leave the islands. Years later, after the bonus system had been instituted, planters found that it had indeed provided the financial means for many laborers to free themselves from plantation employment. In a letter to the manager of the Hawaiian Agricultural Company Plantation dated 1 December 1917, C. Brewer and Company stated: "The Bonus money we note has disrupted the labor for the time being, and the same reports came to us from everywhere. We trust that none of your Portuguese or Spaniards will leave you; they are leaving other plantations for the Coast we hear."[29]

In addition to monetary inducements, planters also tried persuasion to keep their laborers on the plantation. The HSPA hired M. A. Silva as a social worker to "get in closer touch with the Portuguese and Spanish families on the plantations" and "to keep more of these people contentedly on the plantation." The manager of the Hawaiian Agricultural Company Plantation informed C. Brewer and Company that he needed Silva's assistance: "Now that Spring is opening in California there will doubtless be some unrest, especially amongst those who have relatives up there." Managers also sought help from the consuls of the Korean and Japanese governments. Noting the tendency of Koreans to remigrate to the mainland, planters saw the need to have a "good" Korean consul who would advise Korean laborers to stay in the islands. Planters asked the Japanese Consul in Hawaii to issue circulars in Japanese that would advise Japanese laborers to remain on the plantation. In 1903 the Consul urged his countrymen "to stay at work steadily on the plantations and not go to an uncertainty to the mainland." Two years later, the Consul announced that he had conferred with the planters and that they had agreed to increase their wages. "I hereby request with all the earnestness in my power," he stated, "that the Japanese laborers may be diligent and faithful to their various lines of work on the plantations and not to act contrary to the policy of the Japanese Government by going to the mainland." On 10 June 1907 the Consul again advised Japanese laborers that it was better for them to remain where they were. Planters were hopeful the circulars would help check the exodus, and posted the circulars in conspicuous places on the plantation—in the offices, stores, and camps. But even these methods of persuasion were ineffective: Japanese laborers did not heed the advice of the representative of their home government and continued to migrate to the mainland, offering their labor to the highest bidder.[30]

Determined to keep their laborers on the plantation, some frustrated planters even refused to return passports to their workers. In a letter to all planters, the secretary of the HSPA wrote: "It has come to our knowledge that when these passports have been sent to certain of the plantations, they are held by the managers . . . and not delivered to the laborers, with the idea, perhaps, of inducing the people to stay upon the plantation." The secretary advised the planters to discontinue the practice, for it had generated complaints that were jeopardizing the relationship between the association and recruiting companies.[31]

Unable to stem the tide of laborers rushing to the mainland, planters turned to the government for assistance to bring the situation under control. Under the prodding of the sugar companies, the Territorial Legislature in 1905 passed a law that required an emigrant agent to pay a $500 annual fee for a license. The law defined an emigrant agent as one who hired or induced laborers to be employed beyond the limits of the Territory. It also specified that any person engaged in business as an emigrant agent without a license would be guilty of a misdemeanor and fined $500. Clearly, the purpose of the law was to harass labor recruiters from the mainland and restrict their activities. On 28 April 1905 the director of H. Hackfeld and Company sent copies of the licensing act to plantation managers, and sternly stated: "In case, therefore, there are any men prowling around your place trying to entice Japanese to leave, you may have them arrested if they cannot show the license required by this law." Such harassment led Japanese newspapers like the *Hawaii Shimpo* to protest against police efforts to stop Japanese from going to the coast.[32]

Planters were offered a final solution to the problem of remigration in 1907: on March 14 President Theodore Roosevelt issued an executive order that prohibited the passage of Japanese from Hawaii to the mainland. "And Whereas," the President declared, "upon the sufficient evidence produced before me by the Department of Commerce and Labor, I am satisfied that passports issued by the Government of Japan to citizens of that country or Korea who are laborers, skilled or unskilled, to go to Mexico, to Canada and to Hawaii, are being used for the purpose of enabling the holders thereof to come to the continental territory of the United States to the detriment of labor conditions therein; I hereby order that such citizens of Japan or Korea, to wit: Japanese or Korean laborers, skilled and unskilled, who have received passports to go to Mexico, Canada or Hawaii, and come therefrom, be refused permission to enter the continental territory of the United States."

On the Makaweli Plantation, Baishiro Tamashiro received the discouraging news about the executive order. He already made arrangements to remigrate to the mainland. Years later, as an old man of ninety-two years living in Hawaii, he vividly recalled: "On March 20th there was a change in the law, and I was prohibited to go to America. It was written all over in the newspapers. We were planning to go on April 9; however, the rule came on the 20th of March. So I could not go to America, and all my planning was *pau.*" At a mass meeting in Honolulu, Japanese laborers denounced the executive order and angrily declared: "It enslaves us permanently to Hawaii's capitalists!" Denied access to the mainland and confined to plantation employment and the islands, Japanese laborers began to realize they were trapped. Unable to seek higher wages and improved working conditions on the West Coast, they saw they had no choice but to struggle for a better life in Hawaii.[33]

Early Plantation Labor Strikes

From the very beginning of the sugar industry in the islands, plantation laborers had struggled for a better life. In July of 1841, only six years after the founding of the first sugar plantation in the islands, Hawaiian laborers on the Koloa Plantation challenged the "entering wedge" of the wage labor system William Hooper had introduced. They defiantly refused to work and demanded an increase in wages from 12.5 cents to 25 cents per day. The management firmly denied their demand and broke the strike within two weeks. In a letter to a friend, plantation manager Charles Burnham defended his actions. The laborers were already receiving in effect 25 cents a day, he argued. In addition to the 12.5 cents they were paid in wages, they were also exempted from the taxes commoners were required to pay their chiefs, and received fish, free housing, and land for their taro patches. Claiming victory over the strikers, Burnham boasted: "They have not carried their point and will not until they are more efficient laborers." Though the striking Koloa plantation workers failed to raise their wages in 1841, they had advanced the labor struggle from recalcitrance and the counterfeiting of coupons to the strike, or from individual to collective protest and action. Theirs was the first of scores of strikes to punctuate the history of plantation Hawaii.[34]

After the 1841 strike, plantation laborers repeatedly went out on strike in order to improve the conditions of their work and lives. But they often learned bitter lessons. Norwegian laborers, for example, never forgot the severity of the punishments they received for striking. On 1 October 1881, forty-two Norwegian workers struck the Alexander and Baldwin Plantation on Maui and refused to serve the terms of their labor contract. They were taken to court, where they were tried for violating their labor agreements. Eighteen of the strikers were sent to prison, and the remaining strikers, threatened with harsh jail sentences, returned to work. Shortly after the strike, one of the punished workers described the terrible and humiliating experience. They had refused to work because the food was poor, he wrote. They were then arrested and tried in court, where the judge reprimanded them and imposed fines. When they objected to the ruling, the strikers were ordered to prison. "We were driven fifteen or sixteen miles through hot desert sands to the Government prison, where we were put to hard labor and mixed with the worst criminals. We concluded the best policy would be to return and allow the fine to be imposed upon us, and were driven back in the same manner, like so many mules, by two mounted officers, armed with revolvers and a large switch or whip."[35]

Meanwhile, on the Big Island, Norwegian contract laborers on the Hitchcock Plantation at Papaikou also went on strike. Food was unsatisfactory and punishments were too severe, they complained. "For refusing to work more than ten hours we were arrested and each fined $3.90, which was deducted from our wages," they bitterly explained, "and the Judge adding that we were obliged to work for our owner whenever he wanted, which clearly violated the contract, but what could we do against the cruel planter and a corrupt Judge?" They found themselves penalized even for being sick. If they were unable to work due to illness, they were required to add to their three-year term of service the number of sick days they had taken. Consequently some of them feared their "bondage" would be an unending one. On October 17 the Norwegian laborers left the Hitchcock Plantation and traveled to Hilo to sue for their freedom. In Hilo, however, they were arrested for desertion and ordered to return to work on the plantation. As a last resort, they appealed to the Supreme Court in Honolulu but again they lost the suit. In a letter to their countrymen in Norway, the strikers expressed their disappointment and despair: "We have at last come to the conclusion that to sue Mr. Hitchcock was useless, and have resigned ourselves to our fate, hoping that something may eventually turn in our favor. . . . Our situation is daily becoming less endurable, and we would advise our countrymen not to listen to tales of eternal summers and tropical fruits." They warned Norwegians to "remain in their snow-capped mountain home."[36]

Ten years later, striking Chinese plantation laborers in Kohala also experienced brutal repression. In August of 1891, two hundred angry Chinese workers gathered around the home of Luke Aseu; they had been recruited as contract laborers by Aseu and felt they had been deceived. Having been told by Aseu that $1.25 would be deducted from their wages each month to reimburse him for passage expenses, they were surprised and shocked to find $5.00 deducted. They had not been informed that the additional monthly deduction of $3.75 would be returned to them only after they had completed their contract and only if they did not run away and were not disobedient or negligent in their work.[37]

Dissatisfied and feeling they had been deceived by Aseu, three hundred Chinese laborers on the Kohala, Union Mill, and Hawi plantations refused to work the next day. They marched to the courthouse in Kapaau and demanded the arrest of Aseu. The plantation managers immediately ordered them to return to their camps, and the discontented laborers finally left the courthouse late in the afternoon. Armed with bullock whips, the deputy sheriff and a large number of natives impressed as special policemen followed the workers as they headed toward the plantations. One or two of the laborers, fearful of the policemen behind them, stooped to pick up stones. According to a correspondent for the *Pacific Commercial Advertiser*, the laborers immediately found themselves "in the midst of a general onslaught, being ruthlessly overridden and welted with the bullock whips." In panic the laborers bolted through the fences and disappeared into the cane fields. The policemen in pursuit then attacked a nearby Chinese camp: they "demolished every window, strewed the premises inside and out with stones, seized every Chinaman they came across, and yanked forty or more by their queues to the leper cells, where they were summarily crowded in. Chinamen were seen with their tails twisted about the pommel of a saddle, dragged at a gallop." In the end, fifty-five Chinese laborers were jailed for assaulting government officers.[38]

In 1894 the protest of Japanese contract laborers on the Kahuku Plantation was even more dramatic. They had suffered from mistreatment and abuse at the hands of the lunas. "Luna huhu; too much hanahana; Kahuku no good," they complained. After a luna had beaten one of the workers, Japanese laborers stopped working. On November 23 over two hundred strikers began a thirty-eight-mile march from Kahuku to Honolulu. They ate lunch in Waiahole and reached Kaneohe at four in the afternoon. Then in the darkness and a cold rain, they started their hike over the mountains. Many strikers wore wooden clogs, slipping on the wet cobblestones of the Pali Road; most of them went barefoot. Around midnight, the chilled and weary strikers straggled down Nuuanu Avenue and into the city. In the morning, they presented their grievances to Goro Narita, Japanese *charge d' affaires* to the Hawaiian Republic. But their bold march and protest ended in disappointment: arrested by police and fined $5 each, the exhausted laborers were forced to walk back to the Kahuku Plantation.[39]

Contract laborers could not legally strike, for they were bound by contract to work for a specified term of years and could be arrested and punished in the courts for violating the agreement. But the Organic Act of 1900, which established Hawaii as a territory of the United States on June 14, abolished the labor contract system.[40]

Months before the Organic Act took effect, plantation laborers anticipated their freedom. On April 4 Japanese workers at the Pioneer Mill in Lahaina struck. Upset over the deaths of three mill hands who had been crushed under a collapsed sugar pan, the laborers blamed management carelessness for the accident and refused to work. The strikers seized virtual control of the mill, as well as the town. According to an investigator, "the strikers for 10 days continued to meet, to parade in the town under Japanese flags, to drill, and even, unhindered by anyone, demolished the house and property of a store clerk who would not give them credit." The Lahaina strikers successfully forced the manager to yield to most of their demands, including $500 payments to the relatives of each of the accident victims and a nine-hour day for all workers. Meanwhile Japanese laborers at the nearby Olowalu

Plantation also went out on strike and secured even greater concessions from their manager: the discharge of all but one luna, abolition of the docking system, a shorter work day, and $1000 to cover
their expenses while on strike. Shortly after the strikes at Lahaina
and Olowalu, the president of the Planters' Association of Maui
warned the HSPA trustees: "Labor strikes have already begun on
Maui, and we have received information from various sources that
as soon as the U. S. laws governing this country go into effect the
Japanese will strike for higher wages." Japanese laborers on the
Spreckelsville Plantation also struck, demanding the termination
of all labor contracts. Swinging clubs and throwing stones, two
hundred strikers fought a posse of sixty policemen and lunas
armed with black snake whips. Though the strikers were "most
thoroughly black snaked" and forced to retreat to their camps,
they won the cancellation of their labor contracts.[41]

Meanwhile, on Oahu, Japanese plantation workers celebrated
the abolition of contract labor by organizing mass demonstra-
tions. In a march through Honolulu, they carried a banner that
declared: "We are free people." On Kauai Japanese laborers
stopped working and sent shock waves into the offices of plantation managers. A distressed manager wrote: "We have been to a
meeting of managers about labor and wages. The Japanese all celebrated the 14th. . . . The free Japanese went to work on the 16th,
the contract workmen would not do so under $20 a month. We
agreed to give them $17.50."[42]

Before the end of the year, over twenty strikes had swept
through the plantations. Altogether over eight thousand laborers
participated in the strikes. They demanded more than the "freedom" granted by the Organic Act: they called for the employment
of Japanese instead of white overseers, the reduction of work
hours, increased wages, and even mandatory local union membership for plantation laborers.

While the 1900 strikes were led and supported mainly by Japanese workers, two of the strikes involved interethnic cooperation.
On June 22 Chinese and Japanese laborers on the Puehuehu Plantation struck to protest the retention of part of their wages, a provision contained in their original labor contracts. Five months later,
on November 23, forty-three Japanese and Portuguese women field
hands on the Kilauea Plantation demanded that wages be raised
from $8 to $10 per month. Though the striking women were

locked out by management, they stood together. Within ten days they were able to win their wage increases.[43]

After 1900 the relationship between plantation managers and Japanese laborers remained tense, often breaking into open, sometimes violent, confrontations. As they organized themselves and initiated strike actions, many workers found themselves facing the power that came out of the barrel of a gun—the licensed violence of the state. Anxious to check the "growing aggressiveness" of Japanese laborers, many planters and police authorities felt the "Japs must be taught a lesson." The lesson they had in mind, according to a commissioner of the United States Department of Commerce and Labor, was "the kind that the militia" could "best teach."[44]

In 1905 Lahaina became the location for this object lesson. On May 22, in the Kaanapali camp, a luna had beaten a Japanese so badly that the worker lost his sight in one eye. His outraged fellow laborers immediately called for the luna's dismissal. Other demands were quickly added as workers from nearby camps and from the mill in Lahaina joined the Kaanapali protestors. On Saturday, May 24, fourteen hundred striking Japanese laborers demonstrated at a mass meeting in Lahaina. Afterward some of the strikers surrounded the home of a cane-planting contractor who refused to join the strike and threatened him. Arriving on the scene, policemen ordered the strikers to disperse and tried to arrest the strike leaders. According to the authorities, one of the strikers fired a shot. Then, firing a volley of bullets, the policemen killed a striker and wounded two others. The next morning Sheriff L. Mansfield Baldwin sent a wireless message to Honolulu: "Fierce rioting last night, two wounded. Rioting continues . . . need assistance." Lahaina was soon transformed into an armed camp: Wailuku sent sixty special officers and Honolulu dispatched forty-five policemen and thirty National Guardsmen armed with field artillery. The strike was finally settled on Thursday when the manager agreed to meet several of the strikers' demands, including the firing of the brutal luna. Gathered in front of the plantation office, the workers shouted: "Banzai! banzai! banzai." Commenting on the lesson planters should learn from the Lahaina strike, the editor of the *Hawaii Shimpo* wrote: "Behind a strike like that at Lahaina, there is always a long list of grievances which have been ignored by managers who usually do not take the trouble to understand them. The management is surprised when a strike begins by a list of fifteen or twenty 'demands' and thinks they are made up for the occasion. If he had kept in touch with the difficulties of his men he would know that they are the accumulation of months, perhaps years, of small troubles which need not have existed." Shortly after the settlement of the strike, two thousand workers attended a memorial service for the slain striker.[45]

The next year Japanese strikers at the Waipahu Plantation of Oahu found themselves subjected to police intimidation and harassment. Demanding higher wages, Japanese laborers struck, and plantation manager E. K. Bull immediately requested police assistance. Forty-seven policemen armed with rifles were assigned to the Waipahu Plantation. Housed and fed in the plantation offices, they functioned as Bull's private army. The policemen maneuvered and marched in review on the plantation grounds to impress the strikers with a show of force; patrolling the camps, they stopped and questioned all stragglers. During a tense moment of the negotiations, Bull threatened to use the police to evict the strikers. "The need of the strong hand," the editor of the *Pacific Commercial Advertiser* declared in his condemnation of the Waipahu strikers, "has been felt at Waipahu for a long time." But the seventeen hundred Japanese strikers stood firm, and Bull was forced to grant some concessions in order to end the strike.[46]

The Waipahu Strike of 1906 underscored the importance of collective labor action. Labor violence and arson were individualistic as well as spontaneous and sporadic actions: they did not seriously undermine planter control. Recalcitrance and drunkenness sometimes slowed down but did not restructure the process of production. Finally, desertion, or ha'alele hana, and remigration to California merely encouraged dissatisfied workers to escape from the plantation and required the importation of more laborers: they actually functioned as safety valves for plantation discontent. But striking constituted a particularly powerful expression of labor resistance, for it could lead to the transformation of the workplace. Moreover striking could enable men and women of various nationalities to gain a deeper understanding of themselves as laborers, to develop an identity or consciousness of themselves as more than members of particular ethnic group—as members of a working class.

This possibility was explored by Milton Murayama in his novel *All I Asking For Is My Body*. During a strike of Filipino workers on a Maui plantation, the manager recruited Japanese boys as scabs. The youngsters viewed the situation as an opportunity to make extra money. But one day a discussion on the strike erupted in an eighth-grade class. "What's freedom?" asked Tubby Takeshita, and the teacher and students agreed that freedom meant being your "own boss," not "part of a pecking order." And they saw that workers were at the bottom of the pecking order and were getting a "raw deal." "You gotta stick together even more if you the underdog," Tubby said. And the teacher asked: "How much together? Filipino labor, period? Japanese labor, period? Or all labor?"[47]

This question confronted plantation laborers during the Great Strike of 1909, and again during the 1920 strike.

VI

The Revolt Against Paternalism: From Ethnicity to Class

The Great Strike of 1909

Like a fire racing across dry cane fields, one of the most massive and sustained strikes in the history of Hawaii swept through the plantations of Oahu in 1909. On the night of May 9, several hundred Japanese laborers gathered at the Aiea Plantation mill camp to demand higher wages. Throughout the evening, "worked up by the beating of empty kerosene tins," the discontented laborers discussed the need for action. At five o'clock in the morning, they decided to strike and three "banzais" thundered through the camps. Two days later Japanese laborers on the nearby Waipahu Plantation followed the lead of the Aiea strikers. Suddenly the strike spread from plantation to plantation—Waialua on the 19th, Kahuku on the 22d, Waianae on the 23d, Ewa on the 24th, and Waimanalo on the 26th. Altogether seven thousand Japanese laborers acted collectively in a struggle which became known as the "Great Strike."[1]

The strike of 1909 was indeed a great one. Where earlier strikes were usually protests against mistreatment from lunas, the 1909 strike had a definite and singular economic focus: higher wages. Where earlier strikes were confined to individual plantations, the 1909 strike involved all of the major plantations on Oahu. Where earlier strikes lasted only a few days, the 1909 strike was a protracted four-month long conflict. Finally, where earlier strikes were usually spontaneous actions, the 1909 strike was well organized, spearheaded by an articulate and educated leadership, an influential network of Japanese newspapers, and an effective interisland strike support system.

Months before the dramatic May uprisings, Japanese newspapers such as the *Nippu Jiji* repeatedly called attention to the need for wage increases for Japanese plantation workers. Then on 1

December 1908 forty-two concerned individuals met at the Japanese YMCA and organized the Zokyu Kisei Kai, the Higher Wage Association. The leaders of the association were urban and educated men: Yokichi Tasaka was a reporter for the *Nippu Jiji*; Fred Kinsaburo Makino operated a drugstore; Yasutaro Soga, the editor of *Nippu Jiji*, had studied at the Tokyo Pharmacy School and the English Law Institute; and Motoyuki Negoro, the holder of a law degree from the University of California at Berkeley, clerked in a law office.

The Higher Wage Association immediately received enthusiastic support from Japanese plantation laborers. Association members visited plantations, urging workers to petition for higher wages and prepare to strike. "The night we stumped the Ewa Plantation Honouliuli area," Soga recalled, "the plantation police all carried pistols. It is said that an order had been given that if any of us were to as much as put one foot in the canefields, they were free to shoot the intruder dead." Despite such threats, the leaders of the association canvassed the Oahu plantations. "Makino and his friends," the director of H. Hackfeld and Company reported in a general letter to the planters, "are trying to stir up the laborers on the plantations, sending them postal cards with return-answer paid, and in which it is stated that they are in favor of a raise." In addition the association publicized its cause through the Japanese newspapers and through pamphlets (in both English and Japanese) distributed to the public.[2]

On December 12 the Higher Wage Association sponsored a mass meeting at the Asahi Theater in Honolulu. Seventeen hundred Japanese attended the meeting, and adopted resolutions demanding an increase in wages from $18 to $22.50 per month and calling for a meeting between their association and the HSPA. A week later the Higher Wage Association wrote to the secretary of the HSPA requesting a conference.

The request was ignored, however, and several months later the dissatisfied workers took the initiative and struck. "Just as if with the force of wildfire," commented Soga, "7,000 of the compatriots, from each of Oahu's plantations, launched the great strike in the month of May. The die was cast. At last we had crossed the Rubicon."[3]

The strike divided the Japanese community. The *Hawaii Shimpo*, edited by Sometaro Sheba, warned workers not to engage in "reckless action" and assured them that raises would be the "natural" and "inevitable" consequence of increased demands for labor. The Honolulu Merchants Association, composed of Japanese businessmen dependent on plantation purchases, also advised caution. The Reverend Takei Okumura accompanied a group of Japanese businessmen to the Waialua Plantation to pacify the striking laborers. On May 25 the Japanese consul general, Senichi Uyeno, issued a statement against the strike: "It is to my great regret that the people working on the plantations have started to demand higher wages and are leaving the plantations. . . . This act of striking breaks all peace and harmony, and it creates panic in the labor market." The consul general instructed his countrymen to "behave quietly and carefully, and keep on working." But other sections of the Japanese community supported the Higher Wage Association and the Japanese strikers. Organizations such as the Public Bath Operators Association, Carpenters Association, Japanese Hotel and Inn Association, Barbers Association, and the Honolulu Retail Merchants Association publicly backed the strike.[4]

To organize and plan strike activities, the Higher Wage Association established a strike headquarters at the Yamashiro Hotel. The association decided that the storm center of the struggle would be Oahu, and that plantation laborers on Maui, Kauai, and the Big Island would continue working and send part of their wages to support their beleaguered brothers on Oahu. "The strike area was to be limited to Oahu," Soga later explained. "The plantations of each of the other islands were all to continue working, but they were requested to send supporting contributions to the Oahu island strikers who were to make the sacrifice for all." The strikers and their supporters felt an intense nationalistic solidarity. Makino had declared that they had to conduct themselves in the spirit of old Japan: *yamato damashii*, "the spirit that drives everybody away, no matter who the contestants may be." "Yamato damashii" meant, Tasaka stated, "we must do our best, and in order to accomplish that purpose we must stick together."[5]

In their demand for higher wages, the strikers called for equal pay for equal work; they wanted an end to the racially discriminatory wage system. They argued that it was unfair and degrading for Japanese laborers to be paid less than laborers of other nationalities for the same kind and amount of work. The system of differential wages based on nationality, Negoro insisted, indicated that a "pitiable condition" existed in Hawaii where Japanese laborers were assigned "pigsty like homes" and received only $18.00 per month, while Portuguese and Puerto Rican workers doing the same type of work were paid $22.50 and given single family cottages to live in. In a pamphlet on *The Higher Wages Question*, the association eloquently denounced the dual wage system, which was based on a racial hierarchy:

> The wage is a reward for services done, and a just wage is that which compensates [the] labor[er] to the full value of the service rendered by him. It is an unjust wage to pay the laborer less than the real value of the work performed by him. Here we do not propose to discuss whether the planters can afford to pay more than $22.50 a month to ordinary unskilled labor on the plantations, though we are of the opinion that they can pay far more than that sum. Let us take that sum as a just reward for the laborer from Porto Rico and Portugal. If a laborer comes from Japan and he performs the same quantity of work of the same quality within the same period of time as those who hail from the opposite side of the world, what good reason is there to discriminate one as against the other? It is not the color of his skin or hair, or the language he speaks, or manners and customs that grow cane in the field. It is labor that grows cane. . . .[6]

Strikers argued that wages should be calculated in relation to the cost of living; otherwise inflation would silently lower the workers' standard of living. Indeed, in 1909 they found themselves caught between fixed wages and rising prices. Between 1905 and 1908, food and clothing costs had jumped sharply: rice 30 percent, salt 33 percent, soap 28 percent, denim 13 percent, lard 40 percent, canned fish 30 percent. While wages had remained constant, the cost of many basic needs had increased by 25 percent or more. Thus strikers asked for a raise of $4.50 per month, or 25 percent.[7]

To document the case for a higher wage, the *Nippu Jiji* filled its pages with testimonies from the workers themselves. On 4 December 1908 the newspaper printed a Japanese plantation laborer's monthly expenditures and income:

Board	$ 7.00
Laundry	.75
Tobacco, paper, matches	1.00
Bath	.25
Raincoat	.55

Oil	.15
Raincoat oil	.15
Contributions	.25
Shoes and socks	.60
Stamps and stationary	.30
Send-off money	.25
Hat	.08
Haircut	.25
Working suits	.75

Total $12.33

Average monthly income   14.60

Net income $ 2.17

In another financial account published in the *Nippu Jiji*, a worker showed he had a net income of $2.10, which led the editor to ask: "Is it not a cruel spectacle to see a laborer work under this tropical sun, and among the cane bushes, for twenty-one days each month —and no laborer of ordinary health and strength can work more than that each month throughout the year—and he cannot save more than a paltry sum of $2.10 a month?"[8]

Such a sum seemed particularly paltry to Japanese laborers because many of them now had families in Hawaii to support. Earlier, as sojourners and as single men, they had fewer needs and expenses. But by 1908 many of them had become settlers; they were no longer temporary migratory workers. Hawaii had become a place to establish permanent homes and build their communities. "In 1908," Negoro pointed out, "there were 21,000 married [Japanese] women in Hawaii, in addition to 9,500 children between the ages of one to four, 3,000 between five to six years old, and 4,966 children between the ages of seven to fifteen—or approximately 5,000 school age children." Japanese workers needed higher wages in order to support their families and to improve housing conditions in the camps. "Life in the present quarters given to the Japanese laborers," the strike leaders argued, "is utterly unfit for married men or for bringing up their children, both from the sanitary and moral points of view. Laborers need money for building their homes."[9]

In their letter (12 May 1909) to E. K. Bull, the manager of the Waipahu Plantation, ninety-two strikers explained the relationship between their decision to make their homes in the islands and the need for a higher wage: "We have decided to permanently settle here, to incorporate ourselves with the body politique of Hawaii—to unite our destiny with that of Hawaii, sharing the prosperity and adversity of Hawaii with other citizens of Hawaii. Many have families to maintain, children to educate, and most of us will have to not in a very far distant future. And as we are gradually becoming settled laborers, various social relations have sprung up, educational and religious institutions are growing up." In the islands, the Japanese community had to maintain and support a total of fifty-nine churches and temples, sixty-eight schools, and sixty-one ministers and priests and eighty teachers. Plantation workers had new social needs to subsidize. "A large amount of money," the Higher Wage Association declared, "is needed to build respectable churches and schools as worthy of the name of free labor."[10]

But the striking laborers were concerned about the larger society of Hawaii, as well as their particular Japanese communities. Japanese laborers were immigrants and could not even become United States citizens because federal law extended naturalization only to "white" immigrants. Still the Japanese strikers had a certain understanding of the democratic ideals of America. To many of them, the very future of the islands—whether or not Hawaii would become an "American" society—seemed to be at stake in the 1909 strike. In *The Higher Wage Question*, the association argued that the "unsatisfactory and deplorable" conditions of the Japanese laborers perpetuated an "undemocratic and un-American" situation in the islands: a society of "plutocrats and coolies." Such a pattern of social inequality was injurious to Hawaii in general. "If, on the other hand, the wages would be increased," the association predicted, "the laborers would work more industriously; they would become devoted to their employers and more faithful for the work to which they are assigned. . . . Hawaii will enjoy perpetual peace and prosperity with increased production of sugar. . . . Hawaii will have, not in a very distant future, a thriving and contented middle class—the realization of the high ideal of Americanism." As settlers, Japanese strikers felt a responsibility to transform society in Hawaii, to make possible the democratic formation of a "middle class" and thus "Americanize" the islands.[11]

But many planters had their own views of the future of Hawaii and the kind of society the islands should have. Generally they

wanted to maintain the hierarchical social structure of the plantation—White over Asian and capitalist over laborer. A visitor from
the mainland noticed the increasing presence of Japanese children
on the plantations and asked a Maui planter whether he thought
the coming generation of Japanese would make intelligent citizens. "Oh, yes," he replied, "they'll make intelligent citizens all
right enough, but not plantation laborers—and that's what we
want."[12]

Determined to break the strike and defend their hegemony in
the islands, planters secretly mobilized their allies within the Japa-
nese community. One of them was Sheba, editor of the *Hawaii
Shimpo*. The planters had been quietly subsidizing Sheba's newspaper: the Bank of Hawaii, under planter control, had loaned
Sheba $5,000 to establish his newspaper, and the HSPA sent Sheba
$100 a month as a subsidy. Under Sheba's editorship, the *Hawaii
Shimpo* became a leading critic of the *Nippu Jiji* and the Higher
Wage Association. Sheba himself became an informant to the
HSPA, reporting developments within the Japanese community to
the planters. In a letter to all planters dated 7 January 1909, the
director of H. Hackfeld and Company identified Sheba as his
source of information regarding Makino's efforts to stir up unrest
among plantation laborers.[13]

Planters also developed a surveillance system to monitor the
movement for higher wages. The director of H. Hackfeld and
Company advised planters to "get some trustworthy Japanese to
look over the papers (Japanese—*Nippu Jiji*)" distributed in the
camps in order to be informed of the agitators' plans. "As it is
feared," the director added, "that finally the agitators for higher
wages will get the upper hand, we would be pleased, if you would
carefully watch this movement, and to let us know immediately, in
case you hear anything, so that we may be able to notify the
Trustees accordingly."[14]

The trustees of the HSPA spearheaded and directed the drive to
destroy the agitation for higher wages. Two days after the first
group of strikers at Aiea had stopped working, the trustees agreed
to compensate all plantations for property losses incurred during
the strike and required plantations to be guided by the association's policies in dealing with the strike. On May 27, facing an
islandwide strike on Oahu, the HSPA adamantly resolved that the

plantations would make no concessions to the strikers' demand for a wage increase. To intimidate the strikers and to break the strike, the HSPA instructed planters to serve eviction notices to the strikers: "In case of demands by strikers, the laborers are to be paid off and told that unless they return to work they must vacate their quarters." The Aiea and Waipahu strikers were given six days to resume work or remove themselves from camp; the Kahuku, Waialua, and Ewa strikers were allowed even less time—only twenty-four hours.[15]

Fifteen hundred strikers on the Waipahu Plantation responded to the eviction threat by organizing a demonstration march; they cleaned their camps and then paraded into Honolulu, led by the music of a band. Strikers evicted from other plantations also converged on Honolulu. By the end of June, over 5,000 evicted strikers and their families were living in the city, sheltered in theaters and vacant buildings. "The city of Honolulu," Soga wrote, "was just like a battlefield, with everything in extreme confusion. The Wage Increase Association quartered the strikers . . . at both Kakaako and Moiliili, establishing more kitchens everywhere. Women volunteers turned out in full force and helped in caring for them." The Palama kitchen served three meals a day to over 2,200 people, and Aala Park became the central encampment for the evicted strikers. "At headquarters, in Aala lane," the *Pacific Commercial Advertiser* reported, "hundreds of Japanese hung around all day, while thousands . . . were there at meal times. Inside the enclosure, where the kaukau tables are spread, eight long tables were filled several times at noon, the fare served being boiled rice and fish. At four of these tables sat the men, about three hundred at a sitting, while on the Ewa side of the grounds were an equal number of tables for the women and children. Between the sets of tables was the out-of-doors kitchen, a dozen great caldrons boiling away with rice."[16]

Support from the Japanese community was generous. Workers from plantations on the other islands sent rice and truckloads of vegetables, and Makino secured a warehouse to store the donated food. The Physicians Association, an organization of Japanese doctors, gave free medical service to strikers and their family members. The Aiea Merchants Association donated its entire treasury of $1,572.50 to the strike fund, and the Honolulu Retail Merchants Association contributed $1,000. Japanese plantation laborers on the other islands continued working and taxed themselves in order to send money to the Oahu strikers. Individuals also gave magnanimously. "One day," Soga recalled, "an old Japanese woman from another island purposely came to Honolulu to visit the office, carrying something like a bag. She heaped in a row, on my desk, more than four hundred odd dollars she had brought in silver coin."[17]

Frustrated because their eviction strategy had only generated additional momentum for the strike, the planters next targeted the leadership of the Higher Wage Association. On June 10, Makino, Negoro, Tasaka, and Soga were arrested and jailed for conspiring to boycott plantation business. In his account of this unnerving experience, Soga wrote:

> On the night of June 10, 1909, I was being held in solitary confinement in Oahu jail. I did not have complete knowledge of what was happening to the other defendants. That night, about 12 o'clock, I was called out to the jail yard. There were High Sheriff Henry and Interpreter Doyle. We immediately got into a carriage and went to the *Nippu Jiji* office on Hotel Street. I was escorted to . . . the second floor, where stood the safe. I was ordered to open it and take out and hand over all the letters and documents it contained. I flatly replied that I refused to do so until I saw a warrant from the court. But High Sheriff Henry said that if I refused he would be obliged to blast it open.

After Soga had been forced to open the safe, he was taken back to jail. Meanwhile police tried to prevent the publication of the *Nippu Jiji* by arresting its staff members, including reporter Keitaro Kawamura, manager Katsuichi Kawamoto, foreman Hidekichi Takemura, and several clerks. The next day the chief of police prohibited the making of all public speeches for the duration of the strike, and the National Guard was placed on stand-by duty, prepared to impose order by force. After a lengthy trial, the four Higher Wage Association leaders were found guilty of conspiracy and sentenced to ten months in prison.[18]

While the planters harassed the strikers and their leaders, they hired Chinese, Hawaiians, Portuguese, and Koreans as strikebreakers. On 18 May 1909 the director of H. Hackfeld and Company instructed planters to use workers of "other nationalities" to break the Japanese strike. Planters offered strikebreakers $1.50 in

wages per day or twice the regular rate, and recruited and transported to the plantations three thousand Hawaiian stevedores and
workers.[19]

Meanwhile the trustees of the HSPA were developing a long
range strategy to break the strike and control Japanese laborers:
they turned to the Philippines as a new source of labor. On July 28
the labor committee of the HSPA informed the trustees that several
hundred Filipino laborers were en route to Hawaii. "It may be too
soon to say that the Jap is to be supplanted," the committee continued, "but it is certainly in order to take steps to clip his wings," and
to give "encouragement to a new class [Filipinos] . . . to keep the
more belligerent element in its proper place." Three days later
C. Walters, manager of the Hutchinson Sugar Plantation on the
Big Island, wrote to William G. Irwin: "We are pleased to hear that
from present appearances it seems that the worst of the strike situation is about over. . . . We are pleased to learn that the recruiting
of Filipinos is a success." In his address to the annual meeting of
the HSPA in December of 1909, the president of the association
described the new recruiting program and its relationship to the
strike: "The question of immigration has been before your Trustees
more or less during the whole of last year. One of the immediate
results of the labor disturbance was to cause them to take in hand
very vigorously the question of obtaining supplies of fresh labor
from every available source. Messengers Pinkham and Stevens
were sent to the Philippines to revive native immigration from that
point. They have forwarded thus far six or seven hundred people,
who have taken hold of field work in a very satisfactory manner,
being industrious and tractable. There are hopes of obtaining a
goodly number of these people in the near future." Two years later,
due to the vigorous recruitment efforts of the HSPA, over three
thousand Filipinos were working on the plantations of Hawaii.[20]

To accelerate the recruitment of non-Japanese laborers from
"every available source," the trustees of the HSPA offered to pay
the personal taxes of new immigrant workers. In December of
1909, they resolved: "With respect to personal taxes of the Territory (poll, school and road taxes) upon the recently arrived and
presently arriving immigrants, including Portuguese, Russians,
Filipinos, and Porto [sic] Ricans, such taxes shall be paid for three
years by the Plantations, provided such immigrants remain for
three years on the plantations to which they have been or may be

assigned." On 11 February 1910 the director of H. Hackfeld and Company wrote to inform George Wilcox of the Grove Farm Plantation that Russian laborers were en route to Hawaii. The new HSPA recruitment program led to an ethnic recomposition of the plantation labor force: between 1908 and 1915 the percentage of Japanese workers was reduced from 70 percent to 54 percent.[21]

The planter attack on the strikers eventually took its toll on the Japanese laborers. Evicted from their homes and cut off from their leaders, the strikers realized that they would not be able to sustain a protracted struggle for higher wages and justice. They had valiantly confronted the HSPA, a powerful organization that directed the "industrial world" of Hawaii. Amazingly they had successfully held the strike together for four months. But by August they had exhausted their resources, economic as well as emotional. Frustrated and demoralized, many strikers and their supporters felt a profound sense of rage. One of them, young Tomekichi Mori, stabbed and seriously wounded Sheba. On August 5, two days after the assassination attempt, representatives of the strikers and workers from the other islands met at the Japanese elementary school on Nuuanu Avenue and finally decided to end their long and painful ordeal.[22]

But their struggle was not undertaken completely in vain. The strikers had demonstrated their power to organize resistance, and had forced the planters to realize the need to institute reforms and reduce labor discontent. On 29 November 1909, three months after the end of the strike, the HSPA raised the wages of Japanese laborers and abolished the system of wage differentiation based on nationality. Laborers, the HSPA decided, would be "paid in proportion to their individual ability," and would also receive not less than $22 for a month of twenty-six working days. Thus the planters had actually conceded the most important demand of the strike: equal pay for equal work regardless of race.[23]

In effect, the Japanese workers had lost the strike but had won their objectives. Even their leaders were returned to them. On 4 July 1910 Makino, Negoro, Tasaka, and Soga were pardoned by the acting governor, John Mott Smith, and released from prison. Feeling victorious and vindicated, Soga described this momentous day: "At 8 A.M. Head Jailer Asch called us four and those who had come with us, together and held a solemn farewell ceremony. He read the decree issued by Acting Governor Mott-Smith. . . . Before

the jail gate were several hundred persons who had come to welcome us. We four were buried in leis and commemorative photographs were taken. We crossed Aala Park and arrived at the Yamashiro Hotel. Before a crowd of nearly 1,000, Torakichi Kimura,
President of the Nigata Prefectural Association, gave a touching
speech of welcome. We were grateful for the three banzais we
received."[24]

The next day Soga wrote an essay for the *Nippu Jiji* entitled
"Impressions on Leaving Jail." Undaunted by his imprisonment,
he reviewed the great struggle against "the power of wealth and
the oppression of the government authorities," and he reminded
the people of the power they had generated through collective
action. He acknowledged proudly the "various sacrifices sustained
by the full 70,000 Japanese in this strike." Soga had reason to be
proud, for Japanese laborers and their supporters in the Japanese
community had stood together in the struggle of 1909. But this solidarity based on Japanese nationalism had also opened the way for
planters to pit workers from other countries against the Japanese
strikers. To be successful, the labor movement in Hawaii and its
strike actions would have to be based on interethnic working class
unity. This was a lesson workers had to learn from the 1909 strike
and practice in the 1920 strike.[25]

Beyond "Blood Unionism": The 1920 Strike

During the Great Strike, planters developed two long-range strategies to control the laborers—the importation of Filipinos to coun-
terbalance the Japanese workers, and the establishment of the bonus wage system to keep workers "on a string." Eleven years later,
however, the laborers struck again. This time they organized the
first significant interethnic strike, bringing together Japanese and
Filipino laborers and advancing the labor struggle beyond "blood
unionism," the organizing of workers into unions on the basis of
ethnicity. The strikers also called for an end to paternalism, insist-
ing that their earnings be based on fair wages rather than low
wages plus a bonus or "present" from the planters. Aware of the
need for interethnic unity and working class independence from
paternalistic management, the strikers of 1920 provided new directions for the labor movement in Hawaii.[26]

Like the Great Strike, the 1920 strike was not a spontaneous uprising. In October of 1917 plantation workers and their supporters organized the Association of Higher Wage Question to investigate the issue and to submit a "reasonable demand" for a wage increase to the HSPA. The Wage Association sent each plantation a letter requesting information regarding actual wages and bonuses paid to workers, but the HSPA directed all managers not to reply to the letters. Ignored by the HSPA, the Wage Association decided to escalate the campaign for higher wages. At a mass meeting on December 26, the association called for the formation of a labor "union" to "rouse the self-consciousness of Japanese laborers and promote a strong bond of unity."[27]

During the next two years grass roots movements for higher wages sprang up on plantations throughout the islands. On the Big Island, workers organized the Japanese Young Men's Association, which represented laborers on five Hamakua plantations. On 19 October 1919 seventy-five delegates from the Japanese Young Men's Association met in Hilo. Determined to launch a "big labor movement," they demanded an eight-hour day, an increase in wages, and the abolition of the bonus system. A week later, on Oahu, the Young Men's Buddhist Association of the Waialua Plantation declared that it was essential to organize "a big solidified movement of laborers throughout the islands." Within a short span of two months, Japanese workers organized themselves—the Maui Federation of Labor, the Oahu Federation of Labor, the Kauai Federation of Labor, and the Labor Federation of Hawaii on the Big Island.[28]

In early December representatives of the various labor federations met in Honolulu to form an interisland organization, the Japanese Federation of Labor, and formally submitted demands for higher wages to the HSPA. Meanwhile Filipino laborers also organized themselves into the Filipino Federation of Labor under the leadership of Pablo Manlapit and petitioned for pay raises. The demands of both the Japanese and Filipinos were rejected by the HSPA.

The Japanese Federation of Labor immediately asked the HSPA to reconsider its decision, and agreed to declare a strike only after all peaceful methods had been tried. In their internal discussions, the Federation leaders realized striking was the only way to settle the dispute between the workers and the HSPA. "Let's rise and open the eyes of the capitalists," they argued. "Let's cooperate with the Filipinos . . . back them up with our fund [and] our whole force." But the Japanese leaders also thought both labor federations should avoid precipitous action and should prepare for a long strike and plan a successful strategy.[29]

But the Filipino Federation of Labor felt the time for action had arrived. Consequently on January 19 Manlapit unilaterally issued an order for the Filipinos to strike and urged the Japanese to join them. In his appeal to the Japanese Federation of Labor, Manlapit eloquently called for interethnic working class solidarity: "This is the opportunity that the Japanese should grasp, to show that they are in harmony with and willing to cooperate with other nationalities of this territory, concerning the principles of organized labor. . . . We should work on this strike shoulder to shoulder."[30]

Meanwhile, on the plantations, three thousand Filipino workers at Aiea, Waipahu, Ewa, and Kahuku went out on strike. They set up picket lines and urged Japanese laborers to join them. "What's the matter? Why you hanahana?" the Filipino strikers asked their Japanese co-workers. Several Japanese newspapers issued a clarion call for Japanese support for the striking Filipinos. The *Hawaii Shimpo*, which was on the side of the strikers in 1920, scolded Japanese workers for their hesitation: "Our sincere and desperate voices are also their voices. Their righteous indignation is our righteous indignation. . . . Fellow Japanese Laborers! Don't be a race of unreliable dishonest people! Their problem is your problem." The *Hawaii Hochi* advised Japanese laborers to strike immediately, for the best policy to make the strike effective was to have laborers from different countries take "action together." Between Filipinos and Japanese, the *Hawaii Choho* declared, "[there are] no barriers of nationality, race, or color."[31]

On January 26 the Japanese Federation of Labor ordered an immediate general layoff and scheduled a general strike to begin on February 1. From camp to camp, from plantation to plantation, laborers quickly spread the message: "Pau hana. No go work. We on strike." United in struggle, eighty-three hundred Filipino and Japanese strikers—77 percent of the entire plantation work force on Oahu—brought plantation operations to a sudden stop. On the Aiea Plantation, reported a strike leader, the "big chimney" of the mill was "vomitting hardly any smoke. The camps appeared deserted. Only four or five Chinese were seen moving here and there with piles of wood. From the cellar of Waipahu Plantation

WORKERS MARCH TO DEMAND HIGHER WAGES
DURING THE 1920 STRIKE

Between Filipinos and Japanese, "[there are] no barriers of nationality,
race, or color."

hospital about 30 Koreans protected by 15 policemen came out and were slowly moving towards the cane fields. Outside of this small group of men not a single cat or man was seen going to work. Everywhere the camps were shrouded in dead silence."[32]

Again, only eleven years after the bitter 1909 conflict, strikers had shut down the plantations on Oahu. The strike demands represented a broad range of issues: the need for an eight-hour day, an insurance fund to provide for the "hazards of misfortune and the approach of old age," and paid maternity leaves. Women plantation laborers, the strikers insisted, should be excused from work two weeks before and six weeks after the delivery of their babies, and be entitled to a paid maternity leave. The primary issue of the 1920 strike involved wages: in Hawaii, the "Paradise of the Pacific," the strikers declared angrily, laborers were "suffering under the heat of the equatorial sun, in field and factory... weeping with ten hours of hard labor and with a scanty pay of 77 cents a day."[33]

The strikers demanded a wage increase from $.77 to $1.25 per day for men and a minimum wage of $.93 per day for women. Again, as they had in 1909, strikers complained that wages had not reflected the sharp increases in the cost of living. "Rice, miso, and soy, the daily food of laborers are today more than four times the pre-war prices," they declared. "But our wages are not a bit different from pre-war wages." According to a pamphlet published by the strikers, the monthly expenses for workers had risen significantly between May of 1916 and November of 1919:

a single person—from $24.81 to $35.19 or 41%
a married couple—from $46.81 to $57.05 or 27.6%
a family with two children—from $52.36 to $75.72 or 44.5%

The presence of families represented a greater reality on the plantations in 1920 than in 1909. Because the large majority of workers were married and had families to support, the strikers argued, they required higher wages.[34]

In addition to a wage increase, the strikers demanded changes in the bonus system: they wanted the number of workdays required each month for laborers to qualify for the annual bonus to be reduced from twenty to fifteen days for men and from fifteen to ten days for women. "The fact is," strikers argued, "that the twenty-day provision in the bonus regulations excludes about 60 percent of all plantation laborers from participation in the bonus." Due to the punishing conditions of plantation labor and due to illnesses, it was not always possible for a man to work five days a week, four weeks a month. But the bonus had become a part of wages due to inflation. Consequently even when they were actually ill, workers were reluctant to absent themselves from work, fearful they would lose their bonus. Strikers reported that it was for this reason that the influenza patients of the Waialua Plantation in 1918 felt "compelled" to work. Furthermore, strikers demanded that 75 percent of the bonus should be paid to the laborers every month rather than annually, and the remainder of the bonus at the end of the bonus year or whenever the laborers left the employment of the plantation.[35]

While strikers agreed that the reform of the bonus system seemed to be the most realistic and practical way to raise wages, many strikers actually wanted a direct increase in wages from $.77 to $3.00 per day and the abolition of the paternalistic bonus system. They realized that the existing wage arrangement had made them dependent upon a bonus or gift from the planters. Denied fair wages, they had to rely on planter generosity to make financial ends meet, to feed their children. But "if the laborer really earns his basic wage, plus his bonus," the strikers argued, "why not pay him the whole as money earned—and not as a prize, present or bonus?" The strikers also claimed that the bonus system was a "shackle" that prevented workers from changing their occupations or moving to another plantation. Under the "beautiful name of bonus," the planters had devised an "iron fetter."[36]

The planters clearly understood the serious challenge they faced from the striking laborers in 1920 and vowed to "break the strike, no matter how long" it would take, "no matter how much" it would cost. Actually, two years before the strike, planters had confidentially acknowledged the need to raise wages. In a letter to the manager of the Grove Farm Plantation dated 18 October 1917, the vice president of H. Hackfeld and Company wrote:

> The Planters' Association will, sooner or later, have to make a statement to the laborers on what is going to be done, and it seems to us that in a measure the popular demand for higher wages is somewhat justified. While you may not personally approve of this, the signs of the times, if correctly interpreted, point to a determination on the part of the laboring classes to secure higher wages, and is accorded to them nearly all over the world. . . . It must also be born in mind that the living expenses have increased enormously and that it will take some years even after the war in which these are brought down to pre-war conditions. What is best to be done is a very difficult question. It seems very much to us as if an increase in wages of 20% all around is justified. . . .

But planters failed to act in time and found themselves confronted by demands for wage increases in 1920.[37]

In the polarized situation, the planters felt they could not raise wages. To do so would be to give in to the demands of the strikers and open the way for organized labor to gain greater power in Hawaii. A week after the Filipino workers struck, the president of American Factors (formerly H. Hackfeld and Company) stated that the demands for higher wages were "unreasonable." There could be no question of an increase in wages, he explained, for workers were already "very well paid" in terms of the total sum they were receiving from both wages and bonuses. Again, as they had in 1909, the trustees of the HSPA immediately took a hard line against the strikers. On 29 January 1920 the HSPA agreed to bear all losses of property on plantations incurred during the strike and to direct the campaign against the strike.[38]

Determined to "fight to a finish," the HSPA refused to consider a mediation proposal submitted to them by the Reverend Albert W. Palmer of the Central Union Church. Urging both sides to compromise, Palmer had asked the workers to call off the strike and the planters to allow the laborers to elect representatives to negotiate labor issues with management. Representing the views of the planters, the *Honolulu Star Bulletin* dismissed the Palmer proposal, arguing that the strike had to be "utterly defeated and entirely discredited."[39]

To break the strike, the planters employed their time-tested strategy of divide and control. The situation seemed ideal for pitting Japanese and Filipino laborers against each other: though both groups were on strike, they were organized initially into two different unions. On February 3, the president of C. Brewer and Company described the strategy of the management: "We are inclined to think that the best prospect, in connection with this strike, is the fact that two organizations, not entirely in harmony with each other, are connected with it, and if either of them falls out of line, the end will be in sight." Five days later Manlapit of the Filipino Federation of Labor suddenly fell out of line. To the surprise of both the Filipino and Japanese strikers, Manlapit called off the strike and condemned it as a "Japanese" action to "cripple the industries of the Territory of Hawaii" in the hope they might be taken over by "an unscrupulous alien race." Then on February 14 Manlapit abruptly reissued the strike order. As it turned out, the HSPA was involved in Manlapit's maneuvers: the Filipino leader and HSPA attorney Frank Thompson had met to discuss an agreement in which Manlapit would end the strike in exchange for a certain sum of money.[40]

To neutralize both the Filipino and Japanese strikers, the planters hired Hawaiians, Portuguese, Puerto Ricans, Chinese, and Koreans as strikebreakers and paid them $3 per day in addition to the bonus. The HSPA meanwhile directed new importations of Filipino laborers to the Oahu plantations. In a letter to the manager of the Hawaiian Agricultural Company on the Big Island, the vice president of C. Brewer and Company explained why his order for Filipino laborers had not been filled. "A number of Filipinos was on way," he wrote on 2 March 1920, "but in view of the strike, they had to be allocated to Oahu plantations." On 3 March 1920 R. D. Mead, director of the HSPA's Labor Bureau, wrote to the manager of the Hawaiian Agricultural Company: "We have for acknowledgement your Labor Requirement for March requesting fifty laborers, Ilocanos preferred. It all depends upon the strike whether or not we will be able to send anybody to the other islands. We are at present assigning all new arrivals to the plantations on this island to take the places of strikers." Two months later, on May 1, the vice president of C. Brewer and Company again wrote to the manager of the Hawaiian Agricultural Company: "Your requisition for labor is noted, but the situation here is such that any incoming labor must of necessity be diverted to the Oahu plantations."[41]

While planters frantically recruited strikebreakers, they also organized a propaganda attack designed to foment anti-Japanese sentiments and to discredit the Japanese strike leadership. In a letter to a plantation manager dated 13 February 1920, R. D. Mead, director of the HSPA's Bureau of Labor, described the plan for the ideological war to be directed against the Japanese strike leaders. "In order to let the plantation laborers know they are being duped and to make them realize what they are losing by allowing themselves to be misled by the agitating newspapers and strike leaders," Mead wrote, "we have commenced a program of propaganda. . . . There is absolutely no race so susceptible to ridicule as the Japanese, and good cartoons will cause consternation among the members of the Japanese Federation." One of the handbills issued by the HSPA, entitled "Federation Officials Dining," caricatured the Japanese strike leaders. Portraying them as opportunists and manipulators, the handbill depicted the leaders at an elegant dinner and offered the following fabricated conversation:

"This $5 dinner is very good.
"Now bring me a 50 cent cigar.
"Let us get more contributors and have a $10 dinner every night.
"Long live the strike.
"I hope the strike never ends.
"After we finish eating let us go for a joy ride.
"$8 a day and fine meals like this are very nice.

"$5 for a dinner like this is not too much.

"Too bad we have no champagne. Laborers would gladly pay for it.

"If the laborers keep on contributing we can have meals like this for a long time."[42]

But the Japanese strike, the planters claimed, had an even more sinister reality. HSPA President John Waterhouse charged that the action taken by the Japanese Federation of Labor was "an anti-American movement designed to obtain control of the sugar business of the Hawaiian Islands." The two leading newspapers, the *Pacific Commercial Advertiser* and the *Honolulu Star-Bulletin*, repeatedly represented the strike as a racial conflict between loyal Americans and foreign Japanese. "The Japanese Government," the *Advertiser* declared in an editorial entitled "The Hand Across the Sea," "is back of the strike; it is back of the organization of Japanese labor in the American Territory of Hawaii; it reaches out its arms and directs the energies and activities of its nationals here in these American islands." The *Star-Bulletin* warned its readers that "Japanese priests, editors and educators" were seeking to control the twenty-five thousand Japanese plantation laborers in order to be the "masters of Hawaii's destiny." Under the domination of these "alien agitators," Hawaii would be "as thoroughly Japanized . . . as if the Mikado had the power to name our governor and direct our political destiny."[43]

While planters slandered the Japanese and deliberately stressed the racial issue in order to shroud the economic issue, they served eviction notices to the strikers. Given only forty-eight hours to vacate their homes and camps, some twelve thousand strikers and their families were forced to leave the plantations. The Japanese Federation of Labor coordinated the efforts to house and feed the evicted strikers, both Japanese and Filipino. Appealing for assistance from the Japanese Federation, Filipino strikers said: "We no can hanahana. Boss too much huhu." In response, the Japanese leaders agreed to support the Filipinos: "We are duty bound to see that our fellow laborers are well housed and fed. We must realize the principles of justice and love in our actions." The Japanese Federation provided accommodations for the homeless laborers and their families in hotels, Shinto temples, churches, tents erected in vacant lots, and empty factory buildings including an old sake brewery in Kakaako.[44]

Living in congested encampments and temporary quarters in the city, the strikers were especially vulnerable to the killer influenza epidemic, which swept through the islands in 1920. The mass evacuation during the height of the "flu terror" was described as "a pitiable and even frightful scene" by the Hawaii Laborers' Association: "Household utensils and furniture thrown out and heaped before our houses, doors tightly nailed that none might enter, sickly fathers with trunks and baggage, mothers with weeping babes in arms, the crying of children, and the rough voices of the plantation police officers." The influenza ravaged the strikers and their families: over two thousand became ill and one hundred and fifty died.[45]

Under such harsh and chaotic conditions, the strikers could not hold out indefinitely. By the end of June they saw that the odds were against them, the opposition formidable and overwhelming. At ten o'clock in the morning on July 1, seventeen representatives of the Japanese strikers met with John Waterhouse at the Alexander Young Hotel. The president of the HSPA stated that he was willing to meet with them provided they did not represent the Japanese Federation of Labor. Then he told them that the HSPA would not consider any change in the wage or bonus schedule. They should go back to work and resume the relationship of employee and employer. He assured them that after they had done so, they could meet with their managers and discuss their problems. Waterhouse finally shook hands with everyone, saying that the HSPA "bore absolutely no ill-will against the laborers or the Japanese." At ten-thirty the brief meeting was over.[46]

The labor representatives then issued a proclamation to the strikers:

Whereas, an understanding between John Waterhouse, president of the Hawaiian Sugar Planters' Association and laborers on the sugar plantations of Hawaii having been reached over the industrial differences which have existed between them since January, 1920, and

Whereas, the Hawaii Laborers' Association desires to live up to its fundamental principle of cooperation between capital and labor; and

Whereas, the Hawaii Laborers' Association deems it is right and proper that the strike should be settled for the promotion of mutual and harmonious cooperation now.

Therefore, be it resolved by the Hawaii Laborers' Association to
formally call off on July 1, 1920, the strike on the sugar plantations
in Hawaii.[47]

The long, six-month strike was finally over. The laborers returned to work, and the planters claimed a complete victory.
Three months later the HSPA trustees quietly increased wages by
50 percent and allowed workers to collect their bonuses on a
month-to-month basis. The planters also expanded social welfare
and recreational programs for laborers. In November, for example, Donald S. Bowman of the HSPA's Industrial Service Bureau
contracted the Consolidated Amusement Company to supply movie films to the plantations. Planters thought their hegemony was
secure: they had soundly defeated the striking workers. "I doubt,"
boasted Waterhouse, the laborers would care for "a repetition of
the lessons taught them this year."[48]

But many strikers and their leaders had learned other lessons
from the 1920 strike. In their revolt against plantation paternalism, strikers had participated in the first important interethnic
working class struggle in Hawaii. As soon as they struck on January 19, Filipinos found large numbers of Spaniards, Portuguese,
and Chinese laborers striking with them. They were soon joined by
thousands of Japanese laborers. Men and women of different ethnicities, remembering how they had lived and labored together on
the plantations, now fought together to reach the same goal. They
had asked themselves the question which the teacher in Murayama's novel had raised: "How much together?"[49]

Feeling a new sense of cooperation and unity that transcended
ethnic boundaries, the leaders of the Japanese Federation of Labor
questioned the viability of "blood unionism" and the existence of
two separate labor unions, one for the Japanese and another for
the Filipinos, and suggested the consolidation of the two federations into one union. They insisted that Japanese workers must
affiliate with Filipino, American, and Hawaiian workers, for as
long as all of them were laborers they should mutually cooperate
in safeguarding their standards of living. On April 23 the Japanese
Federation of Labor decided to become an interracial union and
to change its name to the Hawaii Laborers' Association, a name
which gave the union a regional rather than an ethnic identity and
which emphasized the class thrust of the new organization.[50]

STRIKERS AT A MASS MEETING
(Aala Park, April 1920)
"Even the laborers of the utterly isolated islands of Hawaii were moved
by this world spirit."

One of the leaders of the Hawaii Laborers' Association expressed the new class consciousness emerging among plantation laborers of all nationalities. The fact that the "capitalists were haoles" and the "laborers Japanese and Filipinos" was a "mere coincidence," explained Takashi Tsutsumi. Japanese and Filipinos had acted as "laborers" in "a solid body"; as workers, they were aware of "capitalistic tyranny over industry, the general awakening of labor throughout the world." Noting that the Russian working class had "conquered a nation," the American Federation of Labor had become a powerful force on the mainland, and workers in Europe had struck for their rights, Tsutsumi declared: "Even the laborers of the utterly isolated islands of Hawaii were moved by this world spirit."[51]

What the workers had learned from the 1920 strike, Tsutsumi continued, was the need to build "a big, powerful and non-racial labor organization" that could "effectively cope with the capitalists." Such a union would bring together "laborers of all nationalities." The 1920 strike had provided the vision—the basis for the new union: in this struggle, Japanese and Filipino laborers had cooperated against the planters. "This is the feature that distinguished the recent movement from all others," Tsutsumi observed.

"There is no labor movement that surpasses the recent movement of Japanese and Filipinos." Tsutsumi predicted that the "big" interracial union would emerge within ten years and be guided by a "Hawaiian-born" leadership. "When that day comes," he declared, "the strike of 1920 would surely be looked upon as most significant."[52]

Epilogue:
Whisper to the Winds

As they sit on park benches and "talk story," old plantation laborers still vividly remember the 1920 strike—the influenza epidemic and the mass evictions. "My brother and mother had a high fever, but all of us were kicked out of our home." The oldtimers laugh as they tell stories about catching crabs to feed themselves and eating "mongoose hekka" during the strike. Looking backwards, they know that it took longer than ten years after the 1920 strike to bring together "laborers of all nationalities" into a "big" interracial union. They know that plantation workers finally organized themselves into the International Longshoremen's and Warehousemen's Union in 1945 and then successfully struck for collective bargaining and higher wages. And they also know that both strikes belong to a long history of labor struggles in the islands and that much of the history of modern Hawaii belongs to them.[1]

But they are not sure about the future of the islands. They go into town, old country villages like Lahaina and Haleiwa, and find a tourist boutique where the old shaved ice store used to be. "No can buy shaved ice there no more," they complain. "And the store used to make em real ono—with azuki beans." They anxiously wonder what is going to happen to the islands. "You know, Castle and Cooke, they went go shut down all the plantations in Kohala —Hawi, for example, on the Big Island." "They not producing cane over there anymore. The cane fields, they getting overgrown with weeds." "One of the mills over there, it looks like a big rusty steel skeleton." "So what do the people now do for a living?" "Oh, one bus comes early in the morning each day and takes them to work at the Rockefeller Mauna Kea Beach Hotel." The oldtimers realize sugar is no longer king in the islands.

Indeed, the world of the Sugar Kingdom and the plantation

laborer belongs to a passing era, one reaching back over a hundred years to Koloa where Hawaiian and Chinese workers cleared the land for the first plantation in the islands. Under the direction of William Hooper, they had produced sugar as a cash crop for export and ushered in a new Hawaii. As an "entering wedge," the Koloa Plantation opened the way for the sugar industry—the enthronement of King Sugar and the recruitment of laborers from Japan, Portugal, Norway, Germany, Korea, the Philippines, and other countries.

And so they came—over three hundred thousand of them—to Hawaii. Brought here as "cheap labor" for the plantations, they filled the orders of the planters—requisition forms which itemized the needs of the plantations for Japanese and Portuguese laborers, as well as macaroni and fertilizer. Brought here from Asia and also Europe, workers of different nationalities were pitted against each other to keep wages low and prevent strikes. In Hawaii, the immigrants found themselves in a new world of labor, and their hopeful visions of "Terra Nova" and "kasla glorya" vanished as they experienced the strict supervision of the lunas and the regimentation of plantation labor. Peasant farmers in the old country, they were thrust into a process of modern agricultural production, plantation sirens awakening them in the morning and sending them to bed at night. Homesick for the places they had left, they wept:

> Hawaii, Hawaii
> Like a dream
> So I came
> But my tears
> Are flowing now
> In the canefields.

But theirs was an indomitable spirit, fiercely hopeful and resilient. Gradually, in the plantation camps, far away from their homelands, they created new communities. Over the years, they came to feel a love for the land, the '*āina*, and accepted Hawaii as a place to settle and raise their families. No longer sojourners, no longer strangers in the islands, they expressed their new sense of belonging in song as they labored in the fields:

> With one woven basket
> Alone I came

> Now I have children
> And even grandchildren too.

Making their homes in the islands, they introduced different customs and traditions from the old countries and established a society of rich cultural and ethnic diversity.[2]

On the plantations, laborers developed a working class culture and consciousness—an identity of themselves in relationship to the process of production. While Hawaiians, Chinese, Japanese, Koreans, Portuguese, Filipinos, and laborers of other nationalities retained their sense of ethnicity, many of them also felt a new class awareness. As they worked together in the fields and mills, as they built working class communities in their camps sharing their different ethnic foods and speaking pidgin English, and as they struggled together against the bosses on the picket lines, they came to understand the contribution they had made as workers to the transformation of Hawaii into a wealthy and profitable place. "When we first came to Hawaii," they proudly observed, "these islands were covered with ohia forests, guava fields and areas of wild grass. Day and night did we work, cutting trees and burning grass, clearing lands and cultivating fields until we made the plantations what they are today."[3]

And, as the laborers grow old and enter their years of pau hana, they occasionally hike down worn dusty red roads through fields of waving green cane to visit the plantation cemetery. There a warm gentle rain falls on them, and a rainbow arches over the steep corrugated slopes of ancient volcanoes. The showers do not bother them, for they know the sun will soon shine again and chase away the dampness on their bodies as it did in the old days when they labored in the fields on rainy days. In the distance, they see the mill and the camps clustered around the smoking stack. But they are too far away to hear the throbbings of the machinery—the presses, the rollers, the centrifugal drums—sounds which had seemed so deafening when they worked in the caverns of the mill.

Slowly they turn towards the sea, and they remember the long voyage they had taken to the islands many years ago. Old images flash before them: they see themselves as frightened young men and women standing on the crowded decks of the ships and turn-

PLANTATION CEMETERY
Their lonely and weathered tombstones stand like erect and voiceless guards.
(Author's photo)

ing to take one last look, with tears in their eyes, at the shores of China, Portugal, Japan, the Philippines, and Korea. And old voices echo from the past:

> Ngai k'iou gnia,
> (I beg of you)
> Li k'oi ho,
> (after you depart,)
> Fei saa fui li
> (To come back soon)
>
> Yokohama deru tokya yo
> (When I left Yokohama)
> Namida de deta ga
> (I cried as I sailed out)
>
> Longe da minha terra
> (Far from my land)
> E aqui sem consolacao
> (And here without consolation)

But nostalgia does not overwhelm the oldtimers. "This is home, our home," their hearts tell them. Standing among the grave sites of their fellow workers, they whisper to the trade winds: "Look at the silent tombstones in every locality." And the winds seem to reply softly: "Few are the people who visit these graves of our departed friends, but are they not emblems of Hawaii's pioneers in labor?"[4]

Notes

Abbreviations

BLS   Bureau of Labor Statistics
ESOHP   Ethnic Studies Oral History Project
HA   *Honolulu Advertiser*
HSPA   Hawaiian Sugar Planters' Association
PCA   *Pacific Commercial Advertiser*
SB   *Honolulu Star-Bulletin*

Prologue

1. Talk story quotes and paraphrased quotes were taken from Ethnic Studies Oral History Project (hereafter abbreviated 'ESOHP'), *Uchinanchu: A History of Okinawans in Hawaii* (Honolulu: ESOHP and United Okinawan Association, 1981), 508, 520; Virgilio Menor Felipe, "Hawaii: A Pilipino Dream," unpublished Master's thesis, University of Hawaii, 1972, v.

I. *The Sugar Kingdom*

1. James J. Jarvis, "Sketches of Kauai," in *Hawaiian Spectator* (January 1838): 66–68; Jarvis, *Scenes and Scenery in the Sandwich Islands* (London: E. Moxon, 1844), 95–102.

2. See William Hooper Diary and William Hooper Correspondence, William Hooper Papers, Hawaiian Collection, University of Hawaii, Honolulu, Hawaii.

3. See Frances O. Jackson, "Koloa Plantation under Ladd and Company, 1835–1845," Master's thesis, University of Hawaii, 1958, 46–47.

4. Hooper, quoted in Arthur C. Alexander, *Koloa Plantation, 1835–1935* (Honolulu: *Star Bulletin* [hereafter abbreviated '*SB*'] 1937), 17; Hooper Diary, 11 September 1835; 12 September 1835; and 14 September 1835.

5. Hooper Diary, 12 September 1836.

6. David Malo, *Hawaiian Antiquities* (Honolulu: Bishop Museum Press, 1951), 56–64.

7. Hooper Diary, 15 September 1835.

8. Ibid., 12 September 1836; Hooper to Ladd and Company, 15 November 1837, 23 February 1836, and 1 January 1839; Hooper, quoted in Alexander, *Koloa Plantation*, 16.

9. Jarvis, *Scenes and Scenery*, 102; Hooper Diary, 29 January 1838; Hooper, quoted in Alexander, *Koloa Plantation*, 16.

10. Hooper Diary, 7 January 1837; Hooper to Ladd and Company, 12 June 1838, 6 March 1839, and 8 March 1839.

11. Jarvis, quoted in Ethel M. Damon, *Koamalu: A Story of Pioneers on Kauai* (Honolulu: *SB*, 1931), 183–184; Hooper to Ladd and Company, 29 April 1836.

12. Hooper Diary, 14 September 1835 and 14 June 1836; Jarvis, *Scenes and Scenery*, 96; Hooper Diary, 25 November 1835, 20 June 1836, 9 August 1836, 27 March 1837, 13 November 1837, 16 November 1837, and 2 December 1837.

13. Hooper Diary, 9 May 1836, 11 May 1836, 28 May 1836, 31 May 1836, 4 August 1836, 10 November 1836, and 10 December 1836.

14. Hooper Diary, 12 September 1836; Hooper to Ladd and Company, 28 April 1836; Hooper Diary, 4 May 1836; Jarvis, *Scenes and Scenery*, 104.

15. Hooper to Ladd and Company, 29 April 1836; Ladd and Company to Dr. Lafore, 16 October 1837, Hooper Papers.

16. Hooper Diary, 15 September 1835, 18 September 1835, and 12 September 1836; Hooper to Ladd and Company, 23 February 1836, 21 September 1836, 3 October 1836, 26 October 1836, 10 December 1836, and 12 May 1838.

17. Jarvis, *Scenes and Scenery*, 102–103.

18. Hooper to Ladd and Company, 1 December 1838.

19. Hooper to Ladd and Company, January 1838.

20. Hooper to Ladd and Company, 28 March 1835 and 16 November 1836.

21. Hooper to Ladd and Company, 1 December 1838 and April 1838.

22. Hooper Diary, 28 January 1837 and 31 January 1837; Jarvis, *Scenes and Scenery*, 97.

23. Ladd and Company to William Henry N. Hooper [printer and brother of William Hooper], 15 November 1837, Hooper Papers; Hooper to Ladd and Company, 5 January 1839 and 7 April 1839.

24. Hooper Diary, 30 September 1835 and 18 October 1835; Hooper to Ladd and Company, 25 June 1838.

25. Daniel Dole to Dwight Baldwin, 10 June 1850, quoted in Alexander, *Koloa Plantation*, 50–51; *De Bow's Commercial Review*, 22 (March 1857): 294.

26. Elizabeth Leslie Wright, *The Memoirs of Elizabeth Kinau Wilder* (Honolulu: 1909), 136; *Pacific Commercial Advertiser* (hereafter abbreviated 'PCA'), 9 April 1864.

27. *PCA*, 21 January 1864; 27 June 1877 issue of *Hawaiian Gazette*, quoted in Ralph S. Kuykendall, *The Hawaiian Kingdom: The Kalaukaua Dynasty 1874–1893*, third of 3 vols. (Honolulu: University of Hawaii Press, 1967), 47.

28. William Henry Taylor, "The Hawaiian Sugar Industry," unpublished Ph.D. diss., University of California, Berkeley, 1935, 6, 7; Lawrence H. Fuchs, *Hawaii Pono: A Social History* (New York: Harcourt, Brace and World, 1961), 251, 258.

29. Damon, *Koamalu*, p. 19; *Royal Hawaiian Agricultural Society Transactions*, 1, no. 1 (February 1852): 6.

30. *PCA*, 9 June 1877.

31. Taylor, "Hawaiian Sugar Industry," 19–20, 170; Fuchs, *Hawaii Pono*, 259; Damon, *Koamalu*, 857–858.

32. Taylor, "Hawaiian Sugar Industry," 66, 166; *Hawaiian Annual for 1904* (Honolulu: Thrum, 1903), 31; *Hawaiian Annual for 1921* (Honolulu: Thrum, 1920), 24; J.A. Mollett, *Capital in Hawaiian Sugar: Its Formation and Relation to Labor Output, 1870–1957* (Honolulu: Hawaiian Agricultural Experiment Station, 1961), 13, 16, 27, 28.

33. Taylor, "Hawaiian Sugar Industry," 66; Fuchs, *Hawaii Pono*, 259; Gavan Daws, *Shoal of Time: A History of the Hawaiian Islands* (Honolulu: University of Hawaii Press, 1977), 312.

34. Commissioner of Labor, quoted in Ray Stannard Baker, "How King Sugar Rules," *American Magazine*, 73 (November 1911): 28; Baker, ibid.

II. *The Uprooted*

1. *PCA*, 25 April 1874; Alexander, *Koloa Plantation* (see chap. 1, no. 2) 198; 1850 law, quoted in Curtis Aller, "The Evolution of Hawaiian Labor Relations: From Benevolent Paternalism to Mature Collective Bargaining," unpublished Ph.D. thesis, Harvard University, 1958, 121; *PCA*, 2 April 1869.

2. Royal Hawaiian Agricultural Society, quoted in Katherine Coman, *The History of Contract Labor in the Hawaiian Islands* (New York: American Economic Association, 1903), 11; *Royal Hawaiian Agricultural Society Transactions*, 1, no. 5 (June 1852): 6–7; *PCA*, 26 March 1864; *Report of the Secretary of the Hawaiian Immigration Society* (Honolulu: 1874), 11; *Planters' Monthly*, 1, no. 2 (February 1883): 277.

3. Theo. H. Davies and Company to C. McLennan, 22 August 1889, 2 July 1890, 3 January 1898, Laupahoehoe Plantation Records, microfilm, University of Hawaii Library; William G. Irwin and Company to George C. Hewitt, 12 October 1894, Hutchinson Plantation Records, microfilm, University of Hawaii Library; vice president of H. Hackfeld and Company to G. N. Wilcox, 5 May 1908, Grove Farm Plantation Records, Grove Farm Plantation, Kauai.

4. Robert Hall, George F. Renton, and George H. Fairfield, in Republic of Hawaii, *Report of the Labor Commission on Strikes and Arbitration* (Honolulu: 1895), 23–24, 28, 36, respectively.

5. *Planters' Monthly*, 2, no. 11 (November: 1883): 177, 245–247; A. S. Cleghorn, in Republic of Hawaii, *Report of the Bureau of Immigration* (Honolulu: 1886), 256–257.

6. Theo. H. Davies and Company to C. McLennan, 24 September 1894, Laupahoehoe Plantation Records; U.S. Commissioner of Labor, Carrol Wright, quoted in *Honolulu Record*, 12 January 1950; G. C. Hewitt to W. G. Irwin and Company, 16 March 1896, Hutchinson Plantation Records; H. Hackfeld and Company to George Wilcox, 26 September 1896, Grove Farm Plantation Records.

7. H. Hackfeld and Company to George Wilcox of Grove Farm Plantation, 22 December 1900, Grove Farm Plantation Records; *Honolulu Advertiser* (hereafter abbreviated '*HA*'), "Sixty Years Ago," 19 September 1960; *Maui News*, 21 January 1961, reprint of article published originally on 19 January 1901.

8. Theo. H. Davies and Company to C. McLennan, 19 November 1896, Laupahoehoe Plantation Records; Walter Giffard to Manager of the Hutchinson Sugar Plantation, 3 October 1898, quoted in Wayne K. Patterson, "The Korean Frontier in America: Immigration to Hawaii, 1896–1910," unpublished Ph.D. thesis, University of Pennsylvania, 1977, 100; Giffard to William Irwin, 18 December 1901, quoted in ibid., 129; Giffard to Irwin, 25 February 1902, quoted in ibid., 134; Giffard to Irwin, 30 April 1902, quoted in ibid., 146; J. P. Cooke to Rithet, 14 October 1902, quoted in ibid., 169–171.

9. *Report of the Commission of Labor*, reprinted in *Planters' Monthly*, 22, no. 7 (July 1903), 296; Giffard to Irwin, 3 February 1903, quoted in Patterson, "Korean Frontier," 225; director of Theo. Davies and Company to C. McLennan, n.d., Laupahoehoe Plantation Records; manager of the Hutchinson Sugar Plantation to W. G. Irwin and Company, 11 April 1905, Hutchinson Sugar Plantation Records.

10. *PCA*, 22 January 1906 and 21 December 1906; *Honolulu Evening Bulletin*, 21 February 1907.

11. *Board of Immigration Report* (1909), quoted in Mary Dorita, "Filipino Immigration to Hawaii," unpublished Master's thesis, University of Hawaii,

1954, 11; manager of the Hawaiian Agricultural Company to C. Brewer and Company, 1 July 1920, 7 and 27 August 1913, Hawaiian Agricultural Company Records.

12. Elizabeth Wong, "Leaves from the Life History of a Chinese Immigrant," *Social Process in Hawaii*, 2 (1936): 39–42.

13. Quoted in Clarence E. Glick, *Sojourners and Settlers: Chinese Migrants in Hawaii* (Honolulu: University of Hawaii Press, 1980), 26.

14. *Hawaiian Gazette*, 3 November 1869.

15. Quoted in Glick, *Sojourners and Settlers*, 27.

16. *HA*, "Hundred Years Ago," 18 December 1961; *Saturday Press*, 11 September and 11 December 1880; Clarence E. Glick, "The Chinese Migrant in Hawaii," Ph.D. Diss., University of Chicago, 1938, 36.

17. *PCA*, 5 September 1868; Labor contract, in Glick, *Sojourners and Settlers*, 29–30.

18. Hakka folksong, translated by Tin-Yuke Char, in Char, *The Sandalwood Mountains: Readings and Stories of the Early Chinese in Hawaii* (Honolulu: University of Hawaii Press, 1975), 67; translation into Hakka by Wei-Chi Poon.

19. Hideko Sasaki, "The Life History of a Portuguese Immigrant," *Social Process in Hawaii*, 1 (May 1935): 26–27.

20. William Hillebrand, report, *PCA*, 21 July 1877; *PCA*, 5 October 1878.

21. Joao Baptista d'Oliveira, "Journal of a Portuguese Immigrant," translated by Lucille de Silva Canario, in *The Hawaiian Journal of History*, 4 (1970): 3–51.

22. Advertisement, reprinted in Eleanor H. and Carl D. Davis, *Norwegian Labor in Hawaii—The Norse Immigrants* (Honolulu: Industrial Relations Center, 1962), 1.

23. Drammen *Tidende*, 15 September 1880, quoted in ibid., 1.

24. Oslo *Dagen*, 20 November 1880, quoted in ibid., 14.

25. Letter to S. T. Alexander, 17 March 1881, Castle and Cooke files, quoted in ibid., 9; translation of letter from Honolulu written by a Norwegian immigrant to the San Francisco *Valkyrien*, reprinted in the San Francisco *Chronicle*, 5 April 1882.

26. *Hawaiian Gazette*, 2 March 1881.

27. C. A. Olsen, 10 November 1881, reprinted in Davis, *Norwegian Labor*, 11.

28. Drammen *Tidende*, 19 September 1880, quoted in ibid., 6–7.

29. Yukiko Kimura, "Social-Historical Background of the Okinawans in Hawaii," report no. 36, Romanzo Adams Social Research Laboratory, University of Hawaii, December 1962, 9; "Information regarding Emigration," pamphlet distributed by the Foreign Ministry, quoted in James H. Okahata, ed., *A History of Japanese in Hawaii* (Honolulu: United Japanese Society, 1971), 90.

30. Japan *Weekly Mail*, in Francis Hilary Conroy, *The Japanese Expansion into Hawaii, 1868–1898* (Berkeley: University of California, 1953), 89.

31. Japan *Weekly Mail*, 20 December 1884, reprinted in Nippu Jiji, *Golden Jubilee of the Japanese in Hawaii, 1885–1935* (Honolulu: Nippu Jiji, 1935).

32. Alan T. Moriyama, "Japanese Government-Sponsored Emigration to Hawaii, 1885–1894," unpublished paper, 11–12.

33. Jiro Nakamura, quoted in Okahata, *Japanese in Hawaii*, 94–95.

34. Ibid., 96.

35. Ibid.

36. Yamato Ichihashi, *Japanese in the United States* (New York: Arno, 1969), 9; poems quoted in Kazuo Ito, *Issei: A History of Japanese Immigrants in North America* (Seattle: Japan Publications, 1973), 19, 34.

37. Lee Houchins and Chang-su Houchins, "The Korean Experience in America, 1903–1924," *Pacific Historical Review*, 43, no. 4 (November 1974): 552; quoted in Patterson, "The Korean Frontier in America," 252.

38. Quoted in Patterson, "Korean Frontier," 460–461, 467.

39. Quoted in ibid., 453; Bong-Youn Choy, *Koreans in America* (Chicago: Nelson-Hall,1977), 77.

40. Quoted in Patterson, "Korean Frontier," 275, 284–285, 440; quoted in Harold and Sonia Sunoo, "The Heritage of the First Korean Women Immigrants to the United States: 1903–1924," paper presented at the 10th Annual Conference of the Association of Korean Christian Scholars of North America, 8–10 April 1976, Chicago, 11; quoted in Morris Pang, "A Korean Immigrant," reprinted in Hyung-chan Kim and Wayne Patterson, eds., *The Koreans in America 1882–1974* (New York: Oceana, 1974), 118.

41. Quoted in Patterson, "Korean Frontier," 386; quoted in Choy, *Koreans in America*, 293, 321.

42. Quoted in Patterson, "Korean Frontier," 398.

43. Felipe, "Hawaii: A Pilipino Dream" (see prol., n. 1), 121, 155–156.

44. Ibid., 68, 142–143.

45. Carlos Bulosan, *America Is in the Heart* (Seattle: University of Washington Press, 1979), 58; H. Brett Melendy, *Asians in America: Filipinos, Koreans, and East Indians* (Boston: Twayne, 1977), 22; Dolores Quinto, "Life Story of a Filipino Immigrant," *Social Process in Hawaii*, 4 (1938): 71–72.

46. Bulosan, *America Is in the Heart*, 38.

47. Quinto, "Filipino Immigrant," *Social Process in Hawaii* , 72–73; Melendy, *Asians in America*, 38.

48. Felipe, "Hawaii: A Pilipino Dream," 158.

49. Ibid., 160, 163–164.

50. Bulosan, *America Is in the Heart*, 93.

51. Ibid., 97, 98; Ruben R. Alcantara, *Sakada: Filipino Adaptation in Hawaii* (Washington, D.C.: University Press of America, 1981), 11; Quinto, "Filipino Immigrant," *Social Process in Hawaii*, 75.

52. Felipe, "Hawaii: A Pilipino Dream," 165–167.

III. *A New World of Labor*

1. "The Five O'Clock Whistle," in the.*Kohala Midget*, 27 April 1910; Sasaki, "Portuguese Immigrant," (see chap. 2, n. 19), 29; Jack Hall, *A Luna's Log* (Kohala: 1927), 5; Felipe, "Hawaii: A Pilipino Dream, 189; ESOHP, *The 1924 Filipino Strike on Kauai*, 2 (Honolulu: ESOHP, 1979), 662.

2. Minnie Caroline Grant, *Scenes in Hawaii* (Toronto: Hart, 1888), 140–142; George Heber Jones, "The Koreans in Hawaii," *Korea Review*, 6, no. 11 (November, 1906): 401–406, Kim, *Koreans in America*, 92; Pang, "A Korean Immigrant" (see chap. 2, n. 40), 119.

3. Quoted in Melendy, *Asians in America* (see chap. 2, n. 45), 86–87.

4. Ko Shigeta, quoted in Ito, *Issei* (see chap. 2, n. 36), 21; Hall, *A Luna's Log*, 5–6; song, in Yukuo Uyehara, "The Horehore-Bushi: A Type of Japanese Folksong Developed and Sung Among the Early Immigrants in Hawaii," *Social Process in Hawaii*, 28 (1980–1981): 114; quoted in Bernhard Hormann, "The Germans in Hawaii," unpublished Master's thesis, University of Hawaii, 1931, 70.

5. Milton Murayama, *All I Asking For Is My Body* (San Francisco: Supra, 1975), 39; ESOHP, *Waialua and Haleiwa: The People Tell Their Story*, 8 (Honolulu: ESOHP, 1977), 167.

6. Anna Choi, interview, in Choy, *Koreans in America* (see chap. 2, n. 39), 321; Mary H. Drout, *Hawaii and a Revolution* (New York: 1898), 237–238.

7. C. F. Gordon-Cumming, *Fire Fountains* (London: Blackwood, 1882), 275–277; Grant, *Scenes in Hawaii*, 140–141; ESOHP, *Uchinanchu* (see prol., n. 1), 369.

8. *PCA*, 30 May 1874 and 7 December 1872; Ray Stannard Baker, "Land and the Landless," *American Magazine*, 73 (December 1911): 210.

9. Quoted in Aller, "Evolution of Hawaiian Labor Relations" (see chap. 2, n. 1), 212; Montague Lord to E. D. Tenney, 21 July 1916, report, Grove Farm Plantation Records.

10. Okahata, *Japanese in Hawaii* (see chap. 2, n. 29), 127.

11. Lord to Tenney, 21 July 1916, Grove Farm Plantation Records.

12. Theo. H. Davies and Company to C. McLennan, 29 March 1901, Laupahoehoe Plantation Records, microfilm in the UH library; vice president of H. Hackfeld and Company to George N. Wilcox, 24 September 1910, Grove Farm Plantation Records; David Bowman to James Campsie, 3 May 1920, Hawaiian Agricultural Company Records, microfilm in the UH library.

13. Republic of Hawaii, *Report of the Labor Commission on Strikes and Arbitration* (Honolulu: 1895), 16; Hawaiian Sugar Planters' Association (hereafter abbreviated 'HSPA'), *The Sugar Industry of Hawaii and the Labor Shortage* (Honolulu: HSPA, 1921), 37.

14. Director of Theo. H. Davies and Company to C. McLennan, 15 February 1904, Laupahoehoe Plantation Records; *Royal Hawaiian Agricultural Society Transactions*, 1, no. 3 (Honolulu: 1852), 6; HSPA, Bureau of Labor Statistics, memo to plantations, 12 February 1918, Grove Farm Plantation Records; Republic of Hawaii, *Report of the Labor Commission on Strikes*, 37, 38; HSPA, *Sugar Industry of Hawaii and the Labor Shortage*, 5, 15, 31, 43.

15. *PCA*, 26 July 1904.

16. Quoted in Glick, *Sojourners and Settlers* (see chap. 2, n. 13), 34–35; quoted in Taylor, "The Hawaiian Sugar Industry," 99.

17. *Royal Hawaiian Agricultural Society Transactions*, 1, no. 5 (June 1852): 6, 7, 70.

18. Experiment Station, HSPA Circular, "The Labor Question," 7 May 1917, in Grove Farm Plantation Records; Felipe, "Hawaii: A Pilipino Dream" (see chap. 2, n. 43), 170, 177.

19. Patterson, "The Korean Frontier in America," 589, 590.

20. Bureau of Labor Statistics (hereafter abbreviated 'BLS'), United States Department of Labor, *Report of the Commissioner of Labor on Hawaii* (Washington: Government Printing Office, 1905), 41; H. Hackfeld and Company to G. N. Wilcox, 21 May 1904 and 29 June 1904; Miki Saito, letter to branches of the Central Japanese League, 2 June 1904, Grove Farm Plantation Records.

21. President of the Branch Japanese League to C. McLennan, 1904; Miki Saito to C. McLennan, 12 October 1904; director of Theo. H. Davies and Company to Miki Saito, 13 October 1904, Laupahoehoe Plantation Records.

22. BLS, *Report of the Commissioner of Labor* (1905), 96–97; quoted in Davis, *Norwegian Labor in Hawaii* (see chap. 2, n. 22), 24; German laborer, interview in Hormann, "The Germans in Hawaii," 124; ESOHP, *Uchinanchu*, 361; Wray Taylor, Report on Olowalu Plantation, June 1897, quoted in *Honolulu Record*, 5 May 1949.

23. Quoted in *Honolulu Record*, 18 October 1951; director of Theo. H. Davies and Company to C. McLennan, 18 January 1902, Laupahoehoe Plantation

Records; quoted in Republic of Hawaii, *Report of the Labor Commission on Strikes*, 37.

24. Charles B. Wilson and G. G. Hitchcock, quoted in *Honolulu Record*, 1 January 1953.

25. *Report of the Subcommittee on Pacific Islands and Porto [sic] Rico on General Conditions in Hawaii* (Washington: Government Printing Office, 1903), 214.

26. Baker, "How King Sugar Rules" (see chap. 1, no. 34), 32.

27. A. Moore, quoted in *Report of the Labor Commission on Strikes*, 11–13.

28. *Hawaiian Gazette*, 11 December 1867; *PCA*, 5 September 1868.

29. George Dole to William G. Irwin, 22 August 1879, letterbook, in Kauai Museum, Lihue, Kauai; Arthur C. Betts, interview notes by Eleanor and Carl Davis, 4 September 1958, in "Norwegian File," HSPA Archives; Kim Hyungsoon, interview, in Choy, *Koreans in America*, (see chap. 2, n. 39), 303; Korean woman, in Sunoo, "The Heritage of the First Korean Women in the United States" (see chap. 2, n. 40), 12; ESOHP, *Uchinanchu* (see prol., n. 1), 484, 513; *Hawaii Herald*, reprinted in *Honolulu Record*, 11 September 1952.

30. Goo Kim, statement, 1897, reprinted in *Honolulu Record*, 18 October 1951; Wray Taylor, report, quoted in *Honolulu Record*, 5 May 1949; Lee Hongki, quoted in Choy, *Koreans in America*, 95–96; Yasutaro Soga, *Reflections on Fifty Years in Hawaii*, translated and reprinted in *Honolulu Record*, 29 October 1949; Baron Yun, quoted in Patterson, "Korean Frontier," 607; BLS, *Report of the Commissioner of Labor on Hawaii* (1910), 25–26.

31. HSPA resolution, 18 November 1904, Grove Farm Plantation Records; HSPA resolution, in director of H. Hackfeld and Company to G. N. Wilcox, 14 June 1911, Grove Farm Plantation Records.

32. *Planters' Monthly*, 1, no. 1 (April 1882): 30.

33. *Planters' Monthly*, 1, no. 7 (October 1882): 242.

34. BLS, *Report of the Commissioner of Labor on Hawaii* (1916), 120–153.

35. ESOHP, *Stores and Storekeepers of Paia and Puunene, Maui* (Honolulu: ESOHP, 1980), 401; Machiyo Mitamura, "Life on a Hawaiian Plantation: An Interview," *Social Process in Hawaii*, 6 (1940): 51.

36. BLS, *Report of the Commissioner of Labor on Hawaii* (1910), 20; BLS, *Report of the Commissioner of Labor* (1916), 122, 124, 143.

37. *Hawaiian Annual of 1895* (Honolulu: Thrum, 1894), 33; BLS, *Report of the Commissioner of Labor on Hawaii* (1916), 124–125; Damon, *Koamalu* (see chap. 1, n. 11), 595; Chen Jay Kim, interview, *SB*, 20 November 1953; R. D. Mead, Memorandum to All Plantations, 15 July 1918, Grove Farm Plantation Records.

38. Sasaki, "Portuguese Immigrant," *Social Process in Hawaii*, 1 (May 1935) (see chap. 2, n. 19), 26–27; Sunoo, "Heritage of the First Korean Women Immigrants" (see chap. 2, n. 40), 10; Melendy, *Asians in America* (see chap. 2, no. 45), 161–162.

39. HSPA to Board of Education, February 1895, Laupahoehoe Plantation Records; C. S. Childs, "Report on Welfare Investigation: Grove Farm Plantation, Kauai," 1919, Grove Farm Plantation Records; Hormann, "Germans in Hawaii," 70; Takashi Tsutsumi, *History of Hawaii Laborers' Movement*, translation (Honolulu: HSPA, 1922), 234.

40. ESOHP, *Waialua and Haleiwa*, 8: 144.

41. Melendy, *Asians in America*, 88; director, Experiment Station, HSPA, to E. H. W. Broadbent, 1 September 1917, Grove Farm Plantation Records.

42. Ko Shigeta and Kanichi Tsukamaki, quoted in Ito, *Issei*, 21, 22; editor

190 / *Notes*

of Japanese newspaper, quoted BLS, *Report of the Commissioner of Labor* (1916), 65.

43. E. P. Adams, Secretary of the Planters' Labor and Supply Company, Circular, 1883, in Laupahoehoe Plantation Records.

44. HSPA to "Our Plantation Managers," 24 July 1901; H. Hackfeld and Company to G. Wilcox, 15 May 1900; H. Hackfeld and Company, 12 June 1900, general letter, Grove Farm Plantation Records.

45. George R. Carter to G. Wilcox, 15 October 1901; H. Hackfeld and Company to Grove Farm Plantation, 21 August 1901, Grove Farm Plantation Records; T. H. Petrie, Acting Secretary, HSPA, to H. Hackfeld and Company, 30 April 1908, Grove Farm Plantation Records.

46. Sasaki, "Portuguese Immigrant," *Social Process in Hawaii*, 26.

47. Theo. H. Davies and Company to C. McLennan, 4 February 1907, Laupahoehoe Plantation Records; H. Hackfeld and Company to G. N. Wilcox, 24 September 1910, Grove Farm Plantation Records; H. Hackfeld and Company to G. N. Wilcox, 9 April 1901, with letter from the trustees of the HSPA attached, Grove Farm Plantation Records.

48. H. Hackfeld and Company to G. N. Wilcox, 9 April 1901, Grove Farm Plantation Records.

49. C. Bolte to Grove Farm Plantation, 23 January 1899, Grove Farm Plantation Records; Statement of the HSPA, 29 November 1909, in BLS, *Report of the Commissioner of Labor* (1910), 89; ibid. (1916), 29–30.

50. *Report of the Commissioner of Labor* (1910), 91.

51. HSPA, circular letter, 22 August 1910, Grove Farm Plantation Records; HSPA, *The Sugar Industry of Hawaii and the Labor Shortage*, 38–39; vice president of H. Hackfeld and Company to George N. Wilcox, 21 December 1911, Grove Farm Plantation Records; manager of the Hawaiian Agricultural Company to C. Brewer and Company, 20 December 1911, Hawaiian Agricultural Company Records.

52. ESOHP, *Uchinanchu*, 360; Yukiko Kimura, "Socio-historical Background of the Okinawans in Hawaii," unpublished paper, University of Hawaii, 1962, 5; Aller, "Evolution of Hawaiian Labor Relations," 212; *Hawaii Herald*, 2 February and 26 October 1973.

53. Uyehara, "Horehore-Bushi," 114; ESOHP, *Uchinanchu*, 382, 406; *Hawaii Herald*, 26 October 1973.

54. ESOHP, *Stores and Storekeepers of Paia and Puunene*, 399; ESOHP, *Uchinanchu*, 488; quoted in Lind, *An Island Community*, 240–241; ESOHP, *Waialua and Haleiwa*, 8:149; 3:11; Uyehara, "Horehore-Bushi," 115.

55. Quoted in Alcantara, *Sakada*, 54; Kimura, "Okinawans in Hawaii," 5; Felipe, "Hawaii: A Pilipino Dream," 189.

IV. *Plantation Camps*

1. Murayama, *All I Asking For Is My Body* (See chap. 3, n. 5), 28, 96.

2. Jared Smith, *Plantation Sketches* (Honolulu: Advertiser Press, 1924), 17; Pang, "A Korean Immigrant, 114; Wray Taylor, report, reprinted in Char, *The Sandalwood Mountains* (see chap. 2, n. 18), 83.

3. Pang, "A Korean Immigrant," 119; R. A. Duckworth-Ford, *Report on Hawaiian Sugar Plantations and Filipino Labor* (Manila: 1926), 2–3; Quinto, "Life Story of a Filipino Immigrant" (see chap. 2, n. 45), 77.

4. Montague Lord to E. D. Tenney, 21 July 1916, Grove Farm Plantation Records.

5. William W. Goodale to E. D. Tenney, 26 January 1903, Grove Farm Plantation Records; Smith, *Plantation Sketches*, 51.

6. Dr. Charles A. Peterson, Circular, 26 October 1899, reprinted in *Honolulu Record*, 1 December 1949; M. Lord to E. D. Tenney, 21 July 1916, Grove Farm Plantation Records.

7. Yasutaro Soga, *Looking Backward 50 Years in Hawaii*, reprinted in *Honolulu Record*, 31 March 1949; ESOHP, *Uchinanchu* (see prol. n. 1), 363; letter by Norwegian laborer, 18 October 1881, published in Norwegian newspaper, translation in notes from Eleanor and Carl Davis, "Norwegian File," HSPA Archives; Taro Yoshitake, quoted in Ito, *Issei*, 24; John Vasconcellos, "Recollections," in John Henry Felix and Peter F. Senecal (eds.), *The Portuguese in Hawaii* (Honolulu: Felix, 1978), 57; Hyun Soon, quoted in Koh Seung-jae, "A Study of Korean Immigrants to Hawaii," *Journal of Social Sciences and Humanities*, no. 38 (June 1973), 27; Lord to Tenney, 21 July 1916, Grove Farm Plantation Records; R. D. Mead to E. D. Tenney, 19 July 1919, Grove Farm Plantation Records; Yojiro Toma, interview, *Hilo Sugar News*, August 1960; Ko Shigeta, quoted in Ito, *Issei*, 21.

8. Alcantara, *Sakada* (see chap. 2, n. 51), 32; Miki Saito to Agents of the Japanese Emigration Companies, 18 September 1899, Grove Farm Plantation Records.

9. Vice president of H. Hackfeld and Company, with circular attached, to G. Wilcox, 24 September 1910, Grove Farm Plantation Records; W. Pfotenhauser, "President's Address," *The Hawaiian Planters' Record*, 4, no. 1 (January 1911): 4; J. P. Cook, "President's Address," *The Hawaiian Planters' Record*, 10, no. 1 (January 1914): 5–6.

10. C. Brewer and Company to W. G. Ogg, 2 August 1916, Hawaiian Agricultural Company Records, microfilm, UH library; Donald S. Bowman to Grove Farm Plantation, 15 September 1920, Grove Farm Plantation Records; Bowman, "Housing the Plantation Worker," *The Hawaiian Planters' Record*, 22, no. 4 (April 1920): 202–203.

11. Pfotenhauser, "President's Address," 4; Bowman, "Housing the Plantation Worker," 203.

12. Ray Stannard Baker, "Human Nature in Hawaii: How the Few Want the Many to Work for Them—Perpetually, and at Low Wages," *American Magazine*, 73 (January 1912): 333; manager of Hawaiian Agricultural Company to C. Brewer and Company, 19 March 1913, Hawaiian Agricultural Company Records; Ko Shigeta, quoted in Ito, *Issei*, 21.

13. ESOHP, *Uchinanchu*, 65; C. S. Childs, "Report on Welfare Investigation: Grove Farm Plantation, Kauai," 1919, Grove Farm Plantation Records.

14. Vasconellos, "Recollection," 58; Murayama, *All I Asking For Is My Body*, 45.

15. Wray Taylor, quoted in *Honolulu Record*, 8 December 1949.

16. Charles A. Davis, "The Plantation Doctor," *Transactions of the Hawaiian Territorial Medical Association* (Honolulu: 1904), 86–89; Yang Choo-en, interview, in Bong-youn Choy, *Koreans in America* (see chap. 2, n. 39), 295.

17. Davis, "Plantation Doctor," 89; Shigeta, in Ito, *Issei*, 21.

18. Taro Yoshitake, quoted in Ito, *Issei*, 24; Soga, *Looking Backward*, in *Honolulu Record*, 21 April 1949; G. C. Hewitt, manager of the Hutchinson Plantation, to A. de Souza Canavarro, Consul General, 22 December 1896, Hutchinson Plantation Records; Norwegian laborer, letter published in Norwegian newspapers, translation, in notes from Davis, "Norwegian File," HSPA Archives.

19. Dr. E. S. Goodhue, in *Honolulu Record*, 9 February 1950; Wray Taylor, report, reprinted in ibid., 5 May 1949.

20. Davis, "Plantation Doctor," 89; Soga, in *Honolulu Record*, 31 April 1949; Theo. H. Davies and Company to C. McLennan, 28 September 1897, Laupahoehoe Plantation Records; Dr. E. S. Goodhue, quoted in *Honolulu Record*, 9 February 1950.

21. Paul Isenberg, letter, August 1896, in Damon, *Koamalu* (see chap. 1, n. 11), 853; Bernice Kim, "The Koreans in Hawaii," unpublished Master's thesis, University of Hawaii, 1937, 118–119; ESOHP, *Waialua and Haleiwa* (see chap. 3, n. 5), 5: 17.

22. Frank Miranda, quoted in *HA*, 10 February 1955; Felipe, "Hawaii: A Pilipino Dream" (see prol. n. 1), 189; ESOHP, *Uchinanchu*, 523.

23. Soga, in *Honolulu Record*, 27 October 1949; Char, *Sandalwood Mountains* (see chap. 2, n. 18), 208; Ewald Kleinau, "Diary of Operations in the Sugar Refinery, Paauhau Plantation, Hawaii," 2 September 1881, Bancroft Library, University of California, Berkeley, California; Okahata, *Japanese in Hawaii* (see chap. 2, n. 29), 122; ESOHP, *Uchinanchu*, 371; Felipe, "Hawaii: A Pilipino Dream," 189; *Hawaii Herald*, 2 February 1973.

24. ESOHP, *The 1924 Filipino Strike on Kauai* (see chap. 3, n. 1), 675.

25. Vice president of H. Hackfeld and Company to George N. Wilcox, 24 September 1910, with circulars attached, Grove Farm Plantation Records.

26. Montague Lord to E. D. Tenney, 21 July 1916, report of investigation, Grove Farm Plantation Records.

27. *PCA*, 21 February 1919; R. D. Mead to Hawaiian Agricultural Company, 14 January 1919, Hawaiian Agricultural Company Records; manager of Hawaiian Agricultural Company to the HSPA, 5 April 1919, ibid.; Donald S. Bowman, Industrial Service Bureau of HSPA, to Grove Farm Plantation, 20 January 1920, Grove Farm Plantation Records; Social Welfare Committee, report, 10 December 1919, Grove Farm Plantation Records.

28. Helen Mather, *One Summer in Hawaii* (New York: Cassell, 1891), 191.

29. *PCA*, 16 February 1867; Hawaiian Evangelical Association, Report for 1882, quoted in Tin-Yuke Char, *The Bamboo Path: Life and Writings of a Chinese in Hawaii* (Honolulu: Hawaii Chinese History Center, 1977), p. 232.

30. Damon, quoted in Char, *Sandalwood Mountains*, p. 216; Mrs. Paul Isenberg, quoted in Damon, *Koamalu*, 762.

31. Reverend Elias Bond, quoted in Char, *Bamboo Path*, 233–234; *PCA*, 11 July 1868.

32. S. P. Aheong, quoted in Char, *Bamboo Path*, 234, 235.

33. Ibid., 235–236.

34. Homer Hulbert, "The Koreans in Hawaii," *Korea Review*, 5, no. 11 (November 1905): 412; *Garden Island*, 5 April 1976; manager of the Hawaiian Agricultural Company to C. Brewer and Company, 12 October 1915, Hawaiian Agricultural Company Records.

35. George H. Jones, "Koreans Abroad," *Korea Review*, 6, no. 12 (December 1906): 451; Jones, "The Koreans in Hawaii" (see chap. 3, n. 2), 401.

36. Director of Theo. H. Davies and Company to C. McLennan, 10 February 1902, Laupahoehoe Plantation Records.

37. Louise Hunter, *Buddhism in Hawaii: Its Impact on a Yankee Community* (Honolulu: University of Hawaii Press, 1971), 72; Yemyō Imamura, *History of the Honwanji Mission in Hawaii*, selection reprinted in Dennis M. Ogawa, *Kodomo no tame ni: For the sake of the children* (Honolulu: University of Hawaii Press, 1978), 70–71.

38. *SB*, 9 March 1940; Hormann, "The Germans in Hawaii" (see chap. 3, n. 4), 98, 99; Okahata, *Japanese in Hawaii*, 152; Warren Kim, *Koreans in America* (Po Chin Chai Printing Company, 1971), 50, 51, 94.

39. *Hawaiian Gazette*, 6 February 1867; Kleinau, "Diary . . . Paauhau Plantation," 17 February 1882; Grant, *Scenes in Hawaii* (see chap. 3, n. 2), 65, 68, 69.

40. *Maui News*, 29 December 1961; *HA*, 29 September 1943; Grant, *Scenes in Hawaii*, 146; Kleinau, "Diary . . . Paauhau Plantation," 7 April 1882.

41. Hormann, "The Germans in Hawaii," 106–107.

42. Manager of the Hawaiian Agricultural Company to C. Brewer and Company, 17 October and 2 November 1911, Hawaiian Agricultural Company Records; H. Hackfeld and Company to George Wilcox, 25 April 1900, Grove Farm Plantation Records; ESOHP, *Uchinanchu*, 383, 472.

43. Director, Bureau of Labor, HSPA, to manager of the Hawaiian Agricultural Company, 4 December 1920, Hawaiian Agricultural Company Records; *Kohala Midget*, 4 January 1911; ibid., 7 December 1910; Felipe, "Hawaii: A Pilipino Dream," 134–135.

44. Char, *Sandalwood Mountains*, 84; Hormann, "Germans in Hawaii," 99; Choy, *Koreans in America*, 96, 97; for orders for Japanese foods, see Laupahoehoe Plantation Records, especially Theo. H. Davies and Company to Laupahoehoe Sugar Company, 1 July 1889 and 10 February 1896; ESOHP, *Uchinanchu*, 387.

45. Mrs. Joe Rapozo, in *HA*, 6 July 1973; ESOHP, *Waialua and Haleiwa*, 8: 64 and 9: 223.

46. Grant, *Scenes in Hawaii*, 150.

47. Bernice Kim Park, interview, *SB*, 7 January 1973.

48. Jones, "Koreans in Hawaii," 403–405; Yang Choo-en, in Choy, *Koreans in America*, 298.

49. William Speer, quoted in Char, *Sandalwood Mountains*, 61.

50. John E. Reinecke, " 'Pidgin English' in Hawaii: A Local Study in the Sociology of Language," *American Journal of Sociology*, 43, no. 5 (March 1938), reprinted in Ogawa, *Kodomo no tame ni*, 209–217; John E. Reinecke, *Language and Dialect in Hawaii* (Honolulu: University of Hawaii Press, 1969), 95.

51. Manager of the Hawaiian Agricultural Company to HSPA, Bureau of Labor, 5 April 1919, Hawaiian Agricultural Company Records.

52. Reinecke, " 'Pidgin English,' " 212.

53. ESOHP, *Waialua and Haleiwa*, 3: 11; Anna Choi, interview, in Choy, *Koreans in America*, 322.

54. Manager of Hawaiian Agricultural Company to C. Brewer and Company, 1 July 1920, Hawaiian Agricultural Company Records.

55. Soga, in *Honolulu Record*, 27 October 1949.

56. *PCA*, 23 April 1864 and 25 August 1877; Frank Damon, in Char, *Sandalwood Mountains*, 204–205; Frank Damon, "Homes for the Homeless: A Plea for Chinese Female Immigration," *The Friend*, 38, no. 11 (1881): 98.

57. H. M. Whitney to Dr. Damon, 21 November 1881, in *The Friend*, 38, no. 12 (1881): 104; Republic of Hawaii, Bureau of Immigration, *Report* (Honolulu: 1886), 256.

58. Manager of Hutchinson Sugar Company to W. G. Irwin and Company, 5 February 1902 and 25 January 1905, Hutchinson Sugar Company Records.

59. S. Halls, acting director, Bureau of Labor, HSPA, to Hawaiian Agricultural Company, 12 March 1918, Hawaiian Agricultural Company Records; C. M. Cooke, letter, 23 September 1904, quoted in Patterson, "The Korean Frontier in America," 487; BLS, *Report of the Commissioner of Labor on Hawaii* (1916), 31; R. D. Mead to H. Hackfeld and Company, 1916, Grove Farm Plantation Records.

60. Choy, *Koreans in America*, 88, 89, 320–322; Patterson, "Korean Frontier," 457–458.

61. *Hawaiian Annual for 1921* (Honolulu: Thrum, 1920), 18; Baker, "Human Nature in Hawaii," 330.

62. ESOHP, *Uchinanchu*, 101; Kazuo Miyamoto, *Hawaii, End of the Rainbow* (Rutland, Vermont: Tuttle, 1968), 23; second generation Korean, quoted in Patterson, "Korean Frontier," 452.

63. *Hawaii Herald*, 2 February and 26 October 1973; Uyehara, *"Horehore-Bushi,"* (see chap. 3, n. 4), 114.

V. *Contested Terrain*

1. Richard Edwards, *Contested Terrain: The Transformation of the Workplace in the Twentieth Century* (New York: Basic Books, 1979).

2. Kimura, "Social-Historical Background of the Okinawans in Hawaii" (see chap. 2, n. 29), 5.

3. *Royal Agricultural Society Proceedings*, 1, no. 4 (1853): 124; *PCA*, 22 July 1866 and 4 May 1867; *Saturday Press*, 12 March 1881; *Hilo Tribune*, reprinted in *Honolulu Record*, 15 October 1952; *PCA*, 27 June 1915; plantation rules, quoted in Edward Lydon, *The Anti-Chinese Movement in the Hawaiian Kingdom 1856–1886* (San Francisco: R & E Research Associates, 1975), 30.

4. *PCA*, 18 November 1865, 13 October 1866, 8 June 1867, 20 August 1870, 4 October 1879, 2 October 1905, 11 November 1899; Masuda Takashi, quoted in Hilary Conroy and T. Scott Miyakawa, *East Across the Pacific* (Santa Barbara: Clio, 1972), 46–47; manager of the Hutchinson Sugar Plantation to W. G. Irwin, 14 August 1904, Hutchinson Plantation Records; *PCA*, 29 April 1915.

5. James Wood, letter to the *Polynesian*, October 1852, quoted in Lydon, *Anti-Chinese Movement*, 23; Wray Taylor to J. A. King, 27 April 1899, in *Report of Subcommittee on Pacific Islands and Porto [sic] Rico on General Conditions in Hawaii*, 43.

6. Uyehara, "The *Horehore-Bushi*" (see chap. 3, n. 4), 116; *PCA*, 14 August 1880; Japanese Consul, quoted in Okahata, *History of Japanese in Hawaii*, 122.

7. G. W. Bates, *Sandwich Island Notes*, quoted in Theodore Morgan, *Hawaii: A Century of Economic Change, 1778–1876* (Cambridge: Harvard, 1948), 188–189; Jack Hall, *A Luna's Log* (Kohala: 1927), 6.

8. *Planters' Monthly*, 1, no. 2 (May 1882): 34; Isabella Bird, *Six Months in the Sandwich Islands* (Honolulu: University of Hawaii Press, 1964), 77.

9. Kleinau, "Diary of Operations in the Sugar Refinery"; manager of the Hawaiian Agricultural Company to Victor S. Clark, Commissioner of Immigration, Labor and Statistics, 23 September 1911, Hawaiian Agricultural Company Records.

10. *Hawaii Herald*, 2 February 1973.

11. Bird, *Six Months in the Sandwich Islands*, 76–77; Grant, *Scenes in Hawaii* (see chap. 3, n. 2), 64–65; Jose Tavares de Teves, "An Event Which Took Place," translated and reprinted in Edgar Knowlton, Jr., "Portuguese Language Resources for Hawaiian History," *Seventieth Annual Report of the Hawaiian Historical Society* (Honolulu: 1962), 36; Diane Mark, *The Chinese in Kula* (Honolulu: Chinese History Center, 1975), 28; Glick, "Chinese Migrant in Hawaii" (see chap. 2, n. 16), 42.

12. *PCA*, 24 August 1872; Kleinau, "Diary"; Yasutaro Soga, in *Honolulu Record*, 27 October 1949; *PCA*, 2 July 1906; Felipe, "Hawaii: A Pilipino Dream" (see prol., n. 1), 208.

13. Lily Lim-Chong, "Opium and the Law: Hawaii: 1856–1900," unpublished Master's thesis, University of Hawaii, 1978, 11, 45; *Hawaiian Gazette*, 6 June 1877; W. R. Castle, *Shall Opium Be Licensed? Opium in Hawaii* (Honolulu:

1884), 6; Kleinau, "Diary," 25 September 1880; *Planters' Monthly*, 1, no. 1 (April 1882): 20; Aller, "The Evolution of Hawaiian Labor Relations (see chap. 2, n. 1), 126; *Kohala Midget*, 12 July 1911.

14. Glick, "Chinese Migrant," 48; Li Ling Ai, *Life Is For A Long Time: A Chinese Hawaiian Memoir* (New York: Hastings, 1972), 299–302; Felipe, "Hawaii: A Pilipino Dream," 208, 227.

15. *PCA*, 4 January 1897.

16. *PCA*, 14 August 1880; *Hawaiian Gazette*, 28 September 1881; *Honolulu Record*, 1 January 1953.

17. Anton Cropp, Diary, 1892, 4, 12, 13, Grove Farm Plantation Records.

18. H. Horner to H. Center, 21 October 1889; William Goodale to H. Center, 24 October 1889; Hutchinson Plantation Records; J. A. Scott to C. McLennan, 6 August 1889, Laupahoehoe Plantation Records; J. A. Scott to H. Center, 13 February 1890, Hutchinson Plantation Records; W. J. Yates to G. C. Hewitt, 10 September 1894, ibid.; Theo. H. Davies and Company to C. McLennan, 22 June 1894, Laupahoehoe Plantation Records.

19. H. Center to C. McLennan, 12 October 1899, Laupahoehoe Plantation Records; M. McLennan to Theo. H. Davies and Company, 18 June 1894, ibid.; J. A. Scott to H. Center, n.d., Hutchinson Plantation Records; W. G. Irwin and Company to H. Center, 14 November 1890, Hutchinson Plantation Records.

20. Theo. H. Davies and Company to C. McLennan, 25 March 1898, Laupahoehoe Plantation Records; R. Renton Hind, *John Hind of Hawi* (Manaoag, Pangasinan, Philippines: 1951), 92.

21. H. Hackfeld and Company to G. N. Wilcox, 15 June 1891, Grove Farm Plantation Records; C. Bolte, circular to all plantations, 23 April 1894, ibid.; C. Bolte to G. C. Hewitt, 8 September 1894, Hutchinson Plantation Records.

22. L. Chong Company, announcement to plantations, 21 July 1896, Grove Farm Plantation Records; H. Hackfeld and Company to Grove Farm Plantation, 11 October 1898, ibid.; G. C. Hewitt to W. G. Irwin, 5 June 1896, Hutchinson Plantation Records; W. G. Irwin to manager of Hutchinson Sugar Plantation, 29 May 1899, ibid.

23. *Hawaii Herald*, 2 February 1973.

24. *Polynesian*, 3 December 1859; Kleinau, "Diary," 11 January 1882; *Maui News*, 18 August 1900.

25. President of the Board of Immigration to George N. Wilcox, 18 March 1890, Grove Farm Plantation Records; Fuchs, *Hawaii Pono* (see chap. 1, n. 28), 289.

26. Felix and Senecal, *Portuguese in Hawaii* (see chap. 4, n. 7), 81; manager of the Hawaiian Agricultural Company to C. Brewer and Company, 22 March 1913, Hawaiian Agricultural Company Records.

27. *Hawaiian Japanese Chronicle*, 22 March 1905, in BLS, *Report of the Commissioner of Labor on Hawaii* (1905), 22; *Hawaiian Star*, 17 March 1906; S. Sheba to E. Broadbent, 5 February 1906, Grove Farm Plantation Records.

28. *Hawaiian Almanac for 1906* (Honolulu: Thrum, 1905), 188–189; C. M. Cooke, quoted in Patterson, "The Korean Frontier in America," 489–490, 494; BLS, *Report of the Commissioner of Labor* (1905), 22–23; manager of the Hutchinson Plantation to W. G. Irwin, 11 April 1905, Hutchinson Plantation Records.

29. Theo. H. Davies and Company to C. McLennan, 25 October 1904, Laupahoehoe Plantation Records; J. F. Hackfeld to G. N. Wilcox, 10 April 1905, Grove Farm Plantation Records; manager of the Hutchinson Sugar Plantation to W. G. Irwin and Company, 11 April 1905, Hutchinson Plantation Records; C. Brewer and Company to Jas. Campsie, 1 December 1917, Hawaiian Agricultural Company Records.

30. Manager of Hawaiian Agricultural Company to C. Brewer and Company, 5 March 1913, Hawaiian Agricultural Company Records; Patterson, "Korean Frontier," 493; Miki Saito, Circular, 21 September 1903, Grove Farm Plantation Records; Japanese Consulate General, Notice, reprinted in BLS, *Report of the Commissioner of Labor* (1905), 41–42; Miki Saito to H. Hackfeld and Company, 10 June 1907, Grove Farm Plantation Records; director of H. Hackfeld and Company to Grove Farm Plantation, 16 March 1903, Grove Farm Plantation Records.

31. W. O. Smith, secretary of HSPA to all planters, 11 December 1903, Grove Farm Plantation Records.

32. Act 57, Law of 1905, "Licensing of Emigrant Agents," copy in Grove Farm Plantation Records; director of H. Hackfeld and Company to Grove Farm Plantation, 28 April 1905, Grove Farm Plantation Records; *Hawaii Shimpo*, quoted in A. L. Wills, *History of Labor Relations in Hawaii* (Honolulu: Industrial Relations Center, 1955), 5.

33. President Theodore Roosevelt, Executive Order of 14 March 1907, quoted in Patterson, "Korean Frontier," 669–670; John Reinecke, *Feigned Necessity: Hawaii's Attempt to Obtain Chinese Contract Labor, 1921–1923* (San Francisco: Chinese Materials Center, 1979), 22.

34. Charles Burnham to Levi Chamberlain, 23 July 1841, quoted in Alexander, *Koloa Plantation* (see chap. 1, n. 4), 37.

35. Letter from Norwegian immigrant to *Valkyrien*, translated and reprinted in *San Francisco Chronicle*, 5 April 1882.

36. Letter dated 1 February 1882, signed by thirty-nine Norwegian laborers, translated and reprinted in the *San Francisco Chronicle*, 11 May 1882.

37. Deputy Sheriff Charles H. Pulaa, report to the president of the Bureau of Immigration, 14 September 1891, reprinted in Char, *The Sandalwood Mountains*, 76–79.

38. *PCA*, 7 September 1891.

39. *Honolulu Record*, 25 August 1950.

40. Ibid., 12 August 1948.

41. Ibid., 28 April 1949; president of the Planters' Association of Maui, letter to the trustees of the HSPA, May 1900, Grove Farm Plantation Records.

42. Governor Stanford B. Dole, report for 1900, quoted in Alex Ladenson, "The Japanese in Hawaii," unpublished Ph.D. thesis, University of Chicago, 1938, 108; Karl Yoneda, *History of Japanese Labor in the U.S.*, translation (Tokyo: 1967), 167; Paul Isenberg, quoted in Damon, *Koamalu* (see chap. 1, n. 11), 871; *Hawaiian Star*, reprinted in *Honolulu Record*, 12 August 1948.

43. BLS, *Report of the Commissioner of Labor on Hawaii* (1901), 112–115, 254, 257.

44. *Honolulu Record*, 27 November 1951.

45. *Honolulu Record*, 8, 15, 22 November 1951.

46. *PCA*, reprinted in *Honolulu Record*, 19 January 1950.

47. Murayama, *All I Asking For Is My Body* (see chap. 3, n. 5), 34.

VI. *The Revolt Against Paternalism*

1. *Nippu Jiji*, translated and reprinted in *PCA*, 10 May 1909.

2. Soga, *Looking Backward 50 Years in Hawaii*, in *Honolulu Record*, 7 July 1949; director of H. Hackfeld and Company to planters, 7 January 1909, Grove Farm Plantation Records.

3. Soga, in *Honolulu Record*, 14 July 1949.

4. *Hawaii Shimpo*, reprinted in *PCA*, 12 October 1908; Takie Okumura, *Seventy Years of Divine Blessing* (Kyoto: Naigai, 1940), 55–56; *Hawaii Herald*, 27 May and 3 June 1909.

5. Soga, in *Honolulu Record*, 7 July 1949; Makino and Tasaka, quoted in Take and Allan Beekman, "Hawaii's Great Japanese Strike," reprinted in Ogawa, *Kodomo no tame ni* (see chap. 4, n. 37), 158.

6. Negoro, quoted in J. Okahata, *Japanese in Hawaii* (see chap. 2, n. 29), 173–174; *The Higher Wage Question*, excerpts reprinted in BLS, *Report of the Commissioner of Labor on Hawaii* (1910), 76.

7. Negoro, quoted in BLS, *Report of the Commissioner of Labor in Hawaii*, (1910), 63–64; Negoro, quoted in Okahata, *Japanese in Hawaii*, 173; table showing price increases, in BLS, *Report of the Commissioner of Labor* (1910), 70.

8. *Nippu Jiji*, reprinted in *Honolulu Record*, 18 November 1948; *Nippu Jiji*, reprinted in Ernest K. Wakukawa, *A History of the Japanese People in Hawaii* (Honolulu: Toyo shoin, 1938), 177–178.

9. Negoro, quoted in Okahata, *Japanese in Hawaii*, 173; Higher Wage Association, statement, reprinted in BLS, *Report of the Commissioner of Labor in Hawaii* (1910), 68.

10. Letter to E. K. Bull, signed by ninety-two strikers, 19 May 1909, reprinted in BLS, Report of the Commissioner of Labor in Hawaii (1910), 80; Higher Wage Association, statement, ibid., 68.

11. *Higher Wages Question*, reprinted in *Report of the Commissioner of Labor* (1910), 77–78.

12. Planter, quoted in Baker, "Human Nature in Hawaii," (see chap. 4, n. 12), 330.

13. Beekman, "Hawaii's Great Japanese Strike," in Ogawa, *Kodomo no tame ni*, 155–156; director of H. Hackfeld and Company to planters, 7 January 1909, Grove Farm Plantation Records.

14. Director of H. Hackfeld and Company to planters, 7 January 1909, Grove Farm Plantation Records.

15. Director of H. Hackfeld and Company to all plantation managers, 11 January 1909, Grove Farm Plantation Records; Resolution of HSPA, 10 May 1909, ibid.; Resolution of HSPA, 27 May 1909, ibid.; director of H. Hackfeld and Company to G. N. Wilcox, 2 June 1909, ibid.

16. Soga, in *Honolulu Record*, 21 July 1949; *PCA*, 11 June 1909.

17. Soga, in *Honolulu Record*, 4 August 1949.

18. Soga, in *Honolulu Record*, 4 August 1949.

19. Director of H. Hackfeld and Company to G. N. Wilcox, 18 May 1909, Grove Farm Plantation Records.

20. Labor committee of the HSPA to the trustees of the HSPA, 28 July 1909, Grove Farm Plantation Records; C. Walters to William G. Irwin and Company, 31 July 1909, Hutchinson Sugar Company Records, microfilm, UH library; director of H. Hackfeld and Company to Grove Farm Plantation, 24 August 1909, Grove Farm Plantation Records; president's address, in *Planters' Monthly*, 27 (December 1909): 1.

21. HSPA resolution, attached to letter from the director of H. Hackfeld and Company to George N. Wilcox, 30 December 1909, Grove Farm Plantation Records; director of H. Hackfeld and Company to George N. Wilcox, 11 February 1910, ibid.

22. Soga, in *Honolulu Record*, 7 July 1949.

23. HSPA announcement, 29 November 1909, reprinted in *Honolulu Record*, 29 September 1949.

24. Soga, in *Honolulu Record*, 22 September 1949.

25. Ibid.

26. Manager of the Hawaiian Agricultural Company to C. Brewer and Company, 20 December 1911, Hawaiian Agricultural Company Records.

27. K. Shibayama, General Committee, Association on Higher Wage Question, to manager of the Grove Farm Plantation, 16 October 1917, Grove Farm Plantation Records; R. D. Mead, director of Bureau of Labor, to H. Hackfeld and Company, 19 October 1917, Grove Farm Plantation Records; Tsutsumi, *Hawaii Laborers' Movement* (see chap. 3, n. 39), 45.

28. Tsutsumi, *Hawaii Laborers' Movement*, 45, 49, 51–52, 76.

29. Ibid., 194–198.

30. Ibid., 161; Pablo Manlapit, quoted in ibid., 175.

31. Tsutsumi, *Hawaii Laborers' Movement*, 217, 224; *Hawaii Shimpo*, 20 January 1920, reprinted in ibid., 238; *Hawaii Hochi*, 21 January 1920, reprinted in ibid., 240–241; *Hawaii Choho*, 24 January 1920, reprinted in ibid., 242–243.

32. Tsutsumi, *Hawaii Laborers' Movement*, 234.

33. Federation of Japanese Labor in Hawaii, *The Voice of Labor in Hawaii* (Honolulu: February 1920), 2; Hawaii Laborers' Association, *Facts About the Strike on Sugar Plantations in Hawaii* (Honolulu: 1920), 1, 2, 3; Federation of Japanese Labor in Hawaii, *Controversy Between Japanese Labor and the Sugar Planters of Hawaii* (Honolulu: January 1920), 2, 5.

34. Hawaii Laborers' Association, *Facts About the Strike*, 8; Tsutsumi, *Hawaii Laborers' Movement*, 52.

35. Tsutsumi, *Hawaii Laborers' Movement*, 39, 171; Federation of Japanese Labor in Hawaii, *Voice of Labor*, 1, 2.

36. Federation of Japanese Labor in Hawaii, *Voice of Labor*, 2; Tsutsumi, *Hawaii Laborers' Movement*, 39.

37. Fuchs, *Hawaii Pono*, 221, 222; vice president of H. Hackfeld and Company to Grove Farm Plantation, 18 October 1917, Grove Farm Plantation Records.

38. President of American Factors to H. W. Broadbent, 26 January 1920, Grove Farm Plantation Records; HSPA trustees, resolution, 19 January 1920, Grove Farm Plantation Records.

39. John Waterhouse, "President's Address," *Proceedings of the Fortieth Annual Meeting of the HSPA*, 29 and 30 November 1920 (Honolulu: 1921), 5–8; *SB*, quoted in Fuchs, *Hawaii Pono*, 221.

40. President of C. Brewer and Company to James Campsie, manager of the Hawaiian Agricultural Company, 3 February 1920, Hawaiian Agricultural Company Records; Manlapit, quoted in Alan Moriyama, "The 1909 and 1920 Strikes of Japanese Sugar Plantation Workers in Hawaii," in Emma Gee, ed., *Counterpoint* (Los Angeles: University of California, 1976), 175.

41. Vice president of C. Brewer and Company to James Campsie, 2 March 1920; R. D. Mead, director of the HSPA Labor Bureau, to Hawaiian Agricultural Company, 3 March 1920; vice president of C. Brewer and Company to James Campsie, 1 May 1920, Hawaiian Agricultural Company Records.

42. R. D. Mead, director of the Labor Bureau, to manager of Grove Farm Plantation, 13 February 1920, Grove Farm Plantation Records; HSPA handbill, "Federation Officials Dining," 6 March 1920, Hawaiian Agricultural Company Records.

43. Waterhouse, quoted in Fuchs, *Hawaii Pono*, 216–217; *PCA*, 30 January 1920; *SB*, 13 February 1920.

44. *SB*, 13 February 1920; quoted in Tsutsumi, *Hawaii Laborers' Movement*, 334–335.

45. Hawaii Laborers' Association, *Facts About the Strike*, 14.

46. Minutes of a meeting of a certain group of Japanese Laborers called by Mr. Isobe to meet with Mr. John Waterhouse, president of the HSPA at the Alexander Young Hotel on 1 July 1920, at 10 A.M., Grove Farm Plantation Records.

47. Hawaii Laborers' Association, Proclamation, reprinted in Yayoi Kurita, "Labor Movements Among the Japanese Plantation Workers in Hawaii," typescript (Honolulu: University of Hawaii, 1952), 55.

48. Waterhouse, quoted in Fuchs, *Hawaii Pono*, 224; Donald S. Bowman, director of the HSPA Industrial Service Bureau, to Grove Farm Plantation, 19 November 1920, Grove Farm Plantation Records; Waterhouse, "President's Address," *Proceedings*, 9.

49. Hawaii Laborers' Association, *Facts About the Strike*, 11, 12, 16; Murayama, *All I Asking For Is My Body*, 34.

50. Tsutsumi, *Hawaii Laborers'. Movement*, 19; Reinecke, *Feigned Necessity* (see chap. 5, n. 33), 97, 98.

51. Hawaii Laborers' Association, *Facts About the Strike*, 1; Tsutsumi, *Hawaii Laborers' Movement*, 12, 44.

52. Tsutsumi, *Hawaii Laborers' Movement*, 17, 13, 22.

Epilogue

1. Tsutsumi, *History of Hawaii Laborers' Movement* (see chap. 3, n. 39), 13, 17, 22.

2. Hole hole bushi song, in *Hawaii Herald*, 2 February 1973.

3. Hawaii Laborers' Association, *Facts About the Strike*, 1.

4. Ibid.

Glossary

ʻāhina: blue denim dungarees
ʻāina: the land
aliʻi: chief, nobility

bango: number; laborer's plantation identification tag
banzai: cheers

daikon: radish
dekasegi: laborers who would leave their homes temporarily to work in a foreign country

furo: Japanese bath; a large bathtub

Gannen Mono: workers brought to Hawaii in 1868

haʻalele hana: desert service, break labor contract
hana: work, labor
haole: foreigner, outsider; Caucasian
hapai ko: to carry cane
Hawaiiano: Filipino laborer returning to the Philippines, showing off success
hekka: Japanese meat and vegetable dish
hoe hana: to do hoe work in the fields
hole hole: stripping the dry leaves from cane stalks
hore hore-bushi: Japanese plantation work song
huhu: bother, troublesome

ilāmoku: police
issei: first-generation immigrant Japanese

kanaka: a Hawaiian
kapu: forbidden, tabu
kasuri: splash-pattern cloth
kaukau: to eat, food
kim chee: Korean pickled vegetable made with hot red peppers

kō: cane
kompang: to share; work together; pay a share
kyahan: leggings

luna: boss, foreman, overseer, supervisor

maka'āinana: native common people
makai: seaside; in the direction of the sea
manong: older Filipino man
mauka: upland; mountainside; toward the mountains
mochi: Japanese rice cake
musubi: triangular-shaped Japanese rice balls, usually with a pickled
plum *(ume)* in the middle

nisei: second-generation Japanese-American

'ōhi'a: a hardwood tree
okolehao: alcoholic drink distilled from ti root
ono: delicious
'opihi: limpet, a sort of baby abalone

pau: finished, done
pau hana: finished working; retirement
pilikia: trouble
poi: a paste-like food made from taro root
poho: out of luck; too bad
puka: hole
pulapula: seedlings, cuttings of cane

sabe: understand
saimin: Japanese noodle soup
sakada: Filipino migrant laborer
sake: Japanese rice wine
sashimi: Japanese raw fish dish
shoyu: soy sauce
sushi: Japanese rice roll or ball with fish, crab, etc.

tabi: Japanese cloth shoes
talk story: just sitting and talking, a favorite pastime for locals
tanomoshi: credit-rotating system; mutual financing association

udon: Japanese noodles
ukulele: stringed musical instrument
ume: Japanese pickled red plum

wahine: woman

Bibliography

The documentary record for the study of Hawaiian plantation history is incomplete: plantation laborers have not left behind an abundance of written documents, oral history research is fragmentary, most of the non-English language sources have not been translated, and many plantation files are missing or closed to scholars.

But recovery efforts are underway. The Plantation Village and Cultural Park at Waipahu is gathering artifacts of plantation life and labor, such as tools, hats, and bangos. The Ethnic Studies Oral History Project, under the coordinatorship of Chad Taniguchi, has collected literally scores of interviews of old plantation workers and has transcribed and published them in *Waialua and Haleiwa: The People Tell Their Story* (Honolulu: Ethnic Studies Oral History Project, 1977), *Stores and Storekeepers of Paia and Puunene, Maui* (Honolulu: Ethnic Studies Oral History Project, 1980), *The 1924 Filipino Strike on Kauai* (Honolulu: Ethnic Studies Oral History Project, 1979), and *Uchinanchu: A History of Okinawans in Hawaii* (Honolulu: ESOHP and United Okinawan Association, 1981). Minoru Urata has spent over ten years visiting plantations to record old *hole hole bushi*, or Japanese labor songs, and has an impressive collection of these songs on tape.

The Grove Farm Plantation Museum, under the directorship of Barnes Riznik, has a veritable gold mine of plantation documents, including timebooks, financial records, reports, diaries (the Anton Cropp diary), and business and personal correspondence. Included in its holdings are letters and memoranda to and from the Hawaiian Sugar Planters' Association and the corporate agencies in Honolulu. The Grove Farm Plantation collection contains hundreds, perhaps thousands, of cubic feet of primary data, which have only recently been made available to the public.

The University of Hawaii's Hamilton Library has the Hawaiian Collection, which has the most complete holding of secondary works on plantation Hawaii and also an extensive collection of primary documents such as government reports, annual reports of plantations, magazines, journals, and so forth. The Hawaiian Collection also has a photocopy of the William Hooper diary and his correspondence with Ladd and Company. The Hamilton Library has stored on microfilm the most extensive collection of Hawaiian newspapers. More importantly, it houses miles (it seemed so) of microfilm of plantation records for the Kohala Sugar Company, the Kohala Ditch Company, the Hutchinson Sugar Plantation, the Hawaiian Agricultural Company, and the Laupahoehoe Sugar Company. Professor Ed Beechert deserves our thanks for microfilming these records.

The Hawaiian Sugar Planters' Association Archives in Aiea has a very useful collection of scrapbooks on various ethnic groups— Chinese, Japanese, Korean, Portuguese, Filipino, Norwegian, and others. Included in the Japanese scrapbooks are translations of the Japanese press. The archives also has scrapbooks for the various plantations. A translation of Takashi Tsutsumi's *A History of Hawaii Laborers' Movement* (Honolulu: Hawaiian Sugar Planters' Association, 1922), originally written in Japanese, is in the HSPA Archives. The Kauai Museum has the original letterbook of George Dole, manager of the Makee Plantation.

The University of California Library at Berkeley possesses important primary holdings. The Agricultural Library has a complete set of the *Planters' Monthly*. The Bancroft Library has files of old Hawaiian newspapers, including the *Pacific Commercial Advertiser*, the *Saturday Press*, the *Polynesian*, and the *Sandwich Island Mirror and Commercial Gazette*; it also has the diary of Ewald Kleinau, manager of the Paauhau Plantation.

The Bishop Museum and the Hawaii State Archives have hundreds of old photographs of plantations, mills, camps, and laborers, which give a visual understanding of plantation life and labor.

Much more remains to be done to collect and preserve plantation documents. Already several plantations have been shut down due to cutbacks in sugar production, and others are scheduled to be closed. Valuable files may be lost or destroyed unless state and private archives make systematic and active acquisition efforts. In addition, it will be important to support oral history activities, particularly the work of the Ethnic Studies Oral History Project, as well as the translation of non-English language primary sources such as the Japanese press.

Hopefully the expansion of data will encourage and make possible the emergence of new scholarship that will analyze in-depth specific areas of the plantation experience, develop and test new theoretical constructs, and study plantation Hawaii comparatively in relationship to other plantation societies in the world.

While the most valuable sources for the study of plantation history are the plantation records, other sources—primary and secondary—are also useful.

1. Labor in Hawaii

Aller, Curtis. "The Evolution of Hawaiian Labor Relations: From Benevolent Paternalism to Mature Collective Bargaining." Unpublished Ph.D. thesis, Harvard University, 1958.

Baker, Ray Stannard. 1911a. "How King Sugar Rules." *American Magazine*, 73 (November): 28–38.

———. 1911b. "Land and the Landless." *American Magazine*, 73 (December): 201–214.

———. 1912. "Human Nature in Hawaii." *American Magazine*, 73 (January): 328–339.

Coman, Katherine. *The History of Contract Labor in the Hawaiian Islands.* New York: American Economic Association, 1903.

Hall, Jack. *A Luna's Log.* Kohala: 1927.

Honolulu Record, 1947–1953.

Ikeda, Kiyoshi. "Unionization and the Plantation." *Social Process in Hawaii,* 15 (1951): 14–25.

Johannessen, Edward. *The Hawaiian Labor Movement: A Brief History.* Boston: Bruce Humphries, 1956.

Liebes, Richard A. "Labor Organization in Hawaii: A Study of the Efforts of Labor to Obtain Security Through Organization." Unpublished Master's thesis, University of Hawaii, 1938.

Lim-Chong, Lily. "Opium and the Law: Hawaii, 1856–1900." Unpublished Master's thesis, University of Hawaii, 1978.

Reinecke, John E. *Feigned Necessity: Hawaii's Attempt to Obtain Chinese Contract Labor, 1921–1923.* San Francisco: Chinese Materials Center, 1979.

Smith, Jared G. *Plantation Sketches.* Honolulu: Advertiser Press, 1924.

Thrum, Thomas G. *Hawaiian Almanac and Annual.* Honolulu: Thrum, 1884–1922.

Planters' Views and Concerns

Hawaiian Planters' Monthly. Honolulu, 1882–1909.
Hawaiian Planters' Record. Honolulu, 1910–1920.

Hawaiian Sugar Planters' Association, *Proceedings of the Annual Meeting.* Honolulu, 1904–1920.
Royal Hawaiian Agricultural Society Transactions. Honolulu, 1850–1856.

The Koloa Plantation

Alexander, Arthur C. *Koloa Plantation, 1835–1935.* Honolulu: Star-Bulletin, 1937.
Jackson, Francis O. "Koloa Plantation under Ladd and Company, 1835–1845." Unpublished Master's thesis, University of Hawaii, 1958.

The 1920 Strike

Federation of Japanese Labor in Hawaii. 1920a. *The Controversy between Japanese Labor and the Sugar Planters of Hawaii.* Honolulu.
_____. 1920b. *The Voice of Labor in Hawaii.* Honolulu.
Hawaii Laborers' Association. *Facts about the Strike on Sugar Plantations in Hawaii.* Honolulu: 1920.
Hawaiian Sugar Planters' Association. *The Sugar Industry of Hawaii and the Labor Shortage: What It Means to the United States and Hawaii.* Honolulu: 1921.
Moriyama, Alan. "The 1909 and 1920 Strikes of Japanese Sugar Plantation Workers in Hawaii." In *Counterpoint,* edited by Emma Gee, Los Angeles: University of California, 1978, 169–180.

Government Reports

Republic of Hawaii. *Report of the Labor Commission on Strikes and Arbitration.* Honolulu: 1895.
United States Bureau of Labor. *Report of the Commissioner of Labor on Hawaii.* Washington: Government Printing Office, 1902, 1903, 1906, 1911, 1916.

2. The Chinese in Hawaii

Char, Tin-Yuke. 1975. *The Sandalwood Mountains: Readings and Stories of Early Chinese in Hawaii.* Honolulu: University of Hawaii Press.
_____. 1977. *The Bamboo People: Life and Writings of a Chinese in Hawaii.* Del Mar, California: Publishers, Incorporated.
Glick, Clarence. *Sojourners and Settlers: Chinese Migrants in Hawaii.* Honolulu: University of Hawaii Press, 1980. (Originally a Ph.D. thesis entitled "The Chinese Migrant in Hawaii: A Study in Accommodation," University of Chicago, 1938.)
Lydon, Edward C. *The Anti-Chinese Movement in the Hawaiian Kingdom, 1852–1886.* San Francisco: R & E Research Associates, 1975.

3. The Germans, Norwegians, and Portuguese in Hawaii

Davis, Eleanor H. and Carl D. *Norwegian Labor in Hawaii: The Norse Immigrants.* Honolulu: Industrial Relations Center, 1962.
Felix, John Henry, and Peter R. Senecal, eds. *The Portuguese in Hawaii.* Honolulu: Felix, 1978.
Hormann, Bernhard. "The Germans in Hawaii." Unpublished Master's thesis, University of Hawaii, 1931.
Sasaki, Hideko. "The Life History of a Portuguese Immigrant." *Social Process in Hawaii,* 1 (May 1935): 26–31.

4. The Filipinos in Hawaii

Alcantara, Ruben. *Sakada: Filipino Adaptation in Hawaii.* Washington, D.C.: University Press of America, 1981.

Cariaga, Roman R. "The Filipinos in Hawaii." Unpublished Master's thesis, University of Hawaii, 1936.

Dorita, Mary. "Filipino Immigration to Hawaii." Unpublished Master's thesis, University of Hawaii, 1954.

Felipe, Virgilio. "Hawaii: A Pilipino Dream." Unpublished Master's thesis, University of Hawaii, 1972.

Quinto, Dolores. "The Life Story of a Filipino Immigrant." *Social Process in Hawaii*, 4 (1938): 71–78.

5. The Koreans in Hawaii

Choy, Bong-youn. *Koreans in America.* Chicago: Nelson-Hall, 1979.

Kim, Bernice B.H. "The Koreans in Hawaii." Unpublished Master's thesis, University of Hawaii, 1937.

Kim, Hyung-chan. *The Korean Diaspora: Historical and Sociological Studies of Korean Immigration and Assimilation in North America.* Santa Barbara: ABC-Clio, 1977.

Kim, Hyung-chan, and Wayne Patterson. *The Koreans in America, 1882–1974.* Dobbs Ferry: Oceana, 1974.

Lyu, Kingsley K. "Korean Nationalist Activities in Hawaii and America, 1901–1945." Unpublished paper, University of Hawaii, 1950.

Pang, Morris. "A Korean Immigrant." *Social Process in Hawaii*, 13 (1949): 19–24.

Patterson, Wayne. "The Korean Frontier in America: Immigration to Hawaii, 1896–1910." Unpublished Ph.D. thesis, University of Pennsylvania, 1977.

6. The Japanese in Hawaii

Conroy, Hilary. *The Japanese Frontier in Hawaii, 1868–1898.* Berkeley: University of California, 1953.

Ichihashi, Yamato. *Japanese in the United States.* New York: Arno, 1969.

Ito, Kazuo. *Issei: A History of Japanese Immigrants in North America.* Seattle: Japan Publications, 1973.

Kimura, Yukiko. "Social-Historical Background of the Okinawans in Hawaii." Romanzo Adams Social Research Laboratory Report No. 36. Honolulu, 1962.

Ladenson, Alex. "The Japanese in Hawaii." Unpublished Ph.D. thesis, University of Chicago, 1938.

Miyamoto, Kazuo. *Hawaii: End of the Rainbow.* Tokyo: Tuttle, 1964.

Murayama, Milton. *All I Asking For Is My Body.* San Francisco: Supa, 1975.

Ogawa, Dennis M. *Kodomo no tame ni—For the sake of the children: The Japanese American Experience in Hawaii.* Honolulu: University of Hawaii Press, 1978.

Okahata, James, ed. *A History of Japanese in Hawaii.* Honolulu: United Japanese Society, 1971.

Uyehara, Yukuo. "The Horehore-Bushi: A Type of Japanese Folksong Developed and Sung Among the Early Immigrants in Hawaii." *Social Process in Hawaii*, 28 (1980–1981): 110–120.

Wakukawa, Ernest K. *A History of the Japanese People in Hawaii*. Honolulu, 1938.

7. General Studies of Hawaiian Society

Daws, Gavan. *Shoal of Time: A History of the Hawaiian Islands*. Honolulu: University of Hawaii Press, 1974.

Fuchs, Lawrence H. *Hawaii Pono: A Social History*. New York: Harcourt, Brace and World, 1961.

Kuykendall, Ralph. *The Hawaiian Kingdom*. 3 vols. Honolulu: University of Hawaii Press, 1938, 1953, 1967.

Lind, Andrew. 1938. *An Island Community: Ecological Succession in Hawaii*. Chicago: University of Chicago Press.

_____. 1974. *Hawaii's People*. Honolulu: University of Hawaii Press.

Kelly, Marion. "Changes in Land Tenure in Hawaii, 1778-1850." Master's thesis, University of Hawaii, 1956.

Kent, Noel. *Hawaii: Islands Under the Influence*. New York: Monthly Review Press, 1983.

Melendy, Brett. *Asians in America: Filipinos, Koreans, and East Indians*. Boston: Twayne, 1977.

Morgan, Theodore. *Hawaii: A Century of Economic Change, 1778-1876*. Cambridge: Harvard, 1948.

Taylor, William Henry. "The Hawaiian Sugar Industry." Unpublished Ph.D. thesis, University of California at Berkeley, 1935.

Index

About the Author

Ronald Takaki grew up in Palolo Valley, Honolulu, where his neighbors were Japanese, Portuguese, Hawaiian, and Chinese. He has made regular trips home to the islands since moving to the mainland after graduating from Iolani High School in 1957. Takaki received his B.A. degree from the College of Wooster and his Ph.D. in history from the University of California at Berkeley, where he is now a professor of ethnic studies. He is the author of several books, including *Iron Cages: Race and Culture in 19th Century America* and *A Pro-Slavery Crusade: The Agitation to Reopen the African Slave Trade*. Takaki has been awarded fellowships from the National Endowment for the Humanities, the American Council of Learned Societies, and the Rockefeller Foundation. He is also a recipient of a Distinguished Teaching Award at the University of California at Berkeley.

HAWAI Production Notes

This book was designed by Roger Eggers. Composition and paging were done on the Quadex Composing System and typesetting on the Compugraphic Unisetter by the design and production staff of University of Hawaii Press.

The text typeface is Compugraphic Caledonia and the display typeface is Compugraphic Palatino.

Offset presswork and binding were done by Vail-Ballou Press, Inc. Text paper is Writers RR Offset, basis 50.